Comprehending Math

The design on the front cover is a stylized version of the Borromean Rings, so named as they appeared on the family crest of the Borromeo family of Italy in the fifteenth century. They represented an inseparable union of three families through intermarriage. The rings do not go through one another and if one ring is cut and removed, the other two will fall separately to the ground. What holds the three rings together? If you look closely at one ring, let's say the red, it is outside the blue ring but inside the green. Similarly, the blue ring is inside the red ring, but outside the green. Finally, the green is outside the red ring, but inside the blue. Imagine you were an ant crawling along on the red ring. Starting the upper left part of the ring and moving to the right you'd go over the blue ring, then under the green, over the blue again, under the green, and finally back to where you were. Does "over, under, over, under" remind you of anything? How about *braiding* hair? The rings stay together because they are braided.

In this book, I have *braided* together mathematics (especially problem solving) and language (especially reading) together with thinking (cognition and metacognition) to help elementary school students become more powerful mathematical problem solvers. I chose the term braiding because *three things* are being woven into a tightly knit entity like a rope that is stronger than the individual strands. When thinking, language, and math are braided, the result is stronger, more durable, and more powerful than any one could be by itself.

Those who have purchased a copy of *Comprehending Math* may go to its accompanying website, www.braidedmath.com, where they will find supplementary materials, updates, and other resources. As they use the strategies in the book, teachers will be able to share ideas and suggestions with one another via the website.

Comprehending Math

Adapting Reading Strategies to Teach Mathematics, K–6

ARTHUR HYDE

Foreword by Ellin Oliver Keene

HEINEMANN
Portsmouth, NH

Heinemann
A division of Reed Elsevier Inc.
361 Hanover Street
Portsmouth, NH 03801–3912
www.heinemann.com

Offices and agents throughout the world

The author and publisher wish to thank those who have generously given permission to reprint borrowed material:

ISAT Math extended response items (Figures 6.8 and 6.9) by Forness, Megan, et al. Copyright © 2003 by the Illinois State Board of Education. Reprinted with permission.

Library of Congress Cataloging-in-Publication Data
Hyde, Arthur A.
Comprehending math : adapting reading strategies to teach mathematics, K–6 / Arthur Hyde ; foreword by Ellin Oliver Keene.
p. cm.
Includes bibliographical references and index.
ISBN-13: 978-0-325-00949-0
ISBN-10: 0-325-00949-X (pbk. : acid-free paper)
1. Mathematics—Study and teaching (Elementary). 2. Reading comprehension. 3. Reading (Elementary). I. Title.

QA20.R43H93 2006
372.7—dc22 2006014780

Acquisitions editor: Emily Michie Birch
Production: Lynne Costa
Cover design: Jenny Jensen Greenleaf
Cover illustration: Jenny Jensen Greenleaf
Typesetter: Drawing Board Studios
Manufacturing: Steve Bernier

Printed in the United States of America on acid-free paper
10 09 08 07 EB 4 5

CONTENTS

FOREWORD

Sometimes, in schools and classrooms, we simply confuse the help. By help I mean those pesky kids that show up every day expecting to be taught. In our best effort to teach the curriculum, use best instructional practices, create warm, inviting spaces in which kids can learn, prepare them for the tests, respond to individual needs, engage kids in the excitement of learning, integrate around themes, respond to parents, weave in resources from the community, get excited about our principal's latest project, share and plan with our colleagues, read the latest in educational research and practice, go to the best conferences, write thoughtful report card comments, sit on the hospitality committee, and (whew) enjoy children—we just end up confusing the help.

We are trying to apply all we know about teaching and learning and, instead, find ourselves running around the classroom trying to do a little bit of this and a little bit of that. Eventually, we realize through our utter exhaustion that the kids have been watching us fly around like they're enjoying a great tennis match, heads swaying as they follow us (or try to). They must be thinking, "Wow, look at her go!" We are trying to do so much, we are trying to do it well, we are trying to keep them engaged, and, in the end, we are probably confusing the help and it is we who end up doing the heavy lifting—cognitively speaking. I've always wondered: If we understand the basic principles that underlie human learning—the ability to retain and reapply concepts in new contexts—why is everything so difficult, so different, from class to class, discipline to discipline?

I had something close to an epiphany about all this while watching a lesson in a first/second-grade classroom years ago. The brilliant teacher, my friend and colleague, Colleen Buddy, was teaching inference, and on this particular day was trying to help the children understand that predictions are one form of inference. A young man raised his hand with a simple inquiry. "Why, Mrs. Buddy," he said, tongue thrusting wildly through the space where front teeth are usually found, "why do you call it predicting when we're talking about reading, hypothesizing [which came out as hypothethithing] when we're in science, and estimating [ethimathing] when we're in math? Aren't they really all the same thing?"

We might just be confusing the help. Our young friend was merely saying, "Teachers, please! If we're talking about the same kinds of thinking, though we are in different subject areas (your inauthentic scheduling needs, not ours), might we do the common-sense thing and refer to *thinking into the future*, for example, as the same process, no matter what time in the day we happen to discuss it?" Pick one term, they seem to be saying—hypothesizing, estimating, predicting—pick one and stick with it—it will make so much more sense to us.

Well! Of all the outrageous suggestions! But, wait a minute. Why *do* we compartmentalize learning and thinking throughout the day? Why does this segmentation increase as students get older? Why do we refer to one set of thinking processes during reading and another altogether during math? In the words of our precocious first grader, "Aren't they really all the same thing?" Perhaps if we're in the math or cognition departments at a major university, we may quibble a bit with our first grader's notion. Perhaps there are subtle and important differences between estimating and predicting when one is working at the highest levels of theoretical research. But for our purposes in kindergarten through twelth-grade classrooms, might we confuse the help less if we used the same language to describe similar thinking processes throughout the learning day and around the school?

Arthur Hyde has also had this epiphany, and the reader of this important book will be the richer for it. Hyde has woven together—no, **braided**—the concepts of thinking, language, and math, and has made a crystal-clear case for the application to math of the language and learning processes many teachers incorporate routinely into their literacy instruction. Why, he reasons, if we ask kids to construct meaning in reading, wouldn't we ask them to do the same in math? Why not create a mathematically literate environment in the same way we strive to create literate environments for children learning to read, write, speak, and listen? How, he asks, can we fail to incorporate such a critical concept as revision into children's mathematical lives? Revision is indelibly woven into our language and literacy classrooms, but do we, in Hyde's words, *forgive* math mistakes, encouraging children to revise their mathematical thinking?

When reading this superb volume, you will be tempted, numerous times, I'm afraid, to strike your forehead with the heel of your hand and say, "Oh, why on earth didn't I think of that?" The very concepts that have led to a revolution in reading comprehension instruction are here applied, with tremendous clarity, to the teaching of mathematics. Hyde relies on his rock-solid understanding of human cognition in order to relate thinking and language to the process of learning mathematics, a connection a certain first grader made years ago, but one which we educators have been slow to grasp.

This book reminded me of my worry that we elementary teachers may have had less than stellar experiences in learning mathematics in our own K–12 experience. As a result, we tend to draw conclusions about our efficacy as teachers of math and to make some very subtle, perhaps subconscious, decisions about our students' propensity (lack thereof) to learn and to *love* the science of patterns—mathematics. Hyde provides a way through those obstacles for teachers like me who were less than excited about math. He helps us understand critical concepts in mathematics by way of our well-developed knowledge of comprehension strategies. Now, there's a novel idea—how about helping us learn new ways of approaching math instruction by resting new concepts on our existing knowledge?!?! Is that a text-to-self connection, by any chance? Might someone have had the common sense to apply what we know about student learning to professional learning? Read on and be amazed!

In each of Hyde's chapters on major comprehension (thinking) strategies, he lays out, with great good humor and insight-provoking examples, the thinking and language applications to mathematics in our classrooms. He makes the case, not only for using the language of the literacy classroom throughout the day, but to apply well-proven research concepts such as schema theory and metacognition to the fundamentally important problem-solving processes on which mathematical understanding rests.

As I was reading, I remembered an eighth grader named Tony who approached me at a middle school in Bridgeport, Connecticut, several years ago and asked if I was aware that there was a conspiracy going on at that school. Amused, but trying to keep a straight face, I asked him to tell me about the conspiracy. He glanced around him, checking for listening devices, I suppose, and said, "I just think you should know that the teachers around here are all teaching the same thing at the same time." I asked him what he meant and he said, "Well, when I go to language arts, she's teaching determining importance, and when I go to social studies, *she's* teaching determining importance, and when I go to science, *he's* teaching determining importance, only just in science, and when I go to math . . ." Ever prescient, I guessed it. "She's teaching how mathematicians determine importance, right?" I asked. "Yep," he said, with the smug satisfaction of having revealed a vast, school-wide conspiracy. I smiled and said, "Tony, my friend, it's not a conspiracy, it's called good planning. It's called teaching in a way that kids will learn." Disappointed, Tony turned away, shaking his head, and said, "Okay, I just thought you better know."

If *Comprehending Math* were around when I was learning math, I might have become a lover of the science of patterns. If *Comprehending Math* had been around a few years ago, Tony would have had all his conspiracy theories realized much earlier in his education. If *Comprehending Math* had been around when I was teaching math, my students might have had a chance to do something other than watch me run around trying to do a little bit of everything. They might have sensed a conspiracy. They might have made all-important thinking connections between and among the concepts that mattered most to them—throughout the day. They might have had more opportunities to use language, to create representations, to revise, to visualize as they approached math problems. They might have had a chance to understand their own thinking, not only about the books they read, but about the mathematical concepts I so wanted them to grasp. But *Comprehending Math* is here now and, for those who devour it, as I did, their teaching will be clearer, bolder, more connected. And for the ultimate beneficiaries, the help, they will have a chance to understand just how integrally our world is connected.

—*Ellin Oliver Keene*

ACKNOWLEDGMENTS

This book has been a long time percolating. The coffee pot started up in 1970 when I was teaching six sections of general mathematics in an inner-city high school in Philadelphia. Can you imagine how deadening that course was to my students—the same arithmetic that had beaten them down for the previous seven years repeated again and again?

I was very fortunate to get to know two wonderful English teachers at that time who were experimenting with a "reading/writing workshop." Yes, this was 1970. Lynne Miller is now a professor at the University of Southern Maine and Jolley Bruce Christman is the Founding Director of Research for Action, a research and evaluation organization in Philadelphia.

After a series of conversations and visits to each other's classes we conducted a little experiment. In the next quarter, Lynne and I got back-to-back classes with the same students and scheduled them in for a double period with us to team-teach a reading, writing, and math workshop. It was a profound learning experience for me; it changed how I taught mathematics in several significant ways. I got my first taste of how reading, language, and writing should be taught. As a student, I was perpetually on the brink of disaster in my English classes from seventh grade on through college. I am sure that all my English teachers didn't know what to do with me. I know I never quite understood what they wanted me to do. But when Lynne taught, she *played* with language and ideas in much the same way I played with mathematical materials and concepts. The powerful connections between language and thought that my psychology professors had emphasized suddenly became very real. Before reading, Lynne asked her students a million questions, some of which seemed pretty personal. She got them to imagine what the story was going to be about. Sometimes as they were reading she would ask them to stop and talk about what they saw in their minds. She got them to write! First they talked a lot about what they knew, what they thought, how they felt. Then they wrote heart-breaking stories about their lives.

While many of our contemporaries were preaching the need for "relevance" in the curriculum for inner-city kids, Lynne and Jolley had their students—regular inner-city high school students—reading Greek mythology. I remember them helping the kids study the Orpheus myth. A fancy, high-society women's league was screening the film *Black Orpheus*, in which the myth is set in Brazil during Carnival. Lynne called and asked if they could bring about thirty high schoolers. The society ladies agreed but were a little nervous when the students arrived and all were black. To their credit, the ladies welcomed the students, and they all watched the film, totally entranced. When the film ended, the ladies embarked on their usual discussion of the film, the genre, the meaning of the symbols, and so forth, all done while tea and pastries were served. The students jumped right in and discussed their interpretations of the film, especially in light of the Orpheus legend they'd been studying. The ladies were impressed and as the students were leaving, the grand dame of the women's league thanked Lynne for bringing her wonderful *gifted class*. Lynne laughed and assured her that this was just her regular third-period English class.

And that's one of the key points in this book. Good teaching with powerful language and thinking is for all children. It is not just for the gifted; it's for all the "regular third-period" kids that every teacher has.

Since that time with Lynne and Jolley, I have had the pleasure of collaborating with a number of truly fabulous reading, language, and writing teachers and professors: Rebecca Barr, Donna Ogle, Camille Blachowicz, Marilyn Bizar, Smokey Daniels, and Steve Zemelman. Along the way I have devoured the books written by Keene and Zimmermann, Harvey and Goudvis, and Miller, all from Denver's Public Education and Business Coalition (PEBC). All of these people have helped me take the most powerful strategies for teaching reading comprehension, the development of language, and the process of writing and combine them with the cognitive approaches to mathematical problem solving that I love. That is what this book is all about.

Some early pieces of this approach to teaching mathematics can be seen in the book on problem solving that my wife and I wrote in 1991, *Mathwise*. As an elementary school teacher, Pam had encouraged me to see what teaching younger kids is all about. When I came to National Louis, I did just that. I taught my university courses in the evenings and spent many of my days in elementary school classrooms. What an eye-opening, mind-boggling experience! I could not possibly name all the wonderful teachers who have invited me into their classrooms to try my home-made manipulatives, activities, problem solving, and the different versions of the language/thinking/mathematics that I will share in this book. These teachers have helped me test and refine this approach over the past fifteen years. They incorporated my rough-hewn ideas and adapted them to work in their circumstances. They have given me feedback that I could share with others. Because they span the K–8 grades, I can say that what follows works for students in that grade range. The examples in this book focus on grades one through six. It works for most of the kids most of the time when the teacher adapts it into her conscious repertoire of teaching mathematics. Nothing works all the time with every student. If any professor says his way of teaching math does, hold on to your checkbook.

My special thanks go to my wife Pam and all her third graders with whom I played math before she became a principal. She continues to be my touchstone for inspiration. And with great affection I must also thank Beverly Kiss, Mary Fencl, Carole Malone, Susan Gittings, Christina Hull, Michelle Habel, Katie George, Lynn Pittner, Cheryl Heck, and Shari and Pat Watson for sharing their teaching wisdom with me. Thanks to another fabulous teacher, Marie Bartolotta, for her insightful feedback on early chapters. I am very grateful for Emily Birch's editorial skills and to both Leigh Peake and Emily for believing in this project and me. Thank you all.

INTRODUCTION
Braiding Mathematics, Language, and Thinking

[The] human ability—to imagine the future taking several paths, and to make adaptable plans in response to our imaginings—is, in essence, the source of mathematics and language. . . . [T]hinking mathematically is just a specialized form of using our language facility.

—Keith Devlin, *The Math Gene*, 2000

THREE KEY PIECES

I have said to many elementary school teachers over the past fifteen years, "If you have learned ways to help kids to think effectively and understand ideas in reading and language, use them in math and you won't be disappointed." These teachers know quite a bit about reading and language. This suggestion is a good one, but it is only part of the story. Certainly, if you use what you know works in reading, language arts, and writing to teach mathematics, you will get some good results. Teachers enthusiastically report significant involvement and understanding from their students. However, teachers can go beyond simply applying aspects of reading comprehension to mathematics. I have taught hundreds of teachers (and even reading specialists) in scores of courses and workshops how to do more through *braiding* together mathematics, language, and thinking.

If you set out to integrate mathematics and language (or problem solving and reading), what would you put together? What aspects of language fit nicely with mathematics? How about vocabulary? Or writing in math journals? However, the real question is what guides you in determining exactly what the kids should do and how you teach them. Asking the language arts people will only get you what they do in their knowledge domain. Concepts in mathematics are very different from concepts in language. They don't really know the domain of mathematical knowledge or the process of mathematical thinking.

There is one major aspect of human thinking central to both language and mathematics: cognition. There are several key principles from cognitive psychology that can guide us. Therefore, I have used the term *braiding* to indicate that thinking, language, and mathematics can be braided together into a tightly knit entity like a rope that is stronger than the individual strands. When these three important processes are braided, the result is stronger, more durable, and more powerful than any one could be by itself.

For many years, the teaching of mathematics and especially problem solving has suffered from insufficient attention to thinking and language. If you want students to understand mathematical ideas, they must use both language and thought. Trying to put more thinking into the math curriculum or one's teaching without attention to language will be fruitless and so will trying to use language without thinking. The term *braiding* here suggests that the three components are inseparable, mutually supportive, and necessary.

DEATH, TAXES, AND MATHEMATICS

There are two things in life that we can be certain of . . . everyone knows the answer . . . death and taxes. Add another item to that list: at least half of our nation's fifth graders hate story problems. Actually, they dislike math in general, but story or word problems hold a special place of loathing in their souls. This percentage may vary a bit from classroom to classroom. Research has shown that most children start kindergarten with some fairly good ways to solve mathematical problems in the sandbox or with toys and games. However, during their first four or five years of school, they abandon their previously successful ways of dealing with problems involving mathematics.

Have you ever watched three children trying to figure out how to split up a bunch of candies? If the candies are identical, they just give one to each, then another, then another until they run out. Obviously influenced by Long John Silver of *Treasure Island* fame, they refer to this process as "divvying" the candies up. The children have not memorized division facts; they just have a way to do what is necessary. If the candies do not come out evenly (they often check to make sure everyone got the same number of candies), they may use some probabilistic device (e.g., flip a coin, odds or evens of total fingers displayed, paper/scissors/rock) to see who gets the extras. Children can be remarkably resourceful when no adults are around to tell them what to do.

No. I am not advocating *Lord of the Flies*. The question is: what forces are at work to dampen our children's inherent awe and wonder, their excitement about learning, and their facility with mathematics? The early years of schooling present children with a torrent of messages that they must *do* math in one particular way, that there is one right answer, and one right way to find it. They are told what to memorize, shown the proper way to write down problems and answers in symbolic notation, and given a satchel full of gimmicks they don't understand. No matter that they don't understand what they are trying to memorize. Does anyone ask if the symbols make any sense to them? Does anyone notice that they have ceased to trust their own reasoning or intuition borne of experience? Many children (and adults too) see mathematics as arcane, mystical. They believe that understanding mathematics is beyond most mere mortals. Can the children get the answer quickly, efficiently, and accurately? That's all that matters.

Of course, I believe that it is necessary for children to learn the basic math facts of the four operations. As much as I love problem solving, I know that students will be hampered in their problem solving (especially in estimation and determining reasonableness) if they don't know basic arithmetic facts. The question is not *if* those facts are learned, but how and when. All students should understand and be able to use number concepts, operations, and computational procedures. There are several critically important processes, each with a critical cognitive component, that lead to understanding, proficiency, and fluency that need to be developed. When students have many successful experiences using these processes, remembering math facts becomes a simple matter.

These processes are: *counting* (building one-to-one correspondence and number sense); *number relations* (decomposing and recomposing quantities to see relationships among the numbers); *place value* (creating sets of ten with objects and beginning to understand the base ten, positional notation); the *meaning of the operations* (creating mental maps of different situations and realizing that operations have multiple meanings); and *fact strategies* (thinking strategies for learning the facts for the operations).

Acting along with some erroneous beliefs about computation is another perhaps even more sinister force. Most people deny the importance of language in the world of mathematics. An exaggeration? Textbook publishers are very sensitive to the feedback from teachers whose message has been crystal clear for years: too many words on the page will make learning too hard for the kids who can't read well. "Johnny is not a good reader. Math is the only subject he likes (or does well in). Just let him work with the numbers." So what happens when Johnny has to read the story problem? The teacher is ready with a magic trick: just look for the *key* word (*cue* word) that will tell you what operation to use. If you see *sum* or *all together*, you add the numbers. If you see *take away* or *difference*, then subtract the smaller number from the bigger number.

What is the fundamental message the kids get when told to look for the *key/cue* word? Don't read the problem. Don't imagine the situation. Ignore that context. Abandon your prior knowledge. Who cares about metacognition, metaphors, metamorphosis, metatarsals, whatever? You don't have to read; you don't have to think. Just grab the numbers and compute. After all, you've got a 25 percent chance of randomly selecting the correct operation.

This situation, all too prevalent in U.S. schools, discourages kids from thinking. That makes no sense. Both reading and mathematics require thinking. Teachers should use every means possible to encourage students to think, reflect, question, imagine. And how do we do that? With language—with expressive language (speaking and writing) and with receptive language (listening and reading). And they all fit together in a child's life and in the classroom.

There is yet another critical reason to braid language, thinking, and mathematics. When math is taught with the language pruned or purged, who is immediately penalized? Those who use language as their primary means of processing ideas; those who develop their language facility early. *Girls*. Of course, all children can profit from discussing, verbalizing thoughts, talking mathematics, but girls develop language strengths earlier than boys and, when encouraged, can use them effectively to build mathematical understanding. Girls understand the value of braiding language, thinking, and mathematics; they even get the metaphor.

A LITTLE FORESHADOWING

Consider the following ideas, each culled from the literature on reading and language learning and well known to most elementary school teachers. Each of these ideas has a solid foundation in cognition. I have simply played those ideas through mathematics and problem solving. Like the television game show, *Jeopardy*, I have worded the idea in the form of a question.

1. Are students expected to *construct their own meaning* in mathematics?
2. Are students encouraged to have *ownership of their problem solving*—to choose to use mathematics for purposes they set for themselves? What would ownership look like?
3. Are students encouraged to do problem solving for *authentic purposes*? What would *authentic* mathematics look like?
4. Are students encouraged to do *voluntary mathematics*, selecting tasks for information, pleasure, or to fulfill personal goals?
5. How is mathematics instruction *scaffolded*?
6. Does the school help teachers and students build a *rich, mathematically literate environment* or community?
7. Are students encouraged to see the *big picture, important concepts, vital connections* versus isolated pieces of mathematics?
8. Is *forgiveness* granted to students in mathematics? Is making *mistakes a natural* part of learning? Is doing mathematics seen as a dynamic process that incorporates *planning, drafting, revising, editing, and publishing*?

Is it heresy for an unapologetically passionate teacher of mathematics to believe that we could do a far, far better job of teaching children how to understand and love mathematics if we did all of these things?

READING COMPREHENSION

What is reading? Sounds like a silly question, but if you have been following the "reading wars" in the past twenty years (and you may have also followed the "math wars"), there are a whole lot of people who believe that reading *is* decoding, phonics, and word attack skills. No respectable educator would argue that these things are not part of the process of reading and learning to read, but they do not *define* it. By analogy, arithmetic computational proficiency and math facts are part of mathematics, but they do not define it. Mathematics *is* the science of patterns. Neither reading nor math is a collection of skills or subskills. I have no intention of addressing all aspects of reading and language in this book, nor should I. Instead, I will draw selectively from the experts whom I admire.

Reading is the process of constructing meaning from written language. *Reading is thinking.* Constructing meaning does involve decoding, but in greater measure, it is a very dynamic process requiring some very special *thinking* about what one knows already (prior knowledge) and one's experiences (especially with language). Readers *interact* with what they read. They do not passively receive its meaning, they construct it. They use what they know about the content of the text, about the context being described, about how texts of this kind are structured (their format), and about the particular vocabulary (including specialized terms). They must continually draw inferences about the meaning of the words. They must make assumptions about missing pieces, things implied but not there on the page. For proficient readers, this is all done effortlessly and largely unconsciously. As complex as all these processes are, throw into the mix that these things are greatly facilitated by the readers' metacognitive monitoring of what they are doing and a metacognitive awareness of their own ways of operating, being able to reflect on their own ways of thinking (as if looking at your mind in a four-dimensional mirror).

Some people ask: "Do children really do all those things? Don't they just learn phonics and listen to people talk and they figure out how to read?" In psychology, they call that kind of thinking "the black box." We don't know what goes on inside kids' heads. It is a black box. We can't read their minds. We can only go by their behavior. Such an approach is dangerous. And yet, I hear it frequently in both reading and math. A significant portion of adults in this country believe that if they could just memorize the math facts, they'd be fine in subsequent mathematics courses. Ironically, some people who are involved in one of the biggest "reform" curricula in math have said that if teachers just give the kids some good math to do, by "osmosis" they will construct meaning. OSMOSIS!

Those who believe in such osmosis may lack an understanding of cognition and metacognition, and how a teacher can facilitate meaning-making. Teachers model, show, ask questions, make suggestions, and create a safe, supportive, rich, literate environment in which students can explore ideas and interests. Teachers also can mediate between the larger world and the world of the child. Sometimes they explain things. Language, especially oral language, is used continually throughout these processes.

Reading Comprehension Strategies

Research on reading has identified several highly effective cognitive strategies for students to use in reading comprehension. Specific teaching techniques for helping students with these strategies have been developed. With minor differences in terminology among experts in the field, they are:

- *making connections* (activating relevant prior knowledge, linking what is in the text to their own experiences, discerning the context; relating what is in the text to other things they've read, things in the real world, to phenomena around them);
- *asking questions* (actively wondering, raising uncertainties, considering possibilities, searching for relationships, making up "what if" scenarios);
- *visualizing* (imagining the situation or people being described, making mental pictures or images);
- *inferring and predicting* (interpreting, drawing conclusions, hypothesizing);
- *determining importance* (analyzing essential elements);
- *synthesizing* (finding patterns, summarizing, retelling);
- *metacognitive monitoring* (actively keeping track of their thinking, adjusting strategies to fit what they are reading).

When teachers focus on these cognitive strategies in a variety of different text genres, students can learn to use those strategies independently and flexibly. The cognitive strategies are taught most effectively in a reading workshop that includes (1) crafting lessons with direct, explicit instruction and modeling by the teacher, (2) students applying the content of the crafting lesson, and (3) students reflecting at the end of the reading workshop (Public Education and Business Coalition [PEBC] 2004).

During crafting lessons, teachers introduce and explain a new strategy. They think aloud as they read, modeling their own use of that strategy for their students and carefully explaining how they are applying the new strategy to the text. After the crafting lesson, students spend large amounts of time applying the content of the crafting lesson to their own reading experiences. During this time, students might meet in small, needs- or interest-based groups, or read independently. Teachers spend this time guiding small groups of students as they negotiate a common text or a common instructional need, or conferring with individuals as they work to make sense of their reading materials. At the end of the reading workshop, students regularly share their insights about the content of their reading and their use of reading strategies. The format for this reflection can vary, depending on purpose. The teacher participates in the reflecting, offering observations and recording the individual and group needs generated by this process. The goal is for students to internalize these strategies and use them easily.

These seven strategies are fairly broad and incorporate quite a few pieces. Reading experts have also developed more focused strategies. For instance, K-W-L (Know-Want to know- Learn) is a method of having kids think about key ideas before, during, and after reading. QAR (Question-Answer-Relationship) is a method of asking questions while reading. Each chapter of the book addresses one of the broader reading comprehension strategies listed above. It is not my intention to be comprehensive. There are many marvelous books cited in the references list at the end of the book that provide a wealth of examples. In each chapter, I have tried to include only the key elements of reading and language, identified by principles of cognition, that can be braided with mathematics. The chapters will be both cumulative and recursive. Later chapters will incorporate previous ideas into the main strategy being discussed and also will revisit previous ideas to build a deeper understanding of them, in light of the new strategy.

MATHEMATICAL THINKING AND PROBLEM SOLVING

The National Council of Teachers of Mathematics (NCTM) developed a set of principles and standards for mathematics curriculum, teaching, and assessment in 1989. NCTM produced a revised version in 2000 with standards addressing five broad strands of mathematics K–12: *Number and Computation; Algebra; Geometry; Measurement; Data and Probability*. Each of the strands is chock full of powerful mathematical concepts. In order for students to learn those concepts with deep understanding, the NCTM Standards address five processes in which students must be engaged: *problem solving, connections, reasoning and proof, communication,* and *representations*.

Despite their complexity, I infer that the NCTM standards are based on three big (that is, foundational) ideas:

1. Math is the science of patterns; it is much more than arithmetic. Every strand of math has certain patterns that we look for. Probably every concept in mathematics is a pattern of some kind.
2. The goal of mathematics teaching should be understanding concepts, not merely memorizing facts and procedures. Therefore, we must use what we know about cognition.
3. For children to understand mathematical concepts, they must use language, the quintessential characteristic of human cognition.

The five content standards have provoked a lot of dialogue about the concepts of the elementary school curriculum. Less progress has been made regarding the process standards. NCTM views problem solving as *doing* mathematics and as a powerful vehicle for building understanding of mathematical concepts. This would be a shocker for most of my old math teachers, for whom problem solving was an afterthought, something that the kids did after they'd been taught the concept or procedure. Today we can see that by using well-constructed problems, worthwhile mathematical tasks, the use of good strategies, and with the teacher's facilitation, students can construct deeper meaning for concepts by actually using the mathematics they know.

Granted, the majority of classrooms in the United States may be using textbooks that are hanging on to a conception of problem solving as determining what computational procedure to use. The problems may be reminiscent of the settlers leaving Missouri bound for Oregon. For example, "Hattie needs 5 and 7/8 yards of muslin at 27 cents per yard. What will it cost?" They are generally called "routine" problems or "translation" problems (translating the description of the situation into an equation). Somewhat more complex story problems usually entail a string of consecutive computational procedures in order to find the correct answer.

In the 1950s George Polya helped to broaden our sense of problem solving by describing heuristics or strategies that college students could use in their mathematics classes. By the early 1980s the idea of strategies found its way into the school curriculum and most textbooks introduced students to a dozen or so problem-solving strategies. A problem was seen as a task for which the person confronting it wants to find a solution, but for which there is not a readily accessible procedure that guarantees or completely determines the solution. Consider the case of a student confronted with the question, "Sacks of flour cost $4.85 per sack; how much would you pay for ten sacks?" If this student understands that there are ten sacks and each one costs the same amount ($4.85) and realizes that the answer can be readily determined by repeated addition or by multiplication, is this a "problem" for her or him? No, it is a thinly disguised drill exercise, perhaps valuable, but not a problem.

A number of math educators have infused textbooks with problems that require students to do more than merely determine which operation(s) to use, moving beyond what educators see as translation problems. They created "nonroutine" problems, what some called "process" problems, in which a good process of thinking was required. For instance, "How many different ways can a person make change for a quarter?" There is no obvious computation procedure to invoke. You have to figure it out. Try it.

If you tried it, did you find twelve different ways? But how did you work it? Did you make a list? Did you draw a picture? Did you make a table? If so, you chose a problem-solving strategy. Strategies can help students find solutions. They may also help them understand the problem.

In the 1980s some educators came to think of problem solving as an "art" in which mathematicians (as well as regular humans) worked on perplexing problems. They placed problem solving at the heart of mathematics. For many of these educators problem solving required working from an "initial state" to a "goal state" and strategies were to be used when one was "stuck" and did not know what to do next to move toward the end goal.

A serious drawback to this view is that it treats problem solving as a process independent of content. Strategies tend to be seen as generic, applicable to anything, and able to be mastered, like a skill or a procedure. For me, the term *problem-solving skill* is an oxymoron. Skills are physical in nature, requiring a certain amount of innate ability and massive amounts of practice, but with minimal thought or reasoning. In contrast, problem solving is clearly a cognitive venture. How you think and what you think about are intimately related. Analyzing a poem and analyzing a spreadsheet of data are very different processes. That they are similar in that both "break things down" becomes completely irrelevant when one is immersed in the task.

There is yet another way that some math educators are conceiving of problem solving and strategies. Some use a perspective referred to as *modeling* or *creating models* in which problem solving serves primarily to *interpret* the problem. Similar to what some would call *task definition*, this broader approach to problem solving emphasizes the need for interpretation, description, elaboration, and explanation of the nature of the problem. This perspective recognizes the importance of the context, content, and the concepts of the problem. The solution to problems is often the building of a model using particular concepts that are still being developed by the students. In this view, the purpose of the strategies is to help students refine, revise, and extend their ideas, especially through interaction with others.

The point is the kids have to *do* the math. How does a student get better at solving problems? What is the best way to get better at reading? By reading more. Of course, a third grader can't simply pick up Kant and make any sense out of him. (Come to think of it, I can't either.) Problems should be challenging, but not overwhelming.

The dilemma goes even deeper. The NCTM process standard termed *Connections* encourages a wide variety of links within mathematics. For decades the mathematics curriculum has consisted of little, bite-sized chunks of mathematical knowledge. I am not speaking only of narrowly defined skills (as in skill and drill), although some still cling to the erroneous belief that if children crank out a gazillion math facts they know how to do mathematics. I am concerned here with the fragmentation of concepts into isolated compartments that is contrary to the NCTM admonition that students need to see that mathematics is a coherent whole. Many concepts are connected to a multitude of others. Even when teachers go after conceptual understanding, the curriculum treats that concept in isolation from its related concepts. To make matters worse, the curriculum deals with a topic for two weeks and then ignores it for a year.

My wife and I always knew when it was April 1 because the fraction worksheets would come home to be stuck on the refrigerator with magnets. That would go on for two weeks and then as suddenly as they had come, they just disappeared one day (usually at the deadline for filing income tax returns—I am not sure what the connection is).What are kids to make of this phenomenon? Fractions only exist during these two weeks? Nobody thinks about them or uses them at any other time during the year.

What about the highly touted "spiraling" curriculum, which does not expect mastery (or understanding?) the first time a child encounters a concept because it will be back two more times during the year? The issue is not how many times or how often one revisits a concept, but the nature and quality of the experience. Is it conceptually rich? Have the students built a solid initial foundation to begin using the concept in a way that is meaningful to them? Some spiraling math curricula are more like tornados. What happens when the tornado touches down? It briefly stirs things up, and then leaves for an indeterminate time. If its touchdown time is riddled with gimmicks, what do the kids have to show for their brief encounter with the mathematics of that moment?

Another NCTM process standard not fully developed in the United States is *representations*. It was barely mentioned in the 1989 version of the standards. Therefore, in 1991 my wife and I wrote *Mathwise*, in which we made a strong pitch for the critical importance of creating representations in doing mathematics. Furthermore, we asserted that of the ten popular problem-solving strategies, there are five strategies that are based on representations, two that were so broad as to be metastrategies that should be used all the time, and three that were fairly narrow and should be considered supplementary.

When using the five most powerful strategies, students *create their own representations*. Through this creation, they are truly *constructing meaning*. These five strategies are:

- Discuss the problem in small groups (language representations using auditory sense).
- Use manipulatives (concrete, physical representations using tactile sense).
- Act It Out (representations of sequential actions using bodily kinesthetic sense).
- Draw a picture, diagram, or graph (pictorial representations using visual sense).
- Make a list or table (symbolic representations often requiring abstract reasoning).

Language should be used throughout all five of these strategies.

The two common strategies of looking for a pattern and using logical reasoning *always* should be used in problem solving. Mathematics is the science of patterns; every branch of mathematics (e.g., numbers, geometry, measurement, data and chance, algebra) has characteristic patterns. Logical reasoning is essential to doing mathematics. But is it a strategy? Is it something one chooses to do instead of something else? Okay. What is the alternative? "Pay attention, kids; we've been reasoning illogically all year long in math; now it is time for a new strategy. Let's use logical reasoning for a change!"

Children delight in seeing patterns in mathematics or truly understanding a concept. Consequently, I am concerned when children's books present seeing mathematical patterns everywhere as a "curse," mathematics as magic or as witchcraft practiced by the Number Devil. I believe it is a big mistake to tell children that mathematics is magical or incomprehensible while at the same time trying to help them believe in their own capabilities and that they can *expect* it to make sense through diligent work. The books may be cute, but can send a decidedly mixed message.

When students are taught how to look for patterns and reason logically in every activity along with the five representational strategies, the representations they create build understanding of the problem (and lead to a solution). In creating them, students are developing different *mental models* of the problem or phenomena. In rich, meaningful mathematical tasks, students may use several of these representations, moving from one to another to figure out more about the problem. Later they might draw on supplementary strategies (such as the three popular ones: guess and check, work backwards, simplify problem), but these cannot be used effectively unless one *understands* the problem. As students become more mathematically sophisticated, they are able to use more abstract and symbolic strategies (e.g., use proportional reasoning, apply a formula).

Obviously, thinking is critically important in reading and language as well as mathematics and problem solving. It is beyond the scope of this book, let alone this chapter, to adequately address cognition or all the related cognitive issues. Fortunately two wonderful volumes do a fine job of just that. They are *How People Learn* (Bransford, Brown, and Cocking 2000) and its companion, *How Students Learn* (Donovan and Bransford 2005), which uses three main principles to synthesize a tremendous amount of information about human cognition:

1. engaging prior understandings (using prior knowledge, confronting preconceptions and misconceptions)
2. organizing knowledge (developing a deep foundation of factual knowledge organized into coherent conceptual frameworks that reflect contexts for application and knowing when to use which information—referred to as conditionalized knowledge)
3. monitoring and reflecting on one's learning (developing metacognitive processes and self-regulatory capabilities)

HOW DO ALL THESE IDEAS FIT TOGETHER?

Fitting all these ideas together is not an easy task. May I phone a friend? In Figure I.1, I have simply placed the major ideas that need to be braided into three separate clouds. Imagine that each cloud was an overhead transparency that could be placed like a template on top of one of the other clouds. What connects to what?

LANGUAGE
listening speaking reading writing
READING COMPREHENSION STRATEGIES
connecting questioning visualizing inferring
predicting determining importance monitoring
MATHEMATICS CONTENT
numbers computation geometry measurement
data probability algebra
PROCESSES
connections reasoning
problem solving communications representations
REPRESENTATIONAL STRATEGIES
discussing using objects
re-enacting drawing pictures making lists or tables
COGNITIVE PRINCIPLES
engaging prior understanding organizing knowledge
monitoring and reflecting
PRACTICES
preexisting understandings when which knowledge can be used
create multiple representations of increasing abstraction
use multiple contexts for local concept development leading to
generalization scaffolding What if? / on-line thinking

FIGURE I.1

Place the template of thinking over the mathematics and one can see the importance of connecting to prior knowledge, activating relevant schemata, building organized knowledge, and developing self-awareness and monitoring as a learner. Place the template of language over the mathematics and one can imagine some wonderful opportunities for language—expressive, spoken, written, responsive, interactive, dynamic, mercurial, creative, playful, clarifying, metaphoric, defining, and so on. All of these can be a part of the mathematical experience of all students.

From among many ways to organize the braiding of these ideas, this book devotes six chapters to the reading comprehension strategies (asking questions, making connections, visualization, inferring and predicting, determining importance, and synthesizing). The seventh strategy (metacognitive monitoring) involves students becoming increasingly self-regulating when doing the other six strategies. In Chapter 1 I discuss how the strategy of asking questions is essential to metacognition. With these six big ideas to organize the chapters, I explain what each of these strategies contains and then braid in first the cognitive ideas and then the mathematics. No doubt more clever minds than mine would have organized this material differently and better. I am also certain that astute readers will note ideas and relationships that I have overlooked. That is inevitable and I look forward to hearing about them.

Knowing what works is good, but even better is knowing *why*. That is where theory comes in. Two books by mathematician Keith Devlin, *The Math Gene* (2000) and *The Math Instinct* (2005), and one written jointly by linguist George Lakoff and mathematician Raphael Nuñez, *Where Mathematics Comes From* (2000), suggest some rather important linkages between mathematical thinking and language. I could not do these books justice in a hundred pages, let alone one or two. Let me simply say that as the quotation at the beginning of this chapter stated, Devlin believes mathematical thinking is a specialized form of our human language facility. Both developed in humans in parallel tracks from the same source—the ability to reason abstractly in a "What if?" mode. "[M]athematicians think about mathematical objects and the mathematical relationships between them using the same mental faculties that the majority of people use to think about other people. . . . The overall mechanism is the same: a mental capacity developed to handle things in the real world is applied to an abstract world that the mind creates" (2000, 262–63).

Lakoff and Nuñez (2000) have a somewhat different nominee for this mechanism. Humans conceptualize abstract concepts in concrete terms by means of *conceptual metaphor,* "a cognitive mechanism for allowing us to reason about one kind of thing as if it were another. This means that metaphor is not simply a linguistic phenomenon, a mere figure of speech. Rather, it is a cognitive mechanism that belongs to the realm of thought" (p. 6). In fact, they see it as the principal cognitive mechanism: ". . . much of the 'abstraction' of higher mathematics is a consequence of the systematic layering of metaphor upon metaphor, often over the course of centuries" (p. 7).

If you want more theory, these authors will oblige. Bear in mind that they distinguish between arithmetic and mathematics. In our popular way of looking at learning, people often assume that language and mathematics are incompatible or just too different. Yet it seems each day, week, or year we discover ever more powerful and surprising human capabilities!

1 ASKING QUESTIONS

INQUIRING MINDS WANT TO KNOW

Children are natural inquirers; they have a million questions. Most have no trouble asking anyone just about anything. At age four my daughter asked me, "Do some men work alone?" I thought the question a bit odd, but simply told her that some do. After getting the same question four days in a row, I finally asked her why she wanted to know. She said that she just thought men would probably smell better if they wore cologne.

If I had allowed her question to initiate a discussion, instead of just trying to answer her and be done with it, I might have learned sooner what she was thinking. Language and thought go hand in hand (or perhaps, synapse in synapse). The point is a simple one: the more you know yourself and how your mind works, the better able you are to solve problems. The more we teachers can stimulate our students to be aware of their own thinking and monitor it, the better readers they will become and the better mathematical problem solvers.

About a dozen years ago a sixth-grade teacher had attended an intensive week-long summer math problem-solving course I taught in her district. When I ran into her in the supermarket a year later, she said she had enjoyed the course, had read *Mathwise,* and had elected to do her master's degree thesis on problem solving. In her research project, she had found that the most important things that she did with her kids were the suggestions on just two pages of the book. What helped them the most was developing their metacognitive awareness and monitoring through what we are now calling the *KWC*. This little device, which we'll get to shortly, is built around *students asking questions.*

The research literature on metacognition in reading is voluminous, far more extensive than in mathematics. All of the reading comprehension strategies involve metacognition in some way or to some extent. Proficient readers have learned how to use or to adapt various strategies to different purposes. They are able to use strategies to "fix up" or "repair meaning" when they don't understand what they are reading. They are quick to recognize when they have encountered some obstacle to meaning. They stop, go back to clarify, and reread to try to construct the meaning. They *think* and they *ask questions*. They try to determine the author's purpose. They "interrogate the text and the author." They do not passively "receive meaning." They aggressively grab it. They wonder about the choices the author made when composing. They realize that one question may lead to others. They recognize that their questions are important. They believe that their questions will help them understand.

They ask questions about what they read before, after, and right in the middle of reading. They do this to help them understand, to construct meaning, to discover new information, to clarify what is going on, to check their inferences, to help them visualize, and a dozen other purposes, all of which require thinking and metathinking.

Related to the metacognitive purposes for asking questions is the value of consciously surfacing one's prior knowledge so that relevant information can be brought to bear on the text (or problem at hand). In reading circles this is known as "activating relevant schemata." Although many educators and psychologists use that term, they do not all mean the same thing. For some, schema means the knowledge and how it is structured. For others, it means both the way the information is organized and how it is habitually used (like a script). For our purposes here let's just say that a schema is the accumulated background knowledge and experience about something and how aspects of it are connected or organized.

The extensive use of asking questions to activate schemata or prior knowledge in reading contrasts sharply with the typical mode of children working on math story problems in the intermediate grades or middle school. Contrary to educational naysayers, most kids are capable of learning. By the time they get to fourth or fifth grade, they have figured out that the name of the game is memorization and quick recall of facts. The rules of the game are guess-the-operation (and we're not talking about tonsillectomies) and don't make any arithmetic errors.

They passively glance at the words of the story problem and perhaps they might see a cue/key word. The questions they ask are not especially metacognitive: "Can we do this for homework?" "Are we getting graded on this?" Usually followed by, "I don't get it." And then the truly important question: "What do I do?" Ironically, that is the right question, but by asking the teacher, they are asking the wrong person. Instead of asking that of the teacher in the hopes that she will come over and show them what to do (and maybe even do it for them), they should be asking that of themselves. The earlier in their school lives that teachers encourage students to stop and think, "Okay. What do *I* do? And why?" the better off they'll be in mathematics.

My personal belief is that as students experience more and more schooling in math, and continually find teachers emphasizing the one right answer obtained quickly, they consciously or subconsciously think that asking questions is a sign of not knowing. Therefore much of their energy is invested in covering up when they do not know. When I began my pilgrimages to elementary classrooms, I recall being very surprised at how quite a few students in the first grade would "tighten up" during math time. These were very capable students who usually did quite well in math. They were very intent on getting the right answers and even more intent on not making a mistake.

I remember one girl who despite my reassurances that she could simply erase the one thing that she had missed (a trivial error), with tears starting to form in her eyes, insisted on throwing away the entire paper and doing everything again. Over my protestations she crumpled up her paper, threw it in the trash, took a clean sheet of paper and began again. In a third-grade classroom, a teacher handed back a math quiz and complimented the boy who had done the best in the class. He had a nearly perfect paper. But the key word here is "nearly." He looked at his paper, began to cry, and ran into the coat closet. He pulled the door shut and would not come out. He had made a mistake. Were the behaviors of these two children anomalies? Are these two children in therapy today? No, I don't think so on either question. Though they may be at the far end of the anxiety scale, they have plenty of company.

How can we encourage children to ask questions in math class? We can establish a climate of acceptance, where mistakes are a natural part of learning, where successive approximation is valued. The classroom should be a place where students have initial ideas, write drafts, and then think some more, rewite, revise. I do not mean that we don't tell the kid that he's made a mistake or that anyone gets credit for doing it wrong. I simply mean that we promise to *forgive* our students. We let them know that everybody makes mistakes in math. They just need to move on and practice. Use whatever metaphor you want to help them get the point.

ASKING QUESTIONS OF THEMSELVES, THE TEXT, AND THE AUTHOR

The reading comprehension strategies interact and are not independent of one another. There is no absolute sequence implied. The math problem solving of most students by fourth grade suffers from a profound lack of thinking and questioning. Therefore, we think it makes sense to nudge them strongly toward a habit of mind of asking questions as the first strategy to consider. Good questioning by the students will greatly facilitate the other strategies.

There are several ways of helping students learn how to ask questions that the reading folks have found very useful. In general, the teacher does the kinds of things described in the previous chapter on crafting lessons. The teacher thinks aloud as she reads and models her own use of a particular strategy with the whole class. She explains how she is using the strategy. Then the students try doing it in pairs or small groups with the teacher conferring with them. She may also meet with individuals to guide them. The objective is for all students to individually internalize the strategy.

Some teachers read a text out loud and articulate questions that make sense to them as adults. They often record such questions on large sheets of chart paper. Keene and Zimmermann (1997) saw how important their own modeling was. Children needed to see and hear how their teachers read, especially the way they worded the questions they asked themselves while reading (p. 109).

Keene and Zimmermann advise teachers to talk to the children about why readers pose questions, how questions help them comprehend more deeply, and how they use questions in other academic areas.

Debbie Miller (2002) reminds us that through such actions, teachers help students reflect on whether or not the answers to their questions can be found in the text or if they will need to infer the answer from the text, their background knowledge, or some outside source. We need to help students understand that many of the most intriguing questions are not explicitly answered in the text, but are left to the reader's interpretation (p. 140).

These same teacher-moves are echoed by Harvey and Goudvis (2000) and they are always on the lookout for books that generate an abundance of questions from the students. Sometimes they have students list their questions on large chart paper. Sometimes they help students categorize these questions, such as: ones that are answered in the text, ones that are answered from someone's background knowledge, ones whose answers can be inferred from the text, ones that can be answered by further discussion, ones that require further research, and ones that signal confusion.

Taffy Raphael (1982) uses QAR (Question—Answer—Relationship) to help elementary school students see the value of different kinds of questions. She helps them ask "right-there" questions (literal questions that can be answered by finding the answer directly in the text). These contrast with "think-and-search" questions that are inferential, requiring students to put various pieces of information together.

Distinguishing between the literal meaning and inferential meaning is critical in story problems and in fact all of mathematics. Just as some students do not read much of the text in a story problem, others read very selectively and make inferences (and assumptions) without realizing that they are doing so. When questioned, kids often say, "I just figured that . . ." But if they are aware that they are inferring something not literally in the text, then they can ask themselves, "Is this inference accurate?" If they're not aware, they can't ask. Although distinctions among types of inferential questions are fascinating, for our purposes here we can say that we are thrilled when students can distinguish between the literal and the inferential in math problem solving.

To understand literal meaning requires making connections between what is there on the page and what is in your head (prior knowledge). But to understand inferential meaning (drawing an accurate inference) you are making connections among several things in your head and then going beyond the literal; making a connection among those ideas in your prior knowledge to realize something that you didn't see until you made the "leap" of inference. Actually, social scientists distinguish between low inference (small leap) and high inference (a big jump from what is literally there). In Chapter 4 we will address drawing inferences as an important aspect of reading comprehension.

A very well-researched and proven strategy for engaging students in informational text is Reciprocal Teaching, developed by Palinscar and Brown (1984), in which the teacher models each of four different strategies (summarizing, questioning, clarifying, predicting). When the teacher feels that the students have sufficient experience with the strategies, she turns the teacher role over to the students. They must guide the class in the continued use of these strategies with the text. The students learn to ask good questions of the text.

Students learn to think more about who has written a text and how successful the writer was for them as readers through the strategy of "questioning the author" (Beck et al. 1997). According to Blachowicz and Ogle (2001, 116), students "develop a dialogue with the author, just as they would with a person talking with them face to face." Such questions may be: What was the author trying to say? What could the author have said instead? What was the intent of the author? What is the point of view? How could something be stated more clearly?

Donna Ogle developed the K-W-L strategy to help students become engaged in reading informational texts. It is a "frontloaded" strategy, activating schemata to make sure students have the knowledge they need *before* they read (Daniels and Bizar 2005, 41). Prior to reading, the teacher essentially asks the students, "What do you know?" about a particular topic. She models and guides students through a group process of "brainstorming together what they *know* (the K in K-W-L) about the topic. The teacher guides students to probe their knowledge statements and to find conflicting or partial statements" (Blachowicz and Ogle 2001, 108). The teacher writes what the students say without evaluation or correction in the first column (K) of a three-column chart on the chalkboard, overhead transparency, newsprint, or computer. The brainstorming encourages students to think about the topic, to activate their knowledge, and to develop their interest before reading. The teacher can encourage more student engagement by continuing the thinking: "Does anyone know anything [more] about. . . . Can anyone frame a question that may help us find out more?" (Blachowicz and Ogle 2001, 108).

Inevitably, during the brainstorming/discussion process some questions and uncertainties come up. The teacher writes these down under a second column (W) as they signify things they *want* to know. The teacher next has to decide if the students can think more deeply about the topic;

she may ask them to think of ways that experts might organize this information that they have generated. They might also look at the information in the K column and try to find connections. These are recorded also. Next the teacher asks them to come up with real questions for the W column—what we want to know. The teacher can readily extend the questions in this column by asking "I wonder" questions. The third column (L) is for students to summarize what they have *learned* after reading the text. In a follow-up to the K-W-L, K-W-L + (plus) was developed to give students more responsibility for reorganizing the ideas involved in the K-W-L. Graphic organizer sheets are given to students so that they can record the K, W, and L information as it emerges in the brainstorming and discussions. Or they might create semantic maps of the key information. Ogle believes that it is extremely important for retention that each student write down his or her own ideas before, during, and after reading. Also the writing helps them monitor their own thinking and learning. This writing task is a concrete way for all students to continue to participate in the thinking (Blachowicz and Ogle 2001, 111).

SECOND GRADERS USE THE KWC

For more than a dozen years teachers and I have been refining an approach to engage students in understanding word/story problems. Initially we tried applying Donna Ogle's KWL to story problems. Although that worked well sometimes, we realized that it was not a simple application that was needed, but rather a transformation of the KWL into a mathematical tool, one that dealt directly with the essence of mathematical problems. We now use a KWC that becomes a framework for other strategies as well.

Probably the best way to understand what the KWC is would be to experience it as a student would. Come with me into Betty Hogan's second-grade classroom, where as soon as you enter the room your eyes are splashed with bright, vibrant colors. Dozens of posters fill the walls, books overflow their bookcases. And twenty adorable children there reside. Most noticeable are the long, twisted strands of crepe paper hanging in great boughs from the ceiling. We are in the Amazon rain forest. Betty is a veteran teacher with a master's degree in reading and language. Math is her least favorite subject to teach. But she has taken some courses with me and is willing for us to team on a KWC with her second graders.

Betty arranged the twenty kids into pairs and explained that I was going to tell them a story and then they were going to do some mathematics based on the story. We pulled out a large sheet of chart paper that had been rolled up. We taped it up on the wall and covered it with another sheet, revealing only the title, "The Freight Trains."

We asked the class a series of questions. What is a freight train? Have you ever been on a train? What kind of train was it? What is freight? What do you think this short story is about? The kids were eager to tell us things that we asked and to volunteer personal experiences with trains. One offered, "Yesterday we had to wait for a very real long time for a train to go past." I asked about the train and the cars that the engine was pulling and how long did they have to wait for the train to go by. We spent five full minutes just talking about trains, and the students had quite a lot of information to share. Of course, they are second graders and they repeated themselves. Sometimes their answers were a little off the mark, and I thought I was in a movie of an Amelia Bedelia book. But they were definitely trying to answer our questions. As Betty had predicted, most did not know what freight was, but some did and we asked them to explain.

We continued to slide the paper down to reveal the first full sentence:

At the train station there are many different freight trains.

Then the second:

They carry 3 kinds of freight across the US: lumber, livestock, and vegetables.

We again asked the children questions about the trains. They took about ten minutes discussing the three different kinds of freight. We went through each sentence one at a time, asking questions to get the kids to clarify what was meant. Here is the whole problem.

The Freight Trains

At the train station there are many different freight trains.

They carry 3 kinds of freight across the US: lumber, livestock, and vegetables.

Each train has some lumber cars, some livestock cars, and some vegetables cars.

Each train always has 18 freight cars.

There are never more than 10 cars of one kind.

Freight cars that are the same are always connected together.

How many different ways of making trains with 18 cars can you find?

Those familiar with second graders and their level of cognitive abilities may believe this problem too difficult for second grade. Betty thought they would be challenged by it, stretched in a good way. They had done a few KWCs before. They had done multiple addends in math. It was May in the school year, so they were "mature" second graders.

Like the KWL, the KWC expects the students to express their ideas under three big headings.

K: What do I Know for sure?
W: What do I Want to do, figure out, find out?
C: Are there any special Conditions, rules or tricks I have to watch out for?

The students wrote down their thoughts and answers to the questions.

For the K, most copied parts of the original problem (despite Betty gently prodding them to "Say it your own way"). There were a few kids who rephrased information for the K column, such as: "Only 18 cars" or "10 cars per kind." In the W column sixteen of them simply copied the wording of the question asked by the problem. Four were a little different. Two wrote, "Find out how many different ways I can make a freight train." Two wrote, "Find out how many ways I can make 18."

In the C column (special Conditions), most of the students wrote down specific pieces of information from the problem, sometimes things they had mentioned in K, sometimes others things from the problem. Several were reminding themselves, "Remember, only use 18 cars." Sixteen of them referred to either using only 10 of each or 18 altogether. Four were a bit different. One wrote, "I need to remember to put the same

What do you know for sure?	What are you trying to find out?	Are there any special conditions? (Special rules? Tricks to watch out for? Things to remember?)
I know that each train has 18 cars. 10 cars of 1 kind lumber, livestolk and vegtabals	I'm trying to how many ways can you make 18	I need to each train never has more than 18 cars

Show how you solved the problem using pictures, numbers and words.

I learned that you can have niumbers lik 3 + 2 + 5 (3+2+5 = 10) and arange them and they will still = the same thing.

FIGURE 1.1

kind of cars together." Another wrote, "Not take all the same kind." Two girls who sat and worked together both wrote, "Don't do the same thing twice." See four student papers in Figures 1.1–1.4.

Betty handed out to each group 10 Unifix cubes of three different colors that would represent the three kinds of freight cars (green for vegetable cars, yellow for lumber cars, and red for livestock cars). Each group got one sheet of legal size paper with the outlines of four trains of 18 cars the same size as the Unifix cubes. The students took out markers, crayons, or colored pencils of those three colors and began. We encouraged them to make the train, check to make sure it met the conditions of the problem, then color it in. One child ignored these instructions and immediately colored in an all green (vegetable) train. I asked her to look at her KWC sheet and see if that was okay to do. She said, "Oh, oh!" and drew a big "X" over the train, and grabbed the Unfix cubes to make her next try.

The kids charged ahead famously, making trains that met the criteria, and soon asked for more sheets to make more trains. When most of the groups had completed two sheets, Betty told them to write under the train the number sentence that fit with the number of each kind that were

What do you know for sure?	What are you trying to find out?	Are there any special conditions? *(Special rules? Tricks to watch out for? Things to remember?)*
I know that	**I'm trying to**	**I need to**
18 cars	find out how many	only 18 cars
10 cars per kind	ways I can make	can't do the same
livestalk	18.	thing twice
vegtables		don't mix colors
lumber		use all three

Show how you solved the problem using pictures, numbers and words.

I learned that you can make a lot of thing out of eighteen. One of the ways is 6+6+6. I could go on and on and on. But I dont have time and room on this paper.

FIGURE 1.2

What do you know for sure?	What are you trying to find out?	Are there any special conditions? (Special rules? Tricks to watch out for? Things to remember?)
I know that •18 cars, •live stock vechicles and lumber goes across the U.S.A.	I'm trying to find out? how meny diffrint ways can it go, how much colors can it be?	I need to 18 in cars in a train. There is diffrint stuff in it. It is long.

Show how you solved the problem using pictures, numbers and words.

I lernd that there is diffrint ways to make a certinte Number or Color and much more,

FIGURE 1.3

in it. When they had done that, they were to cut out each separate train. They now had a color-picture record of their work.

I asked for all the kids who had made a train where there was the same number of each kind of cars to hold up that train. It was a 6 + 6 + 6 = 18 train. I took one of these from a student near me and taped it on to a sheet of newsprint. It had 6 green cars on the left, 6 brown in the middle, and 6 red on the right. I asked if any one else had exactly this train. Several said yes. I asked them hold the train up and asked if these were the same as the one we had just put on the chart. Several children immediately said no and their classmates were puzzled.

I asked the students holding up 6-6-6 trains to compare and to contrast their train with the one on the chart, "Tell us what is the same and what is different." Several kids gave partial answers; this was tricky for them. They did explain eventually that the numbers were all the same but the colors from left to right were different. Betty told them that we could say that the "order" of the colors was different. I asked them to bring all the 6-6-6s forward and we taped them up. I asked them to figure out how many different trains we had on the chart. They checked carefully and found only six: (B, R, G); (B, G, R); (R, G, B); (R, B, G); (G, B, R); (G, R B). I then suggested that if the order of the colors (kinds of cars) does not matter, we could say these are all from the same "family"—the 6-6-6 family.

Then I asked if anyone had found a 5-6-7 train and we went through much the same "debriefing" as with the 6-6-6s, comparing and contrast-

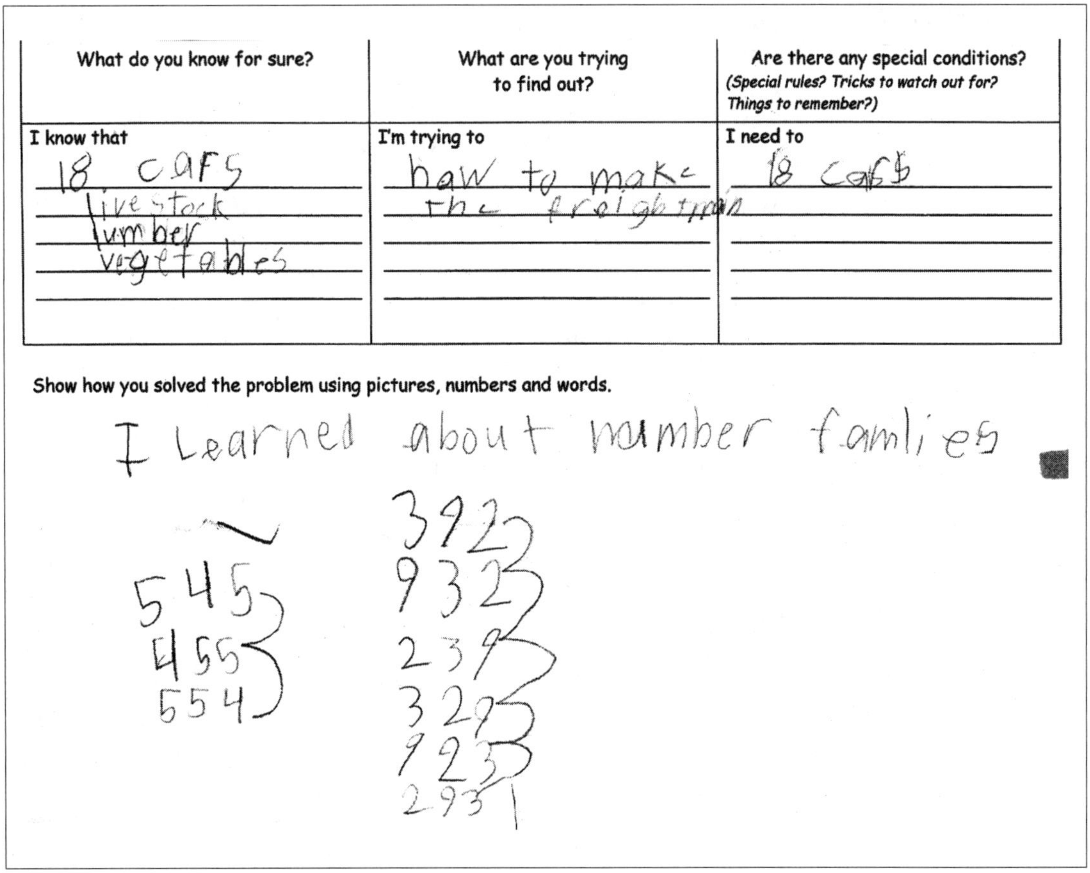

What do you know for sure?	What are you trying to find out?	Are there any special conditions? *(Special rules? Tricks to watch out for? Things to remember?)*
I know that	I'm trying to	I need to
18 cars livestock lumber vegetables	how to make the freight train	18 cars

Show how you solved the problem using pictures, numbers and words.

I Learned about number famlies

545
455
554

392
932
239
329
923
293

FIGURE 1.4

ing trains. This time I suggested that the order of the colors and the order of the numbers really does not matter; we can say these are all from the same family. We talked about it in terms of the number sentences. Betty reminded them that they could add together any of the addends and then add the third one and always get the same sum. I asked, "If we ignore colors and just look at the number sentences, how many members are in this family?" They found six: (5, 6, 7); (5, 7, 6); (6, 5, 7); (6, 7, 5); (7, 5, 6); (7, 6, 5). We decided that they were all in the same family. I told them that mathematicians name this family the 5-6-7 family, listing the numbers in order.

I then told them that we were going to try to determine what the different families were. How many were there? And what were they? At this point a girl who was sitting near me came over to me and very quietly asked, "Do you mean we are supposed to find all the combinations?" I whispered yes to her.

We asked them to save their paper trains and the next day Betty continued to work on finding all the families (combinations) with them.

DEBRIEFING THE ACTIVITY

What follows are my comments on why Betty and I did what we did. She put them into small groups according to her perception about who would work well together on this task. I have done this activity with second graders before and was able to describe the typical behavior and what I hoped to see. The small groups, in this case pairs, would give the students maximum opportunities to talk about their conceptions of the problem. The materials and their use in creating representations (i.e., the Unifix cubes, the paper strips, and the crayons, markers, colored pencils) could be shared more easily with two rather than three students.

We told them that we would read a story aloud and they could read along with us on the newsprint. Then they'd have to answer some questions about it, math questions. They were fine with that. Since math educators call them "story" problems, I give my problems a title. Therefore, the students' first encounter with the problem had the title of "The Freight Trains." By asking them to think about the meaning of the title, we were treating this experience like one of their reading activities, which, if positive, would carry over into the math activity. They had lots to say and many experiences to relate to this reading. They were motivated; they had bought in.

When we introduce the KWC to kids, it is not just to stimulate engagement (although that is valuable). They need to activate the schemata they have that will help them with the problem. For instance, we wanted them to imagine trains with an engine car pulling a great many freight cars. As we slid the paper down to reveal each sentence separately, we posed questions and also asked the kids to explain their responses. When teachers introduce the KWC they often make an overhead transparency of the problem, separating each sentence on different lines. Some kids get overwhelmed by the text of an entire problem. The overhead transparency allows the kids to focus on just one sentence at a time as the teacher covers what comes next.

After we had read and talked through the entire problem, they began to write information on the graphic organizer. Betty had added the second row of "prompts" to the KWC questions: "I know that . . . ," "I'm trying to . . . ," and "I need to . . ." She also added the italicized prompts in the first row under C (*Special rules? Tricks to watch out for? Things to remember?*). I have encouraged teachers to work with their classes to modify wording of the KWC questions in ways that will help their kids.

Writing things down under K is not a problem for kids, except when there is an abundance of information and they have not yet worked with the strategy for determining the most important information. Unlike real-life problems, school-math problems come with a question, usually at the very end. Students know this text structure, and they are on the lookout for a question or a question mark. They have no trouble discerning the W and what to enter onto their sheet. The C is always tricky and this case was no exception.

In mathematical problem solving we have long had "givens, the goal, and the constraints." I will discuss in Chapter 5 how some believe that math story problems are a genre and we will examine alternatives to this genre. "Givens" have been established by the author of the story problem. In technical terms, one is in a "given state" and the problem solver is to figure out/find out how to get to the "goal state." The KWC asks the question, What do I **K**now for sure? so that students will think about the problem and generate the givens. Then the KWC asks, what do I **W**ant to find out or figure out?

Constraints are special conditions, often limitations on what the problem solver/mathematician can do, or what possible values are allowed. These constraints are often the most difficult of the three things to discern. Sometimes they involve drawing an inference or making an assumption. Sometimes they are only obvious to an expert in the context of the problem and hard for a novice to see because they are only implied. On the other hand, sometimes students will generate all the necessary information in the problem, including the constraints, while looking for the K. Students and teachers usually need some examples of what we mean by C.

In the freight train problem the students had the opportunity of oral discussion as a whole group with the teacher modeling the thinking that goes on when we try to answer the three questions: What do you know for sure? What are you trying to find out? Are there any special conditions? They read through each of the sentences of the story one at a time as a class and then they wrote down their answers on their graphic organizer.

However, five of the twenty kids did not mention that each train had three different kinds of cars. Sometimes, kids will pick up a piece of information like that under C rather than K, but in this case they just did not mention it anywhere on their papers. However, all five students did *make* trains that had three different kinds and/or three different colors. They "knew" to do so. These second graders were learning how to write down information. The physical representation of the trains made it easy to realize the need for three colors.

In this problem we scaffolded the multiple representations and helped the kids go back and forth between them. The term *scaffolding* has several meanings. For some it means making sure that the task is challenging, but within their capabilities; I'd say, pitched just right to make them have to stretch to do it. Scaffolding can also mean that the teacher provides some process, structure, or device (tangible materials or a good question to prompt thinking) that enables the students to actually do the task. Scaffolding does not necessarily make the problem easier, and the teacher does not do the work for students or show them how to do it. Like scaffolding along the side of a building that enables the painter to safely work on the outside wall, the scaffolding does not do the work. It enables the person to do it.

In the freight train problem we provided some scaffolding by requiring that: (1) they use oral and written language to describe the situation; (2) they physically make each train, then place it on the paper to check that they had 18; and (3) they had to make a color-picture record of each train. Finally, they counted the squares and wrote number sentences/equations with three addends that symbolically represented what they had done.

This progression of representations was moving from concrete to abstract: language and object (most concrete) to picture to symbols (most abstract). In the final stage, which began on day one and continued into day two, the students found different number families and made a table of them (used an abstract representation to look for patterns). The girl who recognized that we were looking for combinations might have been able to handle a more abstract version of the problem from the beginning. "What are all the combinations of three different addends that sum to 18 with the constraint that none can be greater than 10?"

The girl's insightful question brings up a related issue. There are general questions that kids can ask themselves that would fit with virtually any story problem (e.g., the three KWC questions). There are also questions that are very context dependent. For example, in the freight train problem kids often ask, "Can we alternate the colors like stripes?" Although it does not literally say "alternating colors is prohibited," the prohibition is implied and kids should realize that this is an inference they should have drawn from the statement, "Freight cars that are the same kind are always connected together." We will deal with inferences in a subsequent chapter. Here simply note that to a child who asked about alternating colors, we might ask things like, "What does the problem actually say?" "What do you think that means?" "Are you sure?" "Are you making an inference?" Asking questions keeps their thinking going. When we answer definitively, we give them permission to stop thinking.

Another kind of question is more *content* or *concept* dependent. The girl asked about "combinations," a very slippery concept when approached in the abstract. When kids study the concept of combinations (versus permutations), they use the KWC but we also help them learn to ask themselves several critical questions that are strictly related to the concept.

> *How many different combinations did you find?*
> *Did you check for duplicates/repeats? How?*
> *Did you find all the combinations?*
>
> And the really important question is:
>
> ***How do you know when you've found them all?***

There are many different directions that we could have gone with Betty's second graders once they had generated a good number of trains with number sentences. For instance, this problem can be a very nice basis for the associative and commutative properties of addition. It can help students see the difference between combinations and permutations (where order does matter). A longer discussion of what makes two things "different" might have been profitable. We might have used the paper trains to show the patterns as the numbers of each color were systematically changed in order, which can be a precursor to an organized list—keep one color the same number (start with the most it can be) and change the other two (e.g., 10, 7, 1; 10, 6, 2; and so on). When you place the paper trains side by side in that order the visual impact is considerable.

We chose to focus on making sure that the children were not overwhelmed by the sheer number of trains they had made. We wanted them to have a way of grouping them to be a more manageable number. This also served to lay a foundation for other ideas Betty would address later, such as associative and commutative properties. Just as important, they were developing their cognitive and metacognitive processes. They were learning how to attack problems by breaking them down analytically, by translating between representations they had created, and by talking through with teammates what was going on.

In the KWC, the teacher models for the whole class the process of asking herself the three critical questions. Then the teacher leads the whole class in asking the questions. Then the students work in small groups and ask each other those questions. Finally, each individual student should internalize these questions and use them when solving problems alone (on a test, at home, by oneself).

FRONTLOADING TO UNDERSTAND THE PROBLEM

In the introduction I mentioned George Polya, the grandfather of problem solving. He saw problem solving in four phases:

1. understanding the problem
2. developing a plan/considering various problem-solving strategies
3. implementing a strategy or plan
4. looking back to see if your answer makes sense

For Polya and many others who write on problem solving, the first phase is critically important and deserves to have significant time devoted to it—perhaps up to 75 percent of the time available. Does this sound excessive? Have you ever had a project given to you that was ill-defined or that made you initially uncertain how to do it? That would be a problem. Or have you ever worked on a group project that was not structured, where the participants had to make a lot of decisions about what to do and how to do it? In both these cases, spending initial time on *task definition*—understanding exactly what you have to do—is the smart way to proceed. If one "frontloads" the discussion to gain clarity on the task, it is time well spent because there is always danger in *assuming* one knows what is the problem and charging ahead to solve what was *not* the problem.

The KWC is designed to encourage students to consciously attend to understanding the problem. It is the best device we have found to help with the understanding phase. It requires kids to stop and think, to get their minds around the problem. It is quite versatile and can be used with many different kinds of problems. The reading folks use the expression "activating relevant schemata," in which a reader brings to conscious awareness the prior knowledge that is related to the text at hand. If a student, even a very capable math student, goes charging ahead without really thinking about all elements of the story problem, there is a high probability of misreading or misunderstanding and operating in error. Each of the questions in the KWC asks the students to focus attention on a somewhat different but related part of the problem.

The students use the KWC to sort out basic factual information. In so doing, they must read the problem and think about the information. The teacher may ask them to jot down some notes, or to do it orally for the whole class, and she records the facts on the chalkboard. Although this recording may sound tedious, it establishes that the teacher believes it is important for the students to actively think about what they know to be true. They get the message that this is an important step. Notice that they cannot tell what facts are relevant or important until they have read or seen the question. I'll have more to say about this in Chapter 5. The key idea here is that they read carefully, attending to any information. As we saw in the freight train problem, while they are developing their ability in problem solving, the teacher may require them to consider only one sentence at a time by having the problem on an overhead transparency and by displaying a single sentence to be understood.

After students have read the question, they do the W— What are we trying to find out or prove? They should restate the problem in their own words. Next they must consider the special conditions. For some problems these are very real constraints on the possible values. In other cases, the information is so evident that students glean all they could possibly get from simply doing the K phase. Nevertheless, thinking about possible C statements keeps them thinking. It slows down the impulsive students who like to charge on ahead, willy-nilly, and gets them to be more careful and thoughtful. For those who need more guidance in problem solving, it provides a structure.

HOW THE K AND THE C WORK TOGETHER

The interplay of the K and the C can be seen in a different kind of problem done in the third-grade classroom of Beverly Kiss in Deerfield, Illinois, a number of years ago. We were working on fractions and gave the students what we called the Canteen Problem. As usual we had them ask the KWC questions. The problem was:

> A small plane carrying three people makes a forced landing in the desert. The people decide to split up and go in three different directions in search of an oasis. They agree to divide equally the food and water they have, which includes 15 identical canteens, 5 full of water, 5 half-full of water, and 5 empty. They will want to take the empty canteens with them in case they find an oasis. How can they equally divide the water and the canteens among themselves?

Some kids jumped right in with the KWC. Others seemed perplexed and were hesitant to volunteer K information. They finally asked some questions like, "How much money do they have with them?" "Will the people just follow the highway? Maybe a car will stop for them." Schemata were being activated all right, but not what Bev and I expected. By discussing the problem, their schema for "oasis" surfaced; it was a rest stop on the highway with a Baskin-Robbins and a Wendy's. They lived near an interstate highway with the Deerfield Oasis. The value of activating relevant schemata cannot be overestimated. Often students have in their heads accurate and useful information relevant to a problem, but fail to access it or to connect it to the problem at hand. Good problems, rich in mathematical ideas, often reside in specific contexts or real-life situations. After this incident, we started calling this problem "Meet Me at the Oasis," and before reading the problem, we asked the kids to tell us what they thought the story would be about. The question of what is an oasis always seems to pop up. I have shown a five-minute clip from a video of the movie *Jewel of the Nile* showing actor Danny DeVito cavorting with Sufis at the local oasis. That has started a lively dialogue about oases!

There are always some students who need the C with this problem. The problem includes explicit statements about dividing the canteens, even the empty ones. And it gives an explanation of why. Nevertheless, there are always a few students who do not catch this special condition or constraint. They try to divide only the water. Seriously considering the C question helps most students slow down, go back, read and reread, and catch the other idea. Once the students understand the problem and want to try solving it, we suggest drawing a picture. Some students quickly say, "Just pour half of each full canteen into an empty one. Then you'll have 15 half-full canteens and each person can take 5 of them."

When they tell me this, I respond, "How will you know you have exactly half?" Or "You don't want to pour because you might spill or some water might evaporate. Is there a way to solve this problem without pouring anything?" [A simple solution is for one person to take 2 full, 2 empty, and 1 half full—which is 5 of the 15 canteens, and one-third of the water; a second person does exactly the same thing; that will leave for the third person 5 canteens, each of which has the same total amount of water. They start with FFFFF HHHHH EEEEE (full, half, and empty). The use of manipulatives shows this relationship readily. {F F H E E } {F F H E E} or {F H H H E}.

SURFACING PRIOR KNOWLEDGE

A different type of problem illustrates a variation in using the KWC. In the Eight Shapes Problem, pairs of students (fifth grade and up) are given oaktag cutout versions of the shapes in Figure 1.5. The KWC begins with the W: "What do you know for sure about these shapes?" The question is often followed with, "What are the 'attributes' (or features, characteristics, properties) of these eight shapes?" I tell the kids, "I just gave you some manipulatives. Take a close look at them." Either I write down the information they share on the chalkboard or they write it on their graphic organizers. I will sometimes ask, "How many different shapes do you have?" There are only four different shapes, one pair of each. The key concept is congruence. The kids can discern congruent shapes by laying one on top of another.

Depending on grade level and experience, the students may fill the chalkboard with their prior knowledge. Thus, this little problem may be quite a valuable diagnostic activity. If they do not mention a key attribute that I want them to surface for this activity, I might ask, "What can you tell me about the corners (angles, vertices) of these shapes?" Usually most will realize that all the shapes have one square corner (some say right angle,

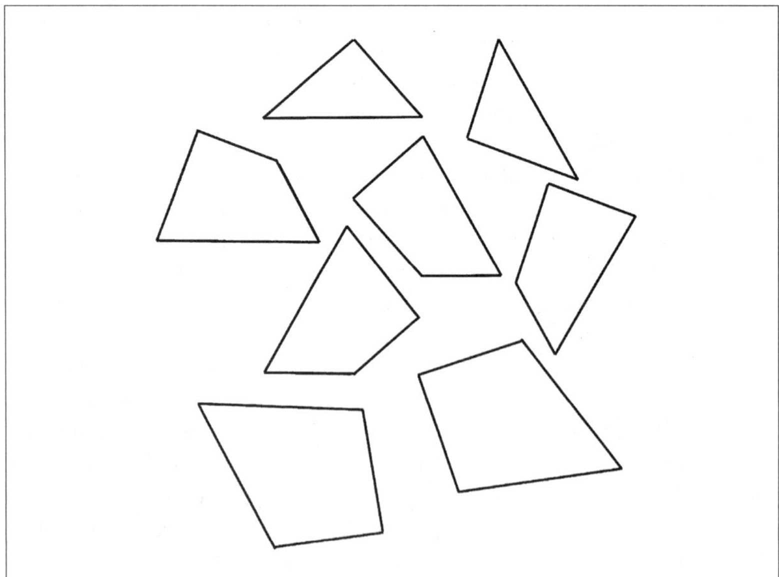

FIGURE 1.5

some say 90-degree angle). With continued questioning the teacher can get a feel for what the students understand about angles and degrees.

There are four different shapes; three are quadrilaterals, of no special name. The fourth shape is a triangle that has one right angle (and is called a right triangle). I ask them, "How would we prove that each shape has a right angle?" They often lay the shapes on top of each other. To this I respond, "That shows me that the angles are congruent, they are the same. But are they right angles?"

The students use various means to compare the four corners to a standard they "know" is a right angle, such as a piece of paper. Others stand two shapes next to one another on a table top with right angles on the table. Or they place the four quadrilaterals down on the table and move four alleged right angles together at a common point. If the four are equal and completely encircle the point (covering the full 360 degrees), all are 90-degree angles. Now comes the question that makes this a problem.

> Can you use these eight shapes to make a square from some and an equilateral triangle out of the others? And the two shapes must have the same area.

When we ask the kids the W question: What do I **W**ant to do, to figure out, to find out? They readily say, make a square and an equilateral triangle. But there are always some (generally less than a third of the class) who ask, "Can we make a square with all eight pieces?" Then we ask them the C question: "Are there any special conditions here?" The problem is not simply asking for a square and an equilateral triangle. The constraint is that they must be of equal area. How can one guarantee that the two shapes have equal area?

Notice that the critical piece of information that needs to be activated and connected to the problem is all about congruence. If each of these four pieces is congruent to these other four pieces, then any polygon you make with the first four MUST have the same area as any polygon made with the other four shapes. If this critical concept does not surface/emerge when discussing the K, the students are rarely able to solve this problem.

The discussion about the right angles of the four shapes frequently leads students to place the four right angles at the four approximate corners and then interchange them or turn them over until they fit nicely together as a square. See Figure 1.6. However, most kids, in fact most adults, have trouble making the equilateral triangle. While discussing the K, some students activate potentially useful triangle schemata: an equilateral triangle has three 60-degree angles. Then after placing the four right angles in the four corners to help them make the square, they try to find three 60-degree angles, a marvelous use of prior knowledge.

By comparing the angles of shapes (laying them on top of one another) they find that the three quadrilaterals each have identical acute

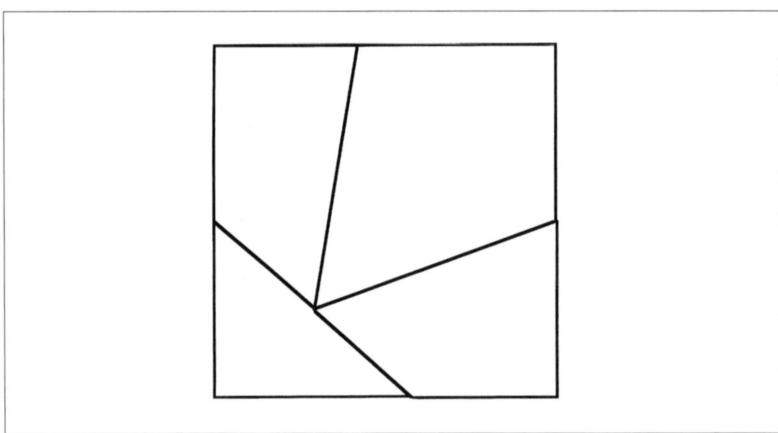

FIGURE 1.6

angles. But are they each 60 degrees? When placed side by side, the three angles will form a straight line against a ruler or piece of paper (three 60s make 180 degrees, a straight line). If some students are having difficulty making the triangle, we provide a little scaffolding in the form of a blackline border of the triangle. See Figure 1.7.

USING REAL-LIFE PROBLEMS: INTERROGATE THE AUTHOR

More and more in recent years, students are asked to work on real problems that are quite different from the often-contrived problems of school math. Some educators applaud this trend and others deride it. In a sense there are two competing philosophies here. One says that children learn mathematics incrementally by working with one piece of the puzzle at a time. And these pieces cannot be as messy as real life. They say that students get too confused by the complexities of real-life situations; there are too many concepts impinging all at once on the children. After they have mastered the skills or understood the concepts from easier, simplified cases, they can transfer their knowledge to other more complex ones and apply their new knowledge to real-life situations. This point of view sounds reasonable, but the transfer of learning from one setting to another is not borne out by research.

The viewpoint that is substantiated by research on transfer is that if students are to use mathematical knowledge in certain situations in their lives, they need to have some experiences that approximate the real setting. If well constructed, those simulations of real situations can not only facilitate subsequent transfers, they can greatly enhance a student's ability to build *initial* understanding. So instead of boiling down the learning of computation to its "naked numbers" that refer to nothing and represent nothing, computation concepts and procedures can be better

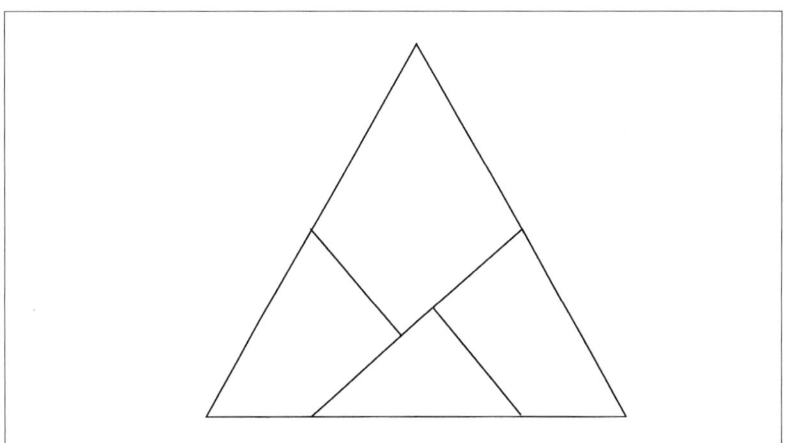

FIGURE 1.7

learned in a context, filled with meaning, where the numbers refer to comprehensible things. Here is an example.

A number of years ago I spotted a data table that I really found fascinating. Ever since, I do a yearly update on the figures to keep it fresh for students. The data table may be seen in Figure 1.8. What do you see?

I let them suggest things. I don't write anything down on the board. I just listen. If no one asks the key questions that I have written on page 36, I will ask the students to consider and respond themselves.

GALLONS OF SOFT DRINKS SOLD IN THE UNITED STATES IN ONE YEAR

	gallons per person		**gallons per person**		**gallons per person**		**gallons per person**
Alabama	59.62	Indiana	46.66	Nebraska	53.30	S. Carolina	63.34
Alaska	47.79	Iowa	46.98	Nevada	55.89	South Dakota	41.31
Arizona	47.14	Kansas	58.16	New Hamp.	46.01	Tennessee	58.97
Arkansas	53.95	Kentucky	57.19	New Jersey	46.49	Texas	58.16
California	52.16	Louisiana	59.45	New Mexico	46.49	Utah	45.36
Colorado	48.60	Maine	47.30	New York	51.35	Vermont	43.09
Connecticut	50.71	Maryland	56.54	N. Carolina	64.64	Virginia	62.05
Delaware	52.65	Mass.	51.19	North Dakota	37.58	Wash. D.C.	58.32
Florida	64.31	Michigan	54.11	Ohio	55.24	Washington	40.66
Georgia	63.83	Minnesota	53.46	Oklahoma	50.22	West Virginia	55.40
Hawaii	50.71	Mississippi	61.88	Oregon	38.56	Wisconsin	46.66
Idaho	33.53	Missouri	58.97	Pennsylvania	42.93	Wyoming	33.37
Illinois	53.78	Montana	37.75	Rhode Island	46.17		

FIGURE 1.8

What is a soft drink?
What is the unit of data in the table?
How was it collected?
What was the raw data? What would it look like?
Who collected this data? Who would want this data collected?
Why would they want it? What would they do with this information?
WHAT DO YOU KNOW FOR SURE?

When students collect their own data, especially when they have designed their own study, they can readily answer these questions. These are the *who, what, were, when*, and *why* questions of reporters from Lois Lane to Bob Woodward and Carl Bernstein. However, when someone else has collected and analyzed the data and then gone to the trouble of creating a very particular representation, it is wise to ask yet another question: *What are they trying to sell me?* We are bombarded daily with data tables, charts, diagrams, and graphs in newspapers and all forms of media. If ever there were a time in mathematics to "determine the author's purpose" or "interrogate the author," this is it. The World Wide Web has created an almost instant capability to electronically gather truly vast amounts of data. So let's take these questions and ruthlessly interrogate someone about the soft drink data. But who? How? The first step is the critical awareness of the need to ask these questions. Next students have to do some digging. Usually there is some kind of fine print somewhere that will give a relentless interrogator some answers.

What is a soft drink? Without the KWC, or some device to ask questions, students will not even think twice; they'll go charging ahead unwittingly assuming that soft drinks mean "soda pop." However, when asked they will debate this question heatedly. Questions about sugar, carbonation, sugar substitutes abound. They will discuss popular fruit drinks, boutique ice tea, and designer water. I have had a student say simply it is the opposite of hard drinks. It is the liquids you put into mixed drinks with the hard liquor. The student's father was a bartender. And that is just about accurate for these data. While mostly consisting of soda pop, soft drink also includes carbonated water and quinine water.

What is the unit of data in the table? Gallons of soft drinks. But note that the table also says "sold" in the United States in one year. It does not say *consumed*. It also says "gallons per person." I ask the kids, "What does this mean?" How did they (whoever "they" are) calculate the statistic of 53.78 gallons of soft drink per person sold in Illinois in one year? What unfolds is a great discussion about statistical concepts and procedures embedded in a real (and admittedly messy) context. Some kids think that this must be from a survey. Perhaps a random sample of Illinoisans. But who buys soft drinks by the gallon? Not individuals, except those who get the "Big Binge" at the local speedy-mart. The source of data was not a survey.

The unit of gallons is a clue to how the data was collected. It came from beverage distributors who obviously keep very accurate records of their sales. A trade periodical for beverage distributors compiled the raw data. With more discussion the students themselves suggest that the magazine collected data from beverage distributors and added up all the gallons of soft drinks sold in one year and then divided by the number of people in the state: gallons per person. So it is an average, the mean.

But wait, some kid says. That isn't fair. My baby brother does not drink any soft drinks and neither does my grandmother! Another fascinating debate occurs among the fifth graders about the concept of mean, what it means in this context, and the procedure for calculating it. They realize that if some people neither buy nor drink soft drinks then there must be people who drink more than 53.78 gallons per year. Frequently two things emerge: (1) the students decide to collect their own data on beverage consumption and (2) someone asks, "How many cans of soda pop is 53.78 gallons? Is that a lot for a year?"

Now imagine if the teacher had asked the kids to open their textbooks to page 114 and do problem 7 which reads, *"If the consumption of soft drinks in Illinois last year was 53.78 gallons per person, how many 12-ounce cans would that be?"* Presented with this cold problem, most students would yawn. But in the context of the debates about the data, this question arose naturally and meaningfully. The kids are intensely motivated to figure out the answer. There are two ways the kids go after this question. If a gallon is 128 ounces, then 53.78 gallons is 6,883.84 ounces, which when divided by 12 (12-ounce cans) is about 574 cans over the year, between 1 and 2 cans per day. If divided by 20 as in a 20-ounce bottle, it is 344 over the year, less than one bottle a day.

The second way is an estimate. Some students reason that a gallon is about 10 cans or 6 bottles (both are low estimates). And each of those 54 gallons (rounding up a little) would hold 10 cans (or 6 bottles); then to multiply 10 times 54 would give us about 540 cans per year (or 6 times 54 would be 324 bottles).

By fifth or sixth grade students are generally able to deal with the realities of numerical information like the soft drink data. Furthermore they are more motivated to attend, reason, and persevere when the context and content are meaningful. With a good structure for problem solving and a teacher helping them ask questions and make connections, the students can succeed and can understand.

POINTS TO PONDER

Research has found that asking questions can help students develop metacognitive awareness and monitoring of one's thinking while working on a task. However, efforts to break down awareness and monitoring into subcomponents of metacognition in reading comprehension have not obtained consistent results. Meanwhile, many math folks have trouble separating metacognition from cognition. They see cognition including self-regulating awareness and "executive control." Most agree that better problem solving comes when students ask themselves questions about

- the conditions, limitations, and constraints
- if there is sufficient information to get an answer
- if there is one answer, more than one, or no answer
- different ways to represent a problem
- if what you are doing makes sense
- what you have done or where you have been already ("Am I making progress?")
- if answers are reasonable

Using the KWC is an excellent systematic way to accomplish this needed process.

As you plan for your kids to do problem solving, there are several critically important things for you to consider. In the next section you will see some considerations related to the material in this chapter. By the term *consider* (or *consideration*) I mean things that you may need to attend to or deal with. They are not prescriptions for how to do things. They are more like, "I need to check to see if I need to address this issue." There are many different ways to address these considerations, and I have given you some suggestions on how I address them. However, you always will modify and adapt anyone else's ideas to fit your own personality, your teaching style, your school circumstances, and the particular students you have.

In this chapter I have begun to show the *Braid Model of Problem Solving* by describing the KWC. Subsequent chapters will add more features to the model. At the ends of Chapters 2 through 4, I will provide a cumulative picture of the model as it becomes more elaborate and also will offer additional considerations in planning. Therefore, you will have a full model and complete set of considerations by the end of Chapter 4 that you can use in thinking about the problems presented in Chapters 5 and 6.

CONSIDERATIONS IN PLANNING FOR PROBLEM SOLVING

Situation

Big Ideas, Enduring Understandings, and Essential Concepts

What is the concept that I want the students to understand?
To what prior knowledge should we try to connect?
Are there different models of the concept?

Should I break down the concept into its underlying ideas?
Is there a sequence of understandings that the students need to have?
What other mathematical concepts are related?

Authentic Experiences

What are the different real-life situations or contexts in which students would encounter the concept?
Will they see it in science or social studies?
How can I vary the contexts to build up a more generalized understanding?
What version of this situation can I present to start them thinking about the concept?
What questions can I ask to intrigue them and initiate problem solving?

2 MAKING CONNECTIONS

"There are more things in heaven and earth, Horatio,
Than are dreamt of in your philosophy."
—William Shakespeare, *Hamlet*, act 1, scene 5

THE NATURE AND FUNCTION OF CONCEPTS

Even a cursory glance at the research and theory in the areas of reading, mathematics, and thinking would reveal the central role of *connections* in each. Connections build conceptual understanding. The more and the stronger the connections are among related ideas, the deeper and richer the understanding of a concept. There are dozens of different psychological theories concerning the connections that humans make. Rather than trying to summarize, compare, and contrast the different theories, I want to briefly address several ideas that are central to the braiding of language, thinking, and mathematics. After all, the purpose of braiding is to make connections. One difficulty in talking about these ideas is the terminology used by various psychologists and educators.

Lest you think I'm exaggerating, psychologists use terms (actually concepts) such as *interiorization*, *condensation*, *reification*, and dozens of others to explain human development and understanding of concepts. Teachers don't need to make all the excruciating distinctions that psychologists do in their books and articles for scholarly journals. What is the difference between *reflective abstraction* and *reflected abstraction*? Instead of answering, let's examine what concepts are and why they are so important.

Concepts are abstract ideas organizing a lot of smaller bits of information (facts) in a somewhat hierarchical fashion. We can see a set of concepts, subsumed under a macroconcept (an even bigger idea). For example, in language arts we encounter concepts such as hyperbole, synecdoche, metaphor, or metonymy that are examples of a bigger concept, *figures of speech*. Each of these fairly abstract ideas explains particular expressions encountered in literature or poetry. In mathematics, the science of patterns, we have branches of mathematics devoted to the study of specific types of patterns such as shape, dimension, change, uncertainty, and quantity. These are certainly big ideas or macroconcepts that can organize a lot of information. Subordinate to quantity we'd find the concept of multiplication, one that subsumes a great many facts.

Consulting the dictionary for the definition (*denotative* meaning) of a concept is a lot like eating non-fat plain yogurt. Concepts are rich and complex, filled with deeper *connotative* meaning. I get nervous when someone talks about students needing to "know" particular terms or vocabulary words. I don't want kids to memorize a definition. I want their lives enriched by deeply experiencing the *context* that surrounds the concept. For instance, the term *revolution* certainly should be defined, but when we examine the "revolutions" in some of the English colonies in North America in 1776, in France in 1789, and in Russia in 1917, these examples in their rich contexts breathe life into the concept. The same issue of rich, meaningful concepts applies to mathematics. How do third graders conceive of multiplication? Something you do to make the amount you've got get bigger? If so, there may be a real problem when the student encounters multiplying by fractions or decimals that are less than one. The product is smaller than the multiplier and mutliplicand (now you don't hear that word every day!). The concept of multiplication and its relationship to division continues to grow more complex each year for about six years as the operation is performed with different kinds of numbers, then with variables, with matrices, with vectors, and so forth. The concept of multiplication can grow richer and more elaborate and more abstract as you experience it in different contexts.

Conceptual understanding is not like an on-off light switch: you don't *understand* a concept in an all-or-nothing fashion. Initially we grasp some aspect of the concept and build upon it, adding and elaborating our understanding. I like to think of it as building a snowman. First, you find some good snow for making a snowman—not too wet and slushy, not too dry and powdery. You make a snowball with your hands and roll it in some good snow. The ball gains size as more snow sticks to it. You do this to make a big sturdy ball of snow for the foundation. You repeat this process for other parts of the snowman. But you must continue to roll it in the right kind of snow; the wrong snow, or worse, rolling it on grass, will not accumulate more snow. In general, the more connections of the right kind, the more examples in different but relevant contexts, the more elaborate the networks of ideas and relationships—the deeper, richer, more generalized, and more abstract is our understanding of a concept.

SCHEMA THEORY, THE FOUNDATION OF READING COMPREHENSION

Since the 1980s most reading researchers have found schema theory to have extraordinary power in explaining how proficient readers understand text, store their knowledge, and remember what they have read and learned. "Teaching children which thinking strategies are used by proficient readers and helping them use those strategies independently is the core of teaching reading" (Keene and Zimmermannn 1997, 53). Harvey and Goudvis (2000) consider the making of appropriate connections of paramount importance and make it the launching point in their approach. They use the apt metaphor, "building bridges from the new to the known" (p. 67). All of their examples of stories are designed to help kids use their personal and collective experience to enhance understanding.

There are several related devices used by the Public Education Business Coalition (PEBC) folks from Denver. The major device is *explicit modeling* of making connections while you read. Starting with young children (beginning readers), they urge teachers to read aloud to the kids, occasionally stopping and telling the kids what they are thinking.

Debbie Miller does extensive "Think Alouds" with her second graders. For her, preplanning is essential. Simply grabbing a book and reading it aloud to children, assuming you will spontaneously come up with wonderful connections, won't work. "Explicit modeling requires thoughtful planning . . . 'winging' it to model our thinking as we read is difficult to pull off" (2002, 54).

Teachers should think carefully about what connections to make. The teacher identifies important concepts and key themes, thinks about how her own experiences relate to the themes, and notes where in the reading of the text to pause and to think aloud about the text, all the while thinking about how to share understanding of her thinking strategy. What are the key concepts in the text that are critical for students to get in order to understand the story? Keene and Zimmermann (1997, 69) report that students often comprehend the words, but lack a schema for the *setting*, which may be critical to understanding the key themes of the book.

Harvey and Goudvis (2000) describe how they begin the strategy instruction in making connections with stories that are similar to the lives and experience of the children. When the students have had experience with a substantial number of stories and narratives, they begin to connect themes, characters, and issues from one book to another. The teacher then tries to broaden their horizons to consider themes and issues of the larger world. When the students move to new and unfamiliar topics and broader issues, some students really struggle. Students with background knowledge have a much easier time. "Our responsibility is to help build students' background knowledge so that they can read independently to gain new information" (p. 75).

Teachers think aloud and model how connections can help activate schemata. Miller and company want the students to relate unfamiliar text to prior knowledge and/or personal experiences. In general, they ask students to think: what does the text remind you of? More specifically:

- Does anything in the text relate to yourself—relating characters to oneself, when something in the story reminds you of your life?

- Does anything in the text relate to other texts—finding common themes in different books by the same author; comparing characters, their personalities, and actions; comparing story events and plot lines; comparing lessons, themes, or messages; across different authors, comparing how different authors handled the same theme; comparing different versions of familiar stories?
- Does anything in the text relate to the world—what is going on in the world, real-world issues or problems—natural disasters, poverty, war, crime, technology?

With beginning readers, teachers read, making a big chart with the connections. After modeling the "think aloud," the students practice thinking aloud, and teachers record their connections on the big chart.

Older students developing proficiency at reading, read the text for themselves and put coded sticky notes onto the pages of books: T-S for Text to Self, T-W for Text to World, and T-T for Text to Text. The students might also code R for Reminds me of. They also may jot down some brief connections on the sticky notes.

These devices help activate schemata in the midst of the reading. But how relevant are they to comprehension? Once kids start seeing connections, they may see them anywhere, regardless of how meaningful they are to the understanding of the text. *(Amelia Bedelia Goes Off on a Tangent!)* Harvey and Goudvis (2000) remind us, "We need to read student work carefully and listen well to conversations to see that kids are making meaningful connections" (p. 77). "We watch for authentic connections that support understanding. Kids are terrific teacher-pleasers and may think that any connection is better than no connection at all" (p. 78). "Although children may initially have trouble articulating more significant connections, with teacher and peer modeling and plenty of time, they gradually begin to refine and limit their connections to those that deepen their understanding" (p. 80).

Miller (2002, 67) describes a postreading activity in which she and the second graders went back to earlier connections they had made, marking the ones that had helped them understand and why. This activity is one of Miller's "Anchor Experiences" (highly effective minilessons used as anchors for students to remember specific strategies). "When I begin to teach children how to think out loud, I have the same expectations for them as I do for myself. I want their think-alouds to be genuine, their language precise, their responses thoughtful. My goal is to give them a framework for thinking, as well as to help them build a common language for talking about books" (p. 55).

Katie George, a middle school math teacher in Lincolnshire, Illinois, identifies some of her more powerful activities as "math anchor lessons." She frequently refers the students back to the anchor lesson as a touchstone for clarity and understanding. Miller's ideas are perfect for mathematics classes: anchor lessons, genuine, precise, thoughtful, and a framework for thinking!

HUMANS ARE PATTERN-SEEKING CREATURES

Humans are pattern-seeking, meaning-making creatures. We have experiences. We encounter people, events, phenomena, circumstances, thoughts, ideas, symbols, music, art, emotions. And what do we do with these things? We classify, organize, sort, group, pull apart, look at little pieces, grab a whole handful of pieces and put them back together. We even look for the pattern in tea leaves, ashes, and chicken bones. We see faces, animals, and many strange shapes, in clouds. For example, we drive down the highway, see a "vanity" license plate, and try to decipher its meaning, [IMAQT2] or [ZUP2U]. More to the point, we see patterns in license plates where none was intended (although I knew [XAG756] was randomly generated, I could not help thinking Xylophones Are Great). Humans of all ages are remarkably equipped to make connections.

Perceiving patterns is essentially an *inductive* process: the child examines a bunch of particular examples and derives a pattern. These perceptions can't be forced. Consider the following sequence of numbers that would challenge any adult to discern the pattern since it is expressed abstractly with no context. It begins 1, 6, 11. What would come next in the sequence? When I ask this question of fifth or sixth graders, I get answers such as: 66 or 16. Some people just say that we need more data, we don't have enough examples. I do not at this time ask them to describe the rule for generating the pattern. The sequence is 1, 6, 11, 4 . . . Now what comes next? Some again say they need more examples. I have a hunch that they can think of possibilities but they do not want to be told they are wrong. Others say, 9 or 24 or negative 3. Here are the next four numbers in the sequence: 1, 6, 11, 4, 9, 2, 7, 12 . . . What comes after the 12?

We are in a "pure induction" process: a bunch of examples with very little feedback (only yes or no, are your guesses correct) and no real-life context to give meaning to the numbers. Have you ever heard the saying, "Deduction is going from the general to the particular and induction is going from the particular to the general"? I must have heard that saying in every math class from sixth grade up through twelfth, but I didn't really understand it until I was 30 (and had my first midlife crisis). No, I finally figured it out in high school.

Pure induction can be amazingly challenging and motivating, if the example or the context is conceivable for the student. However, it can be very frustrating to others. Here is the sequence again: 1, 6, 11, 4, 9, 2, 7, 12, 5, 10, 3, 8, 1, 6, 11 . . . and it continues to repeat. What is the pattern? What is the rule that governs this sequence? Note that you have no hints, no partial explanation, no scaffolding. Yet some people love to intellectually struggle with this pure induction. If you are such a person, stop reading now and try to figure out the rule. However, most humans like to have some scaffolding or hints, or the explanation. Okay.

After 8 it went back to 1 and then continues in an endless *cycle*. What is the smallest number in the sequence? What is the largest number? Are all the numbers between 1 and 12 present in the sequence? But they are not in numerical order. What does create the order? At this point or sometimes earlier someone may say "The pattern is add 5, add 5, subtract 7, add 5, subtract 7, add 5, add 5, subtract 7, add 5, subtract 7, add 5, subtract 7." I ask the one who offered this rule, "How do you know when to add 5 and when to subtract 7?" I explain to the class that what the student recited is an excellent *procedure* for generating the sequence accurately. But it does not explain why. Concepts do that.

What object in your immediate surroundings has all twelve numbers and continues in an endless cycle? A clock. What is the pattern or the rule? Something happens every five hours starting at one o'clock. I didn't trick you: I merely gave you the sequence in its most abstract form, divorced from the real-life example that made it so clearly understandable.

Contrast the way you handled the inductive sequence with what most of us experienced in math class most of the time. Can you remember your math teachers who gave brilliant lectures, explaining the procedures, the principles, and the concepts? They'd explain the rules, the formulas, the theorems and then expect us to apply them, using deductive reasoning. The problem with pure deductive teaching is that most of the time an explanation of the principles does not *connect* to anything in kids' heads because most of the time, most humans (especially young children) need examples. In most cases of mathematics in the elementary and middle school, *simply telling* does not work.

As a teacher, you provide your students with a mixture of *examples* and *explanations*. If you taught purely by an inductive process you'd give the kids lots of examples for them to figure out the rules, principles, concepts by discovering them. But pure inductive experiences, with no feedback, can be frustrating, and many kids just never "discover " what they are supposed to learn. Typically, human beings need both examples and explanations. We all need examples to build the meaning of the concept, principle, theorem, or rule. Examples can clarify what the explanation meant. We construct our personal understanding of the concept through an interaction of inductive examples and deductive explanation.

The key question is, not whether or not, but rather *when* are each of these kinds of teaching and student thinking done?

Most traditional mathematics textbooks start the lesson with an explanation, or a definition of some kind. Then the teacher explains the explanation, developing the main ideas. Finally the students do guided seatwork where they work on the exercises or problems related to those ideas that the teacher and book have shown. This sequence puts the explanation in the wrong place, making it difficult for students to make connections. The students have no experiential referent for it; no schemata are activated; there is nothing to connect it to. During guided practice the teacher bounces back and forth like a ball in a pin-ball machine with the kids hitting the flippers. "Ms. Jones, I don't get it! Show me what to do again." A good rule of thumb for effective math teaching is to make sure that *every* symbol has a concrete reference (an anchor) in their experience that you and they can refer back to when dealing with abstract symbols.

There is a better way than the highly deductive aproach. Here are five phases:

Situation. The teacher presents the problem to the students. Key concepts are embedded in a real-life situation which exists within a **context** that is familiar or imaginable to the students. The KWC is used with some enhancements (described shortly) to help imagine and understand the situation.

Representations. The students create representations of the problem by using one or more of the representational problem-solving strategies.

Patterns. The teacher asks the students to look for patterns in the representations. Some students are able to discern patterns, solve the problem, make all the connections the teacher hoped they would. But some do not.

Connections. The teacher leads the students in a debriefing discussion to ascertain who has understood the problem, who has a good way of looking at the problem, and who has made the right connections. It is *now* that a cogent explanation of the major concepts can be effectively done! Why now? The teacher can tailor-make her explanations to use the conceptions that the *students* have generated. She can *connect* the mathematical concepts directly to what the students have just done, just expressed, and just realized. She explicitly builds bridges between ideas, the new and the known. She explicitly makes connections between and among concepts. She helps them *crystallize* their understandings.

Extensions. As the teacher has just witnessed the students wrestling with these ideas, she now has a feel for what needs to be *differentiated* for whom. For most of the students the appropriate extensions would be doing more of the same challenging problems. For some the problem may have been too challenging and they need extensions that circle back to build some foundation. For others the problem may not have been much of a challenge and they will need to work on more advanced extensions.

These five phases require students to do some hard thinking. In the first two phases, Situation (in context) and Representations, the students are trying to understand the problem. They will activate relevant schemata through asking questions. The teacher should provide her students with a good balance of examples and explanations at the right time. Next we'll examine the power one gets when using examples from real situations that live in a context.

In Chapter 1 we mentioned the four-phase model of problem solving that Polya introduced in the 1950s and is still fairly popular today. Some current descriptive labels are given in parentheses. They are:

- understanding the problem (reading the story)
- planning how to solve the problem
- carrying out the plan (solving the problem)
- looking back (checking)

How are the five phases different from Polya's four phases? Why use five? How do the five relate to the four? Good questions I am frequently asked. Polya's four phases describe a very general approach that the students should follow. Although the five do include things that the students do, their orientation is what the teacher does to facilitate the students' problem solving. Both are necessary and they fit together nicely, as you can see in the summary outline. I have also incorporated the key moves from the reading comprehension strategy, Asking Questions, from Chapter 1. This is the beginning of the Braid Model of Problem Solving. I will continue to add pieces to it throughout the book.

The Braid Model of Problem Solving for the Students

Understanding the problem/Reading the story

Imagine the SITUATION

Asking Questions (and Discussing the problem in small groups)

K: What do I know for sure?

W: What do I want to figure out, find out, or do?

C: Are there any special conditions, rules, or tricks I have to watch out for?

Planning how to solve the problem

What REPRESENTATIONS can I use to help me solve the problem?

Carrying out the plan/Solving the problem

Work on the problem using a strategy.

Do I see any PATTERNS?

Looking back/Checking

Does my answer make sense for the problem?

Is there a pattern that makes the answer reasonable?

What CONNECTIONS link this problem and answer to the big ideas of mathematics?

BUILDING CONNECTIONS IN MATHEMATICS

Two basic types of connections serve somewhat different functions for students in organizing knowledge. These are *context connections* and *concept connections*. Bear in mind that our goal in teaching mathematics is understanding. Making connections, organizing knowledge, and understanding concepts are three things that braid nicely.

As we start by asking questions with the KWC, we enhance the K (What do I Know for sure?) with questions that stimulate students' thinking about the situation or context of the math problem. These are context connections: Math to Self and Math to World. Other questions call for concept connections (Math to Math), which tend to be the most difficult of the three. Of course, this process should engage their prior knowledge and activate relevant schemata. It is fairly easy when the students have used the coding T-S, T-W, T-T in their reading of text. The teacher models it herself. Typical questions are:

Math to Self (connecting to prior knowledge and experience; connecting to preconceptions and misconceptions)
What does this situation remind me of?
Have I ever been in any situation like this?
Math to World (connecting to natural or created structures, events, environment, media)
Is this related to anything I've seen in social studies or science, the arts?
Or related to things I've seen anywhere?
Math to Math (connecting the math concepts: to other math concepts [e.g., big ideas], within and across strands of mathematics; to related procedures; within and across contexts and representations)
What is the main idea from mathematics that is happening here?
Where have I seen that idea before?
What are some other math ideas that are related to this one?
Can I use them to help me with this problem?

For younger students a somewhat different list of questions is done orally and the teacher records their responses on chart paper. These are all essentially Math to Self, but responses could be coded either M-S, M-W, or M-M.

What do you think about that/it?
Tell me about this situation.
What do you know about it already?
What do you think will happen?
Is there anything weird or strange about this?
Does anything surprise you?

The students who are in third grade and up are for the most part able to read and write down connections on a graphic organizer of some kind. Most of the teachers I work with simply incorporate these questions in with their KWC, rather than having a separate graphic organizer.

Local Concept Development

Students are motivated to think when the *context* of a problem appeals to them. Initially they are much more interested in the particular examples, the situation, and the context than they are in the mathematics. Working in a meaningful context can help students build an initial understanding of a concept. When the student considers a bunch of examples from a particular context, an inductive process is at work to create meaning, to derive a pattern and create a particular, and perhaps context-specific, version of a concept that describes or explains the pattern.

A number of educators use the term "internal model" to explain what is going on here. We humans interpret our experiences by comparing them to internal models that are based on our past experiences. These internal models filter, construct, and create how we conceive of the new experiences. Students' knowledge is generally organized around their experiences, not around the abstract concepts of the discipline of mathematics. Similar experiences are grouped together in their internal models. Does this sound like schemata?

Students build up concepts gradually. First they come to understand the concept in a very specific context or situation (i.e., "local"). Their initial understanding is very much grounded in a set of examples in that context. It is not global, not generalized to other contexts. They create a kind of model that explains a particular problem-solving situation. With more experience in somewhat similar situations and with facilitation by the teacher, more elaborate understandings can be built up by experience and inductively derived. Heavy doses of deductive explanations trying to get them to generalize across contexts and to think abstractly about the concept will *not* likely have much effect until they have had experience with those other contexts. We cannot do Mr. Spock's Vulcan mind meld and make a student conceive of a concept the way we do. It does not work that way.

The good news is we know how to build the snowman. We can use the innate, pattern-creating, meaning-making, inductive reasoning that students bring to school. We can provide many examples of the target concept in a particular situation so they develop a solid initial local version of the concept. Then we can deliberately provide experiences of the same concept in a different context. We can help them build a strong local conceptualization of the second situation or context. We can help them discern similarities across the two contexts. We can help them build bridges between the two. The process of generalizing can be facilitated, but not deductively forced.

Working in One Context

Here is an example of helping students in one context to build a very solid *local* understanding. In Beverly Kiss' third-grade classroom, she was helping the students learn the KWC and they had been exploring multiplication as equal groups. She had all the students together as a whole class. She had given them the following problem to read.

> Imagine that you work on a ranch that has 24 horses. The owner of the ranch tells you that you must put all of the horses in corrals. You can fence off the corrals many different ways. The owner says you must put the same number of horses in each corral. What is one way you might do this? How many different ways to do this can you find?

She asked her students what they knew about ranches. Had they ever been to one? Several had. Several said they had been to farms where there were horses. She asked them what was the difference between a ranch and a farm? She did a brief compare/contrast chart on the board. She asked, "Are there any words that you are not sure what they mean?" Three students said they did not know or were not sure what a corral was. Instead of asking the others in the class, she went into the K of the KWC and said to them, "Ask yourself, 'What do I know for sure?'" They responded fairly directly with the information in each sentence.

"There is this ranch with 24 horses." "I work at the ranch."

The teacher asked, "What do you do?"

"I move the cattle around." "We are supposed to put the horses in corrals." The teacher said, "It does say that, but remember that we have a second question. What is it?" The students said, *"What do I want to find out or figure out?"* The teacher said, "Yes and sometimes that might mean, 'What do I want to DO?'" *"Put the horse in corrals."* One of the kids shouted out, *"There are lots of ways to make corrals."* The teacher turned to one of the three who wasn't sure about corrals and asked, "What do you think corrals are?" He wasn't sure. She said, "Put your finger over the word *corral* and read one of the sentences aloud that uses that word. When you get to that word just say 'blank.' Then do the same with the other sentence." He did. And then she asked, "What are corrals made of?" The student said tentatively, *"Fences?"* She asked, "Then what are corrals?" He replied, *"A bunch of fences to keep horses in one place."* Then she asked the class, "What is the second question?" They chimed in, *"What are we trying to figure out or find out?"* "How would you answer that question?" She called on a student who said, *"We have to figure out how to put all the horses in corrals so that every corral has the same number of horses in it."*

Beverly asked if anybody had other things we had to do or find out. No one said anything. Then she asked them about the third question. *"Is there a special condition that I need to look out for?"* She asked them to quietly on their own read the problem again. They did. After about a minute, one of the students said, *"I think we could get lots of different answers."* "Why do you say that?" *"Because the problems says, 'How many different ways to do this can you find?' "*

This dialogue took about five minutes.

Next the teacher gave each pair of children a collection of 24 Unifix cubes. She said that each Unifix cube was going to represent a horse. She asked them to please put them into the groups with the same number in each group. Let's see if everybody can find one way. She circled around the classroom and checked what each pair had done. They all had found a way to do this.

She gave each group a piece of poster paper about 12 inches by 14 inches that had been folded into four rectangular sections on each side. Her instructions were that every time someone found a solution, to draw the 24 "horse" cubes in one of the rectangles of the paper. Make it and draw it. She gave them about ten minutes. Some kids asked if they could turn the paper over. She said, "Yes." Others asked, "Are there eight ways to do this because there are eight sections of the paper?" She said, "We'll find out!" She also told them to draw the corrals before removing the cubes.

They put their names on their papers and labeled their pictures, very carefully, in the following manner. There are 3 corrals with 8 horses in each corral. She displayed an overhead transparency of 24 squares, 8 inside each of three roughly drawn circles. See Figure 2.1.

Each of the student pairs found several ways. As the teacher circulated about the room, kids asked her questions like, *"Can we put them all in one big corral? Do we have all of the ways?"* She just said, "We'll see."

After about ten minutes she asked them to stop and to put away the cubes. "Let's see how many different ones we found as a class." She pulled out a sheet of newsprint that had a big T-chart on it. She asked one pair of students to tell us one way they found. One of the kids said, *"Six horses in each."* She asked him, "How many corrals would you need?" He said,

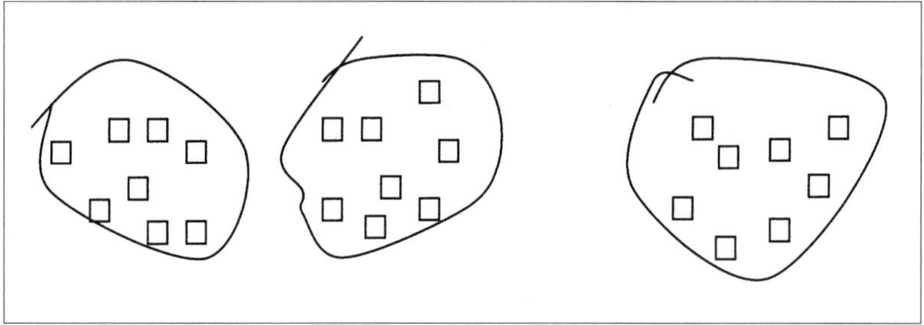

FIGURE 2.1

"*Four.*" She then said, "Can we say it like we did with equal groups last week? How would we say it?" Someone volunteered, "*We have 24 horses in 4 corrals with 6 horses in each corral.*" She acknowledged him and nodded to another student who said, "*Four corrals with 6 horses in each could hold 24 horses.*" Beverly then wrote on the column headings of the T-chart: **[number of corrals] [number of horses in each]**. She explained that as each pair of students described their possible arrangements of horses, she would record it in the T-chart, but they had to tell her what to write by saying it in the order that was left to right. She said, "Say it the way we did in groups. I have 4 groups with 6 in each group, or 4 groups of 6." As pairs responded, she entered their solutions. After the first four, pairs started saying that we had all the ones they had found. Others in the room said there were more. She paused when the chart looked like the table in Figure 2.2. Then she asked one of the students to ask her question again.

The girl asked, "*Can we have all the horses in one big corral?*" "What do you think, class?" A debate began. Some students were adamant: "*The problem said 'put them in corralSSSSS,'*" with great emphasis on the S. (No doubt these children were strict constructionists of the Constitution as well.) Others maintained that you could have one group, so why not one corral? Finally, one of the students asked me (they knew me as Beverly's professor). I suggested that the solutions they had so far were "recorded" but not organized, not in any order, and asked, "Which solution would you put first?" They were about evenly split between 1 corral of 24 and 2 corrals of 12. I suggested they enter both in the chart, but use a different color for 1 corral of 24.

We went down the first T-chart looking for what would come next. After 4 corrals with 6 horses, they paused and I quickly said, "Oh, oh. We missed one. What about 5 corrals?" Some were still thinking while others blurted out, "*You can't do it! You can't have 5 corrals!*" I said, "Sure I can." I drew 5 circles on the chalkboard and put 5 squares into 4 of the circles and 4 squares into the last circle. "There you are. Five corrals, 24 horses." You could hear them on the other side of Lake Michigan: "*The groups*

number of corrals	number of horses in each corral
6	4
4	6
3	8
2	12
8	3
12	2

FIGURE 2.2

number of corrals	number of horses in each corral
1	24
2	12
3	8
4	6
6	4
8	3
12	2

FIGURE 2.3

aren't equal." I said, "Oh, you mean we have a SPECIAL CONDITION?" At least a couple of kids giggled. Most just had expressions that seemed to say, *"Well, duh. Isn't that what you've been teaching us?"*

They used reasoning similar to 5 corrals when we got to 7, 9, 10, and 11 corrals. They stopped at 12 corrals with 2 in each. See Figure 2. 3. I asked, "What would come next?" Some thought we were finished. I asked, "Do you see any pattern in this table or T-chart?" One said, *"One side goes up, the other goes down."* I asked, "Why?" Several kids started to answer but stopped. Finally one said, *"If you've got more corrals, you don't need to put as many horses in each one."*

We went back to the T-chart. And I asked, "Can we have 13 corrals?" They said, "*No.*" I went through 13, 14, 15, 16, 17, 18, 19, 20, 21, 22, 23. They were chuckling. "What about 24 corrals?" Someone said that would be too much work. "But could you?" The same kids who objected to 1 corral, now objected to 24 because, *"The problem says to put the same number of horseSSSSS in each corral."* Beverly and I let the kids argue briefly and then one student interjected, *"Let's just put it in the table in the same color as 1 and 24."* The class liked this idea. I asked them again about the patterns and this time they immediately saw that the same numbers on the left side were repeated on the right, but as one kid said, *"Going the other way."* See Figure 2.4.

I must tell you of an incident a few years earlier in a different classroom when doing an analogous problem. I asked if they saw any patterns. They mentioned the ones cited here. Then one child said, *"The top half is like the bottom half except like upside down and looking in a mirror."* Well, I almost fell off my chair and had him repeat it and show us what he meant (I knew what he meant). See Figure 2.5. He drew a horizontal line

number of corrals	number of horses in each corral
1	24
2	12
3	8
4	6
6	4
8	3
12	2
24	1

FIGURE 2.4

One factor	The other factor
1	72
2	36
3	24
4	18
6	12
8	9
9	8
12	6
18	4
24	3
36	2
72	1

FIGURE 2.5

separating 8 9 from 9 8, and explained that when you get to the middle it *"flips"* and there are four sections that are like mirrors to one another. Thereafter that class referred to *"hitting the flip—that's when you know you've got them all."* For sixth graders, this idea comes in handy because the top half are all the factors of the number and little problems like this reveal another way (besides tree diagrams) to generate all the proper factors. For example, to find all the factors of 72, I would not give the kids 72 manipulatives. That is too many to handle without major trouble. But once they have built up their number sense through these kinds of activities, they can generate the organized table in Figure 2.5.

Do you see the middle of Table 2.5 where it flips from 8 9 to 9 8? We can draw a horizontal line and all 12 numbers above the line in the table are the factors of 72.

Notice in this example of a single problem how easily the students moved across representations. They read the story, and then talked about it (language). They used objects to represent the horses. They drew pictures to record the different solutions that they found with the objects, they labeled the pictures with written language, and then used symbolic notation when generating a T-table. These representations were roughly in sequence from more concrete to more abstract. Yet they were not big intellectual leaps for the kids, they were manageable. *Every representation was explicitly connected to the others.* They were all done in the same context (corrals and horses). Most of the students could easily have done extension problems in this same context, but with different numbers. How about 32, or 40, or 60 horses, but don't use cubes? Can you do it with just a table? Would it help to draw 60 little circles and partition them into corrals? Same context, different examples.

A simple yet powerful way to *differentiate* your instruction is to have a variety of extensions ready to go. You can easily provide the kids with the right kind of next experience. Plan for many of the same kind of problem for practice, some much more challenging, and some quite a bit easier. You can vary the context and the kinds of representations to provide other opportunities for kids with different abilities, cognitive styles, and preferred learning modalities to enter the world of mathematics in a way that makes the most sense to them.

Handling Multiple Contexts

Let's return to Beverly's classroom a few days after she did the 24 horses in corrals. We did a kind of round-robin in the classroom. Beverly had 27 kids in her class. They usually did problem solving (PS) in groups of 3 and she had used this fact to help them see that the 9 groups of 3 were 27 (repeated addition 3 + 3 + . . . nine times). She had spent some time helping them learn how to work together in small groups, for instance, developing social skills of how to listen to one another, how to disagree in a way that did not offend the other person, how to respect one another, how to share materials. She also emphasized task roles for small-group problem solving: supplier, recorder, reporter are three that can fit most problems. As they practiced these roles by using them in problem solving from the first day of school, they became increasingly more successful in cooperative learning tasks.

I have noticed fewer teachers in recent years emphasizing these kinds of skills and roles and actively helping kids learn how to work in groups. Then when the teacher asks them to work in pairs or triads, some of the students fail to share, help one another, and work cooperatively. It is predictable. I also believe that a good structure like the KWC gives them some guidelines on exactly what to do or talk about when in PS groups.

We put them into the 9 regular PS groups. We had 3 PS groups go to math tables we had set up in the northwest corner of the room (NW station). We had another 3 PS groups go to the northeast corner of the room (NE station), and the final 3 PS groups went to the math tables in the southeast corner (SE station). Each station had 3 sets of materials so that the 3 PS groups could work on the problem independently of the other 2 PS groups at a particular station. Each corner station actually took up about one-fourth of the classroom so that the PS groups would have plenty of room to work. At each station there were recording sheets specifically formatted for the task.

Before we started, we designated one member of each PS group as the recorder: one at the NW station, one at the NE station, and one at the SE station. We similarly rotated responsibility for roles of manipulator and clean-up batter. The recorder handled all data entry to the recording sheet. The manipulator was in charge of the materials for the group at one station. The clean-up batter was in charge of making sure that when they left that station, everything was set up for the next PS group exactly as the current group had found it when they arrived at the station. We prepared a chart that showed who was doing what at each station. Here are the roles (R, M, and C) for PS Group I. The other 8 PS groups were included in the chart. See Figure 2.6.

	SE STATION ROLES			**NW STATION ROLES**			**NE STATION ROLES**		
PS GROUP I	**R**	**M**	**C**	**R**	**M**	**C**	**R**	**M**	**C**
	AL	JO	KIT	KIT	AL	JO	JO	KIT	AL

FIGURE 2.6

The SE station had three zip bags each with 36 pennies, one for each PS group. The NW station had three sets of 40 Unifix cubes; each set was a single color. The NE station had three square pegboards that were about 26 inches on a side and zip bags of 48 golf tees. (In the past, I have also used Lite Brites: small, cylindrical plastic pieces). The pegboard leaned against a chalkboard, sitting up in the chalkboard tray.

We presented the students with very simple, situational story problems relating to the tasks.

Task 1

You have been given 3 dozen freshly baked doughnuts. What are all the different ways you could share them evenly with your friends? You have a bag of pennies to help you figure out this problem. Arrange the pennies into groups, with the same number in each group.

Task 2

Your PS group is working with a real estate developer (Arnold Grump) who wants to put up a lot of medium-priced condominiums. He has enough money to build 40 units as condo-towers. Find all the ways to build condo-towers using all 40 Unifix cubes, so that every tower has the same height.

In the preceding week, the students had worked on the concept of *array* and Beverly and I had brought in collections of things that came in arrays (e.g., egg cartons, racks of soft drinks in cans).

Task 3

You are part of a design team for a department store, assigned to find all the ways to arrange the expensive items into a rectangular array of 48 items in a display window. The display items will be represented by golf tees. You will put 48 golf tees into the pegboard holes to make rectangular arrays and then write down the possible solutions.

We gave each PS group about 7 to 8 minutes at each station. All 9 PS Groups moved to the next station clockwise at the same time. So all 9 experienced the 3 stations. All 27 students had the experience of being a recorder, a manipulator, and clean-up batter.

What might have appeared to an outside observer as a three-ring circus actually went very smoothly. Of course, the kids made a lot of noise, but they were amazingly on task. The three groups that had the pegboard arrays as their first station had more trouble getting started. This was a new manipulative for them and I think they wanted to get the feel for it and just play a little. This was a classic mistake on my part. I know full well how kids love to get a feel for a new manipulative by messing around with it. Consequently I always give them five minutes to explore the manipulative before they have to use it.

Probably due to a lack of familiarity with the manipulatives, the three groups did not find very many rectangular arrays at the SE station. I think another problem was that it just took longer to make the displays than it did to create the groups of pennies or the stacks of

Unifix cubes; just the physical act of inserting golf tees into the proper holes in the pegboard took some time. They obviously enjoyed it; squeals of glee were frequent.

As they went through the stations, they did appear to get a bit more adept at doing the tasks. However, I rarely heard any talk that would suggest that they saw the inherent mathematical similarity in these tasks, probably because they were so intent on the materials and the specific task that was in front of them. They were not yet generalizing the math across contexts.

After about twenty minutes, all nine groups had completed three stations. We debriefed one station at a time with the nine recorders reading their solutions from their recording sheets. We started with the three recorders whose groups encountered the pennies that represented doughnuts first. I wrote their solutions on a large newsprint T-chart. They took turns giving me one solution from their group. When these three had finished, we asked the three recorders from the other six groups if they had found any solutions that had not been mentioned by the three groups.

We thoroughly discussed the doughnuts/pennies, repeated these steps with the condo/Unifix cubes, and then with the pegboard arrays. We debriefed the doughnuts/pennies first because this was the most familiar situation of the three and we assumed that it would likely be a good foundation for making connections to the other two. The newsprint allowed us to collect all the data from the nine groups and then to organize it. Two of the nine groups had found all the solutions in the brief time we gave them. In fact, all the groups did very well, getting nearly all. Several gleefully asserted that they had found them all. So I asked them the critical questions about combinations:

How many different ways (solutions, combinations, etc.)?
Did you check for duplicates/repeats? How?
Did you find all the ways?
How do you know that (when) you have found them all?

The kids answered that they had tried all the ways. I asked, "How do you know you tried all? Maybe you missed some." We are leading up to the very important mathematical idea of generating an organized list or table, but as with most ideas in mathematics, kids need to experience the power and meaningfulness of an idea (conceptual understanding) and not simply memorize how to do it (procedural understanding). Even the two groups that had found all nine solutions had not generated them in order. That was fine. We create a second T-table using all the solutions the class had found (see Figure 2.7). We went in order and we considered if some numbers of persons not listed were possible (e.g., 5, 7, 10, etc.). The kids were certain these were not possible and that this was all.

Beverly asked the students what patterns they saw in this table. As before, they noticed the numbers in the two columns were the same but

number of persons	number of doughnuts for each person
1	36
2	18
3	12
4	9
6	6
9	4
12	3
18	2
36	1

FIGURE 2.7

going in different directions. We introduced the words *ascending* and *descending*. A couple of students noticed that the middle answer had the same two numbers (6 and 6). Then others noticed that the answers above 6 and 6 were the same as the ones below it. Another student mentioned that one of these was a *"turn-around fact"* that they'd been talking about in class. Which one, I asked. She said, *"4 times 9 is 36 and 9 times 4 is 36."*

I cannot emphasize too strongly how important the debriefing of any problem is and the critical role played by language in debriefing. Teachers are pressed for time to cover massive amounts of content, but the better the debriefing, the more complete the crystallization of concepts will be, and less reteaching will be needed. There will always be some who don't get it, but that number is cut down dramatically when the five phases are done well by the teacher and the students: situation in context, representations, patterns, connections, and extensions.

Oral language is critical throughout the problem-solving process, and especially so in the debriefing process. When they are doing a KWC, when they are discussing and describing to one another what the picture they drew means to them, when they are telling others about the pattern they see, they are communicating their mental models through the powerful medium of language. Language representations are used to describe and communicate insights into all other representations. It is the first and the last representation we use. We start with KWC and end with students writing or talking about their writing.

As we were winding up the debriefing of the doughnuts, one kid piped up, *"I see something we didn't talk about!"* We asked him to explain. *"If there are 3 people, they each get 12 (that's a dozen); then if you have 6 people (that's twice as many people), they'd only get 6 (that's half a dozen)."* Some of the kids asked him to say that again. He did and then added,

"And if you've got 12 people (and that's twice as many as 6 people), they'd only get 3 doughnuts each (and that's half of the half dozen)." (This kid is headed for MIT or Cal Tech, I figured.)

I asked him if he could say this in a pattern or rule. He wasn't sure, so I asked the class. No one volunteered, so I gave it a try, "How about this: if you have twice as many people as before, then each person gets half of what people got before. Or how about: twice as many, half as much, for short?" They thought that was pretty cool. Later in the year kids spotted other patterns in these multiplicative tables: three times as many, a third as much; four times as many, one-fourth as much. But they were just beginning to understand the meaning of multiplication and division and the twice/half pattern was a great one to start with. It made sense to most of them.

These are subtle relationships that need nurturing. Students need to truly grasp them in their own mental images and models. I would venture that very few of these third graders truly and deeply understood the pattern that this kid perceived, even after he and I told them about it. When a child shares what she or he sees/conceives, it is the sharer who benefits more than the recipient. I am sure that we do get initial foundational ideas from one another; when a person has to explain his or her reasoning, defend a thesis, justify a conjecture, it is he or she who crystallizes understanding.

Next came the 40 condos. The students had used Unifix cubes to model the condo buildings and the number of stories or floors in each. They considered both high-rise and low-rise buildings. Again, we collected the data from each group and then organized them into one table (see Figure 2.8). We discussed patterns and if they'd found all the solutions. They picked up on the previous insight and several said, "*Twice as many buildings, half as high.*" They used 1 building 40 stories high compared to 2 buildings, 20 stories high, and 4 buildings 10 high, and 8 buildings 5 high. They also spotted a couple of turn-around facts.

Finally we got to the rectangular arrays with golf tees in the pegboard holes. Using arrays helps to build a good sense of rows (vertical) and columns (horizontal), size in two dimensions, and rectangles, which is where the teacher was headed next. Arrays are a marvelous bridge from *groups* to *area.* I am not in any way denigrating arrays, but time is precious and a teacher can get many more conceptual connections working with rectangles and area than with arrays. That is what we were doing here, building some bridges. Based on the previous week's work with arrays, the students were able to create arrays of golf tees in the pegboards. In the debriefing we talked about rows and columns.

The pegboards were about 26 inches square and would not accommodate a couple of conceivable arrays (e.g., 1 by 48, and 48 by 1). None of the nine PS groups found all the arrays. But in the debriefing when we listed what ones they had found, several students successfully discovered others that should be there. In this manner they generated the table in Figure 2.9.

number of buildings	number of stories for each building
1	40
2	20
4	10
5	8
8	5
10	4
20	2
40	1

FIGURE 2.8

number of rows	number of columns
2	24
3	16
4	12
6	8
8	6
12	4
16	3
24	2

FIGURE 2.9

The debriefing of the arrays was very similar to the other two in terms of recorders reporting, and so on. One thing that was a bit different was that the pegboard allowed us to easily rotate the array. For instance, when they had found the 6 rows, 8 columns solution, three of the nine groups who were at that station simultaneously then rotated it 90 degrees so it could become an array with 8 rows and 6 columns. The students also caught on that "*twice as many rows means half as many in that row*" (which is the same as the number of columns). We demonstrated it with pegboards.

The final part of the debriefing was about the connections among these three problems and the recent problems of horses in corrals. We asked students to compare and contrast the different problems. We put the sets of newsprint up: all the T-tables side by side. The students discussed the patterns in the tables. It was then that they began to move away from the particular materials, manipulatives, and context and started focusing on the more mathematical patterns, irrespective of color, size, shape, position, order. This process of ignoring some features, characteristics, or properties while attending to others is critical to mathematics. Earlier, when the MIT/Cal Tech-bound eight-year-old kid saw the pattern *twice as many people get half as many doughnuts*, he was creating an abstraction of this kind. He saw it long before others. In this cross-context debriefing we brought this pattern up for discussion. Then others began to see or perhaps to catch a true glimpse of why that worked.

Concepts in mathematics are about relationships; they are not really about concrete objects or contexts. British psychologist and mathematician Richard Skemp refers to *relational* understanding. "Understanding can be defined as a measure of the quality and quantity of connections that an idea has with existing ideas and on the creation of new connections. . . . Understanding is never an all-or-nothing proposition" (Van de Walle 2006). Relational understanding thus has a rich web of interconnected ideas and relationships. I have been using the term *conceptual understanding* in this same way.

All concepts in mathematics, it seems, are about relationships in some way. The more abstract the ideas, the harder to grasp the relationship. For instance, in the soft drink problem in Chapter 1, one thing that was calculated was the gallons per person of soft drink bought. As we explored the data, we found a ratio comparing two quantities (technically a rate, because the two quantities are measuring different kinds of things). A ratio of boys to girls is a ratio because they are both humans. But comparing gallons of soft drinks to the number of people in a state is really a rate.

Beverly wanted to build the richest possible web of interconnected ideas about multiplication and division, so we planned extensive work in number relationships through numbers in problem solving. She started first with the equal groups examples and built on the repeated addition of equal groups begun in the second grade. We tried to elaborate the equal-groups conception of multiplication with the horses and corrals. But you may or may not have noticed that in the version that we did, the teacher initially held back from calling a problem a division problem or a multiplication problem. Her intent was to help the kids see that in this representation of a real situation it could be either or it could be both. Asking if you had eight groups with three horses in each, how many do you have?—that signifies multiplication. But if you ask, "How can I divide these 48 horses into corrals with six in each; how many corrals would I need to build?"—that is more obviously a division question.

We helped the kids work with groups and arrays in the round-robin. They had done some introductory array work prior to the three problems. The following week we gave the kids 24 one-inch-square tiles and asked them to make some kind of array using all 24 tiles. I displayed 24 overhead square tiles on an overhead projector something like Figure 2.10.

I asked them to describe my array in rows and columns. They described the arrays that they had made in a similar manner. "*I have 3 rows and 8 columns and 24 total squares.*" However, when Beverly first introduced arrays, she made connections to the equal groups they had just been doing. For instance, she had them say, "*I have an array with 3 rows with 8 in each row.*" She also said later, "3 rows of 8." After a number of those, she shifted to saying, "I have an array of 8 columns with 3 in each column (or 8 columns of 3)." After a few days, she shifted again to, "I

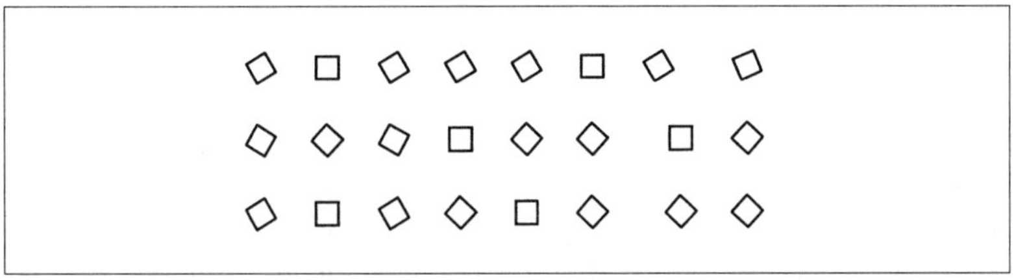

FIGURE 2.10

FIGURE 2.11

have 3 rows and 8 columns." There are two ideas here: (1) the language she's using links to the group language, and (2) she's giving them an overall strategy for moving back and forth flexibly between representations and between contexts.

I asked them to straighten out their arrays into rows and columns. I showed these on the overhead. Then I asked, "What would they look like if we pushed them all together?" And so I did (see Figure 2.11).

We then gave them graph paper with one-inch squares, the same size as the square tiles. We asked them to find as many rectangles as they could with the 24 square tiles. Whenever they found one, they had to draw it on their graph paper. We supplied plenty of graph paper sheets. Some of the kids wanted to make rectangles that would not fit on the paper. We asked them to explain what size these rectangles were and why they wouldn't fit. These questions allowed us to make an important transition and link. Some of the kids realized and stated that the rectangles they had made were 12 inches long and would not fit on the paper, which was 11 inches on its long side. They shared their insight and dilemma with the whole class. The teacher and I from then on talked about the lengths of the two sides as the distance from corner to corner, 3 inches and 8 inches. We explicitly connected the rectangle we called 3 by 8 to the array of squares that was 3 rows and 8 columns.

The next piece of the puzzle was to draw the big rectangles (2 by 12 and 1 by 24) by either taping together two sheets of the one-inch paper or by drawing on a new sheet of centimeter graph paper. Each square centimeter was to then represent one of the square-inch tiles. They made scale drawings of all rectangles they found. It was a little bit of a stretch for some, and we gave them the choice. About half wanted to try the centimeter paper. The kids worked diligently and everyone found at least four different rectangles. We asked them to label each rectangle by the lengths of its two sides, such as 2 inches by 12 inches.

In the days following, Beverly introduced the concept of *perimeter* as the distance around a shape like a rectangle. As a distance they could think of it like a rope that went around and then you'd pull it into a straight line to see how long it was. The kids were given some nonstretching nylon string and used it to measure the perimeter of a variety of objects, including cylinders. Beverly introduced the special name for the perimeter of such circular objects, circumference.

Context	Model	Objects	Visual/Pictoral	Symbolic/Recording
Cookies per person	(Equal groups)	pennies	draw circles	T-table
Horses in corrals	(Equal groups)	Unifix cubes	draw squares	Label picture/ T-table
Condo towers	(Equal groups)	Unifix cubes	———	T-table
Rectangular display	(Arrays)	golf tees/pegboard	———	T-table
Tiles	(Arrays)	1" square tiles	———	Label graph/ T-table
Rectangles	(Area)	1" square tiles	graph paper	Label graph/ T-table

FIGURE 2.12

One day I came in and asked the kids if they had seen my friend, Perry. They looked puzzled. I told them that Perry was from Greece and that he owned a Greek restaurant where he carefully measured all the ingredients. "He really loves to measure things, especially measuring around the outside border of things. His full name is Perry Meter. In Greek *peri* means around and *meter* means measure." Some kids laughed, most of them groaned, but all of them remembered what *perimeter* meant.

About a week later Bev also introduced them to the concept of *area*. Traditionally area has been seen as an application (and a somewhat procedural one at that) of multiplication facts memorized from working with the group model. It is usually introduced much later in the school year than she was doing now. This decision was based on my experience that some kids actually develop an initial local conception of what multiplication is better from working with area, than they do working with equal groups.

Before describing in some detail how area can be conceptualized, related to other topics, and used to teach multiplication, I want to summarize what Beverly has done (see Figure 2.12). She wanted the students to wrestle with examples from several different contexts for multiplication. She wanted to see local concept development of several contexts. She wanted them to generalize across these contexts. She helped them build a complex set of relationships among different models of multiplication (group, array, and area). She wanted to relate multiplication to division. In doing these things she not only used multiple contexts, she also used multiple representations in each context.

Frequently, parents, teachers, and administrators will ask a question, the essence of which is: Won't all these different contexts confuse the students? Not if it is done carefully by the teacher. Experiences should be savored, not hurried. Of course, a teacher can bombard the students with multiple situations so quickly that the kids' minds are reeling. On the other hand, good experiences, good questions, and steady movement without giant leaps to the abstract will pay off. Students will begin to see the basic relationship is similar in each example, and with help can make the necessary connections to generalize across contexts.

POINTS TO PONDER

As you plan for your kids to do problem solving there are several critically important things for you to consider. In the next section you will see some considerations related to the material in this chapter. There are many different ways to address these considerations, and I have given you some suggestions on how I do things. However, you always will modify and adapt anyone else's ideas to fit your own personality, your teaching style, your school circumstances, and the particular students you have. At the end of subsequent chapters I will add additional considerations that come out of that chapter. I will also include here a summary of the features of the Braid Model that have been addressed so far.

CONSIDERATIONS IN PLANNING FOR PROBLEM SOLVING

Cognitive Processes in the Context

How do I scaffold experiences for progressive development from concrete to abstract?

How concretely should I start?

How can I encourage initial play and exploration with the materials or ideas?

How can I make the experiences challenging, but not overwhelming?

What questions can I ask or terms could I use to help them visualize or imagine the context, situation, or problem?

Should they work in small groups and discuss the problem or concept in the specific context?

Grouping Structures to Encourage the Social Construction of Meaning

How can I vary the grouping structures: whole class, small group, individuals (with attention to small groups of 2–5)?

How can I enhance small-group discussions for students to develop, refine, and elaborate their thinking?

The Braid Model of Problem Solving
New entries from Chapter 2 are in italics.

Understanding the problem/Reading the story
Imagine the SITUATION
Asking Questions (and Discussing the problem in small groups)
K: What do I know for sure?
W: What do I want to know, figure out, find out, or do?
C: Are there any special conditions, rules, or tricks I have to watch out for?
Making Connections
Math to Self
What does this situation remind me of?
Have I ever been in any situation like this?
Math to World
Is this related to anything I've seen in social studies or science, the arts?
Or related to things I've seen anywhere?
Math to Math
What is the main idea from mathematics that is happening here?
Where have I seen that idea before?
What are some other math ideas that are related to this one?
Can I use them to help me with this problem?

Planning how to solve the problem
What REPRESENTATIONS can I use to help me solve the problem?

Carrying out the plan/Solving the problem
Work on the problem using a strategy.
Do I see any PATTERNS?

Looking back/Checking
Does my answer make sense for the problem?
Is there a pattern that makes the answer reasonable?
What CONNECTIONS link this problem and answer to the big ideas of mathematics?

3 VISUALIZATION

We would define ***imagination*** *to be the will working on the materials of memory, not satisfied with following the order prescribed by nature, or suggested by accident; it selects the parts of different conceptions, or objects of memory, to form a whole, more pleasing, more terrible, or more awful than has ever been presented in the ordinary course of nature.*

—Webster's Dictionary, 1904

VISUALIZING WHILE READING

I remember being absolutely dumbfounded when my wife told me that some of her third-grade students did not form mental images when they read. They read the words and appeared to understand some of the meaning of text but did not see pictures in their minds. How can this be? The folks from the Public Education and Business Coalition (PEBC) are passionate about helping kids to create images "connected to the senses of sight, hearing, taste, touch and smell to enhance and personalize understandings" (PEBC 2004). Harvey and Goudvis speak of visualizing as "movies in the mind" (2000, 101).

In a workshop setting, extended periods of time are devoted to children reading and to sharing in small groups what they've read. They confer with the teacher and they discuss with their peers. Teachers ask them to process the words and their images, via oral language (to the whole class or in small groups), through writing prose and poetry, by drawing pictures, or through dramatization.

In her second-grade classroom, Debbie Miller uses anchor lessons to deepen children's understanding of the strategy of making mental images, creating and adapting images in their minds. She has children explore how images are created from the readers' own schema and words in the text. They listen to the teacher read aloud and the teacher asks them to consider what are the most vivid images. They each individually read the text and draw something that captures that image. Then they meet in small groups and share what they've drawn and discuss it. She asks them to talk about their images and the pieces of text that inspired that image (Miller 2002, 80–83).

Similarly, Keene and Zimmermann (1997) describe how even jaded junior high schoolers can respond to a teacher's think aloud of a vivid text. The kids initially offered only brief descriptions of their images evoked by the text and the teacher's think-aloud images, but the teacher gently probed, asking questions about the images the kids described. She probed for more details, for the kids to imagine more and to elaborate on their images. "These kids showed us that images come from the emotions as well as the senses. Readers take the words from the page and stretch and sculpt them until the richness of the story becomes the richness of a memory replete with senses and emotions. Words on the page become recollections anchored in an unforgettable image of one's own making" (1997, 130).

They also may dramatize a piece of text, reenacting the story. Readers create images to form unique interpretations, clarify their thinking, draw conclusions, and enhance understanding. Images are fluid and readers adapt them to incorporate information as they read. They are influenced by the shared images of others.

Visualization works best when the text has rich detail or vivid language. When children immerse themselves in the worlds created by these words, visualization helps them perceive and conceive what the author is trying to share with them. "The detail gives depth and dimension to the reading, engaging the reader more deeply and making the text more memorable" (Keene and Zimmermann 1997, 141).

This kind of engagement seems most likely with fiction, biographies, autobiographies, or poetry. They need to be good stories, well told. I believe that we all especially appreciate stories that allow us to share universal human emotions. The PEBC folks urge us to help kids "attend to 'heart' images—feelings evoked while reading" (2004). Although such emotions are universal, our response to literature is intensely personal. The images we create belong to us. *What we own becomes our own.* Making it personal encourages us to persevere with challenging material. When students share their personal images, interpretations, and feelings in discussions or in writing or through drawing they tend to "revise their images to incorporate new information and new ideas revealed in the text. They adapt their images in response to the images shared by other readers" (Keene and Zimmermann 1997, 141).

As students grow older they "begin to censor and limit their images as they read. They focus on literal meanings—narrow, dictionary-type definitions of each word read . . . though when they were younger, their imaginations were intact and they were full of vivid images. Too often in school they've been conditioned to pay attention only to the literal interpretation of text" (Keene and Zimmermann 1997, 140).

THREE TYPES OF VISUALIZATION IN MATHEMATICS

There are two ways that students use visualization in mathematics that should come as no surprise: *creating mental images* as they read and *creating representations* of their mental images. The other way, *spatial thinking*, is quite different and I will review it first.

Spatial Thinking, or Visualizing Spatial Relationships/Orientations

We could say that mathematicians in the United States came late to the game. From the 1930s, Russian psychologists from the former Soviet Union investigated *spatial thinking*, creating spatial images and manipulating them (e.g., *mentally* rotating objects in three-dimensional space) and creating new mental images produced by imagination of something not yet seen.

Soviet psychology was focused on the human potential that *some* could attain under proper conditions. If they could demonstrate that some of their students could go far beyond the typical ability when taught in a particular way, this level of ability was available to humans (not necessarily all humans, but attainable by some nonetheless). In contrast, U.S. psychology has been more oriented toward statistical definitions of what the average students can do or if a teaching technique was statistically significant across a broad population of students.

Yakimanskaya (1991) summarized a vast body of Soviet research on spatial thinking. The value of spatial thinking lies in helping students to identify spatial properties and relations and to use them in solving problems of orientation in real space and theoretical geometric space. Though they found individual differences among school children, a major source of the differences came from the teaching techniques to which students were exposed. Furthermore, students do *not* make the transition from representations of real space to a system of graphical substitutes via maturation or development. Even those who were innately beyond the typical spatial ability (i.e., in U.S. parlance, "gifted") required particular teaching methods to acquire "a specialized conceptual apparatus" enabling them to use various frames of reference and methods of representation.

The training in spatial thinking, creating and manipulating mental images, nurtured several generations of highly proficient technicians, draftsmen, and engineers in applied math and science areas as well as many pure math and science people. These were the people who launched Sputnik (years ahead of the Americans), Soyez, their space station, and Major Tom.

Little attention is paid to spatial thinking in U.S. curricula, teaching, and teacher preparation. It tends to be seen as an interesting topic that teachers never get to in the school year. This trend is likely to continue because of the unfortunate confusion caused by the term *visualization* in one of the more prevalent educational theories about the teaching and learning of geometry (the Van Hiele model), in which visualization is the lowest form of geometric thinking. Their model contains sequential stages beyond visualization: *analysis, informal deduction, deduction, and rigor.* Visualization is merely where space is simply observed, where geometric figures are recognized by their physical appearance as a whole, and not for their properties.

U.S. researchers have investigated how *spatial thinking* compares and contrasts with *verbal reasoning* and how both are used in problem solving. They have studied *spatial visualization* (mentally moving, manipulating, twisting, or transforming a visual representation—rotating cubes or folding paper) and *spatial orientation* (changing only perceptual perspective for viewing an object, comprehending arrangements of elements within a visual pattern; understanding a visual representation or a change between two representations; and organizing/making sense out of visual information). In contrast to the Russians, findings have been mixed and inconclusive. Definite conclusions about these complex distinctions has been further complicated by the discovery of two different types of logical thinking processes: one characterized by step-by-step, analytical, and deductive thinking, often mediated by verbal processes, and the other by more structural, global, relational, intuitive, spatial, inductive processes. I designed a two-part activity for students to explore both kinds of reasoning with the same materials. Part one emphasizes intuitive, spatial, inductive processes; part two analytical and deductive thinking. I have done versions of this activity with four-year-old preschoolers, every grade up through eighth, and even with adults in my college classes, and I am certain that in this spatial thinking activity, as in so many others, everyone gets better with experience.

Twenty-four Shapes

I arrange the students into groups of four, five, or six. I give each group a zip bag containing some specially made geometric shapes that have

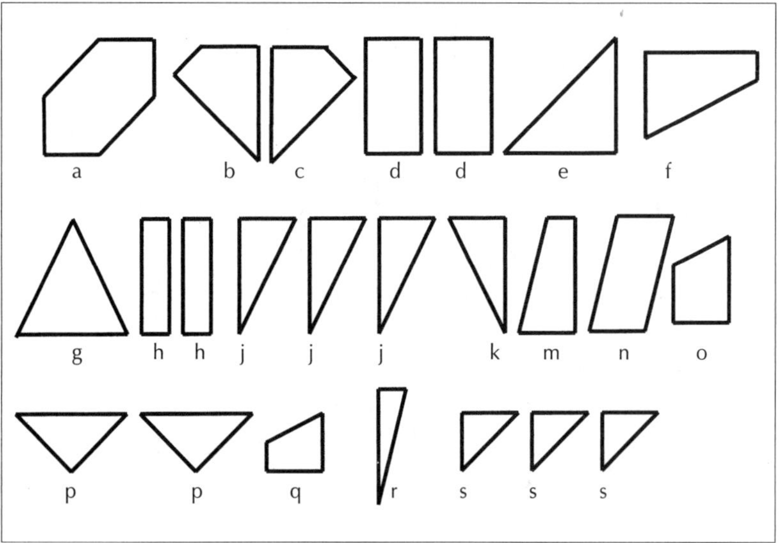

FIGURE 3.1

been photocopied onto bright pink paper, mounted to white, high-density foam boards (from an office supply store), and cut out with a utility knife. Initially, I will describe how I do this activity with the older kids (sixth grade), then how I have modified it for younger students. There are 24 shapes. See Figure 3.1.

Actually there are only 17 different shapes, or 15 if you are allowed to flip mirror pairs (**b** and **c**; **j** and **k**), over onto the other side. Shapes **d**, **h**, **p** are in duplicate; shapes **j** and **s** are in triplicate. As in previous activities, we do a modified KWC and ask them what they can tell me about the shapes. What do you know for sure? If they do not start describing properties very soon, I ask more focused questions about the properties, such as which shapes have right angles.

Then I introduce the first task: Each group has the same 24 shapes from which they are to create 8 congruent squares, that is, 8 squares of the same size using all 24 shapes. This is a challenging task involving structural, global, relational, intuitive, spatial, and inductive processes. We go through the questions of the KWC. Often sixth graders struggle with, "What do I write down for C," the special conditions? The main thing is the requirement that all 24 shapes be used. See Figure 3.2 for how it may be done. (In the appendix I give a blackline version of these in 3-inch squares.) The solution is not unique because one can substitute congruent shapes. These squares are approximately in the order that sixth graders and adults find them, which generally corresponds with their perceived difficulty. Square H is described by students as the most difficult. There are several reasons: very frequently students will combine shapes **o** and **q** to get Figure 3.3.

Once a group has made this rectangle, it is as if the two pieces had been glued together. It seems so logical and it is versatile. It is congruent with shape **d** or with the two **h**'s and several other combinations. It

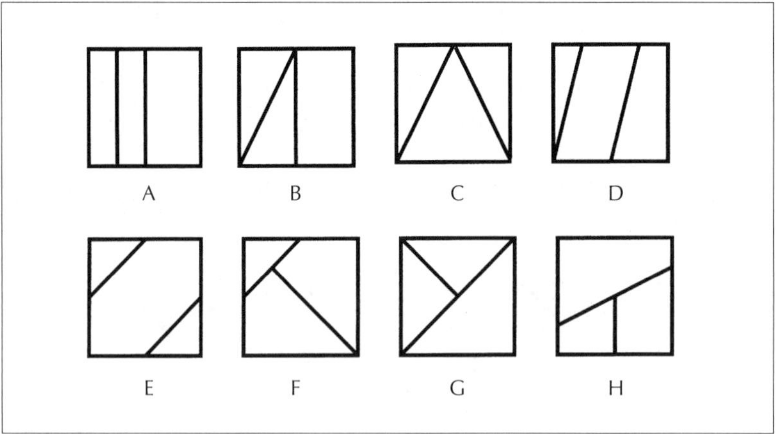

FIGURE 3.2

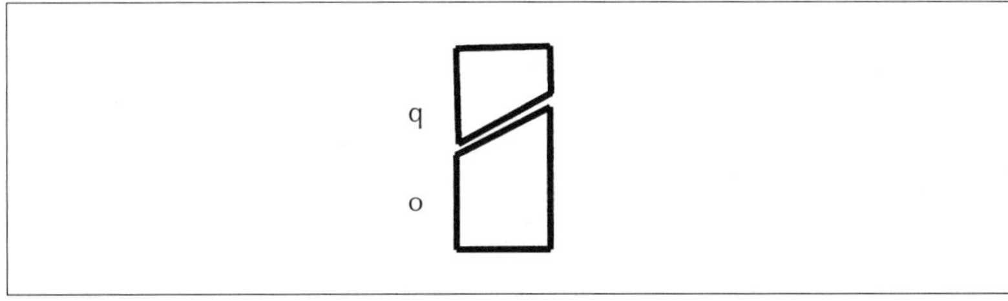

FIGURE 3.3

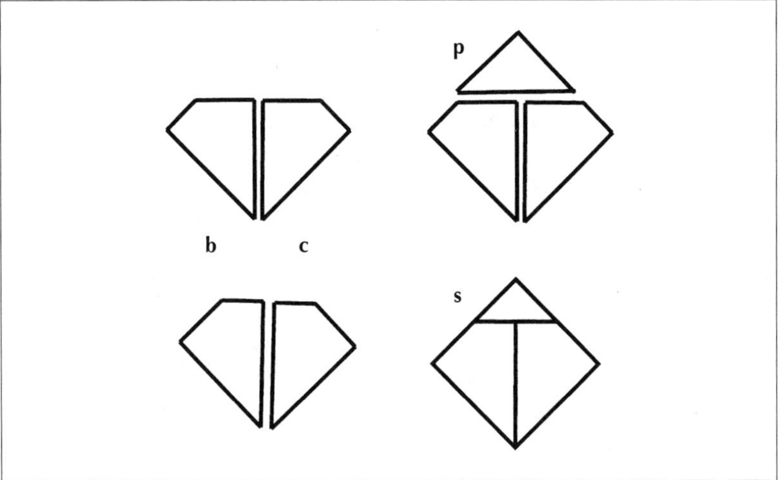

FIGURE 3.4

may be versatile, but it is wrong for this task and will block a solution to the 8 squares.

Similarly, if the mirror pair **b** and **c** are connected in the wrong way, they'll be stuck. Notice that shapes **b** and **c** are not kites; that is, they do not have pairs of adjacent sides congruent. Their long sides are congruent, but opposite them are two different lengths for the short sides. Therefore, **b** and **c** can be connected at their long sides in two ways. Students frequently connected them as shown in Figure 3.4 and then added onto it shape **p**, thinking they had made a square. Actually they have made a rectangle. The proper way to orient shapes **b** and **c** to make a square is shown in Figure 3.4 so that the small triangle **s** is joined to it.

The first task in this activity puts a strong premium on spatial visualization. Even though the students are in groups, they do not talk much about the properties of the shapes as a way to help them solve the task. They do a lot of trial and error, placing shapes next to one another. Most have not had much experience with such tasks.

When a group successfully completes the first part of the activity and creates the 8 squares, I give them a writing prompt to reflect on what they did, such as: which squares did you find the most difficult to make? Why? What did you do to get success? Were there any properties of the shapes that make it easier or harder to go with another shape to make a square? The group may discuss their ideas and answers, but I require individual written statements from every student.

When doing group activities, one group always finishes first and one last. That is logical. But in terms of management, I want the time between the first and last finishing to be as short as possible. So the writing prompt gives a little bit of a cushion. As the quicker groups finish (and quicker does not mean smarter), I have them write while the other groups keep on working. I may intervene a little in the groups that are taking longer, when, for instance, they have "glued" together two pieces in their mind. Or the group may be stuck on how big the square must be (this is more prevalent with younger students than with sixth graders). If so, I may scaffold them a little by providing a border/perimeter showing the size the square must be. It does not do the work for them, but it does help them focus on the gestalt of the square. They can then systematically try a different position for each shape, especially the big shapes. For instance, if you have the border and try to fit shape **a** inside, there is really only one way. Rotations don't count as different. Also, with this border they can check the arrangements shown in Figure 3.4.

I realize that in my way of doing this, the last group may have much less time to write. In fact, sometimes I will take the whole class into the second part of the activity and tell the last group to do the written prompt for homework. It is a trade-off I can live with.

If a group is stuck because they've mentally glued two pieces together in a way that will never work, I do not tell them what is wrong. Interventions are best done with questions that help them rethink and redo on their own. I usually ask questions such as, "Which of these squares that you have made can only be done the way you did it? Put them aside. Of the squares you made that did not have to be made that way, how could those shapes be combined with other shapes differently? Which would you now like to rethink?" Most groups respond well to these kinds of questions. However, if a group places one of those wrongly stuck examples, I may ask, "Are you certain that this is the only way those shapes may be used?" If they still don't get it, I may say, "I suggest you rethink this one also."

When they have found all 8 squares, I give them a paper handout with the solutions drawn for squares A through H. After a group has done some writing, I introduce them to the second part of the activity. I give each person a handout with the border of the square and ask them to look at the shapes and look at the square. "Show me a shape that is exactly half the area of the square." Invariably they show me shape **d**. (See Figure 3.5.) I ask for another, different half. Shape **e** is usually offered. Then I ask them to show me a shape that is one-fourth of the square. Shape **h** is usually the one they pick. "Your task is to take each one of the 15 different shapes and figure out what fractional part of the

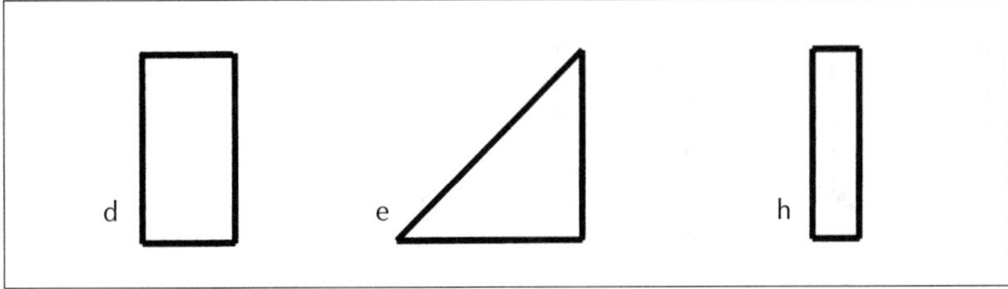

FIGURE 3.5

square it is." I encourage them to use shapes and solutions on paper that are the actual sizes of the shapes. I mention that drawing on the paper will probably help them. This second part of the activity requires more step-by-step, analytical, and deductive thinking. Both parts use the same physical materials, but the nature of the questions and tasks engenders different thinking.

Still in the same work groups in part two, the students talk more about this task (i.e., verbal mediation) than they did about the task in part one. They start with what they perceive to be the "easy" shapes—the halves and fourths. There is always an interesting moment when they consider shape **g** in square C. Some say it is half the square; others say, "No way!" Regardless of age or grade, some students have in their minds the misconception that one-half means two identical pieces that make up the whole shape. They missed the day the second- or third-grade teachers explained or showed how one-half can be the equivalent of half of the whole shape. Someone in the group figures out that shape **g** can be made from shapes **j** and **k** (which are congruent if you flip one of them).

Some younger children say the square C has been cut into thirds, because it is made of three pieces (even though they are not identical). Similarly, some students argue about shape **f**, saying, "It does not look like a half." The ones that look like halves to them are the familiar shapes **d** and **e**; **f**, **g**, and **n** are not often seen in the curriculum and it takes some reasoning for them to figure out that they too are halves. And that is one of the major points here. Part two requires *reasoning*, spatial reasoning, and part one is far more intuitive.

Familiarity with fourths readily allows students to see how two **h**'s as well as 2 **j**'s or **k**'s make shape **d**, the obvious half. Shape **p** always gives some students trouble as does square G. They try to put the right angle of **p** in the corner of the square. Usually one student draws the second diagonal of square G and everyone sees the four identical shape **p**'s.

Drawing lines on the pictures of the solutions (essentially doing geometric dissections) is necessary to finding the fractional parts of the more difficult pieces, **b**, **c**, **o**, and **q**. When doing this activity with younger children, third or fourth graders, I will leave out squares F and H. The way fifth or sixth graders find the shapes is by placing shape **s** (the shape in the upper left-hand corner) in various places in the square and drawing

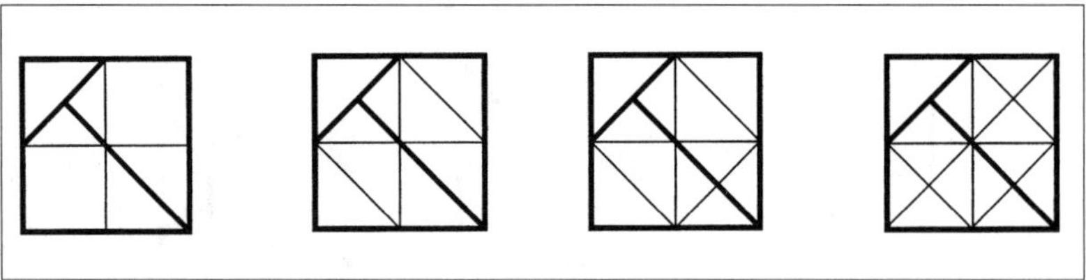

FIGURE 3.6

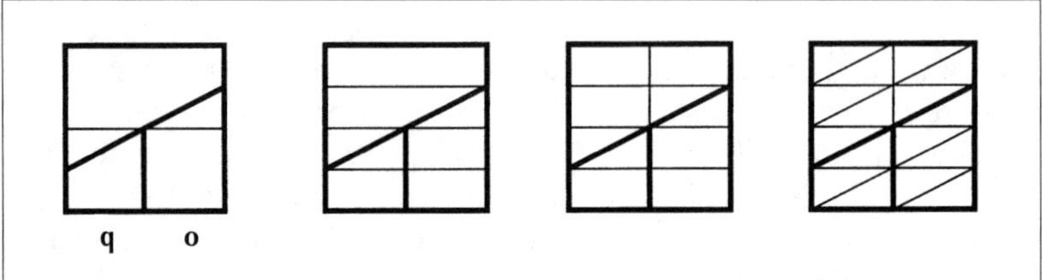

FIGURE 3.7

lines along the shape's sides. The kids say this is like *tracing*. Some kids draw more lines than others before they *see* that the shape they've been tracing is one-eighth. On the far left of Figure 3.6, *this* kid drew relatively few lines, just enough to reason that eighths, fourths, and sixteenths were there. On the far right is that of a child who needed to draw/trace lots of lines so that he could see the sixteenths. When the kids know that shape **r** and shape **s** are eighths, they can use these eighths to fill a square with drawn lines for eight of versions shape **s** and eight versions of shape **r**. When so doing with squares F and H, they see Figure 3.6 and they can reason that half of these eighths would be sixteenths.

In an analogous fashion, Figure 3.7 shows how square H can be dissected in order to find the relationship among the three shapes (trapezoids). I often encourage students to take a shape that they know and use it to help them draw lines. On the far left, a kid took shape **d** (a rectangle that is half of the square) and drew a horizontal line. That was all it took for him to see the one-fourth in the lower right corner. Then he reasoned that shapes **o** and **q** must be bigger and smaller (respectively) than one-fourth by the size of the small triangle. When I asked him what made him think this was true, he replied, "If you cut the little triangle off the top of **o**, you could put it on top of **q** and then they'd both be one-fourth." He did not know how big the little triangle was so he drew some more horizontal lines, which is what most others did. Others needed to take shape **h** and use it for dissecting and tracing lines. Most sixth graders drew lines like the middle two squares in Figure 3.7. Other kids kept drawing lines until they had the 16 sixteenths on the far right.

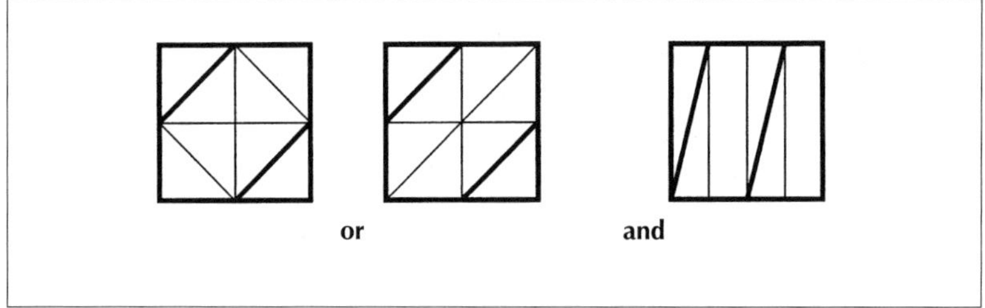

FIGURE 3.8

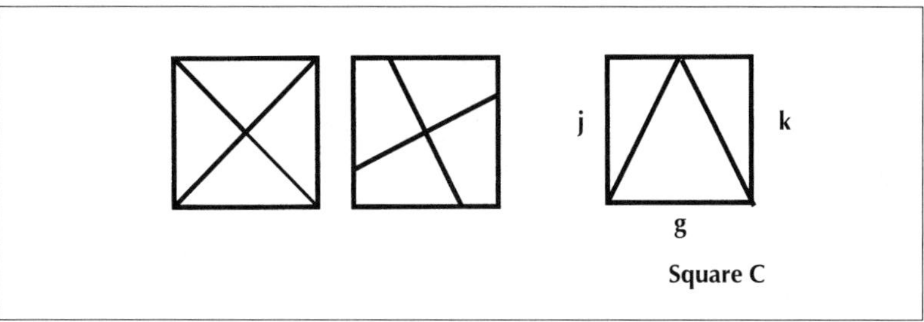

FIGURE 3.9

Dissecting existing shapes with straight lines works wonderfully with some of the easier squares and shapes so that even third graders can use reasoning to discern fractional parts. See Figure 3.8.

When working with kindergartners and first graders, I may use only squares A and B to establish halves and fourths and their relationships, and I also use four of shape **p** and four of a new shape that is half of shape **k** so that they experience the arrangements in Figure 3.9.

With good understanding of the relationship of halves and fourths, they'd be ready to tackle square C and understand that even though they do not have two of shape **g**, a second one can be made with the other two shapes, **j** and **k**.

Both parts of this activity are necessary in the development of good problem solvers and mathematicians. At the very least, the first part of the activity provided a strong experiential base of familiarity with the shapes and their relative size. Even more than "getting the feel" for the shapes, though inherently valuable, the first part develops awareness of some of the properties of the shapes and a motivation for analyzing them. The teacher can definitely weave in selected properties as a very natural extension of what they have been doing. For example, when debriefing the very difficult square H, the teacher can ask the class to compare and

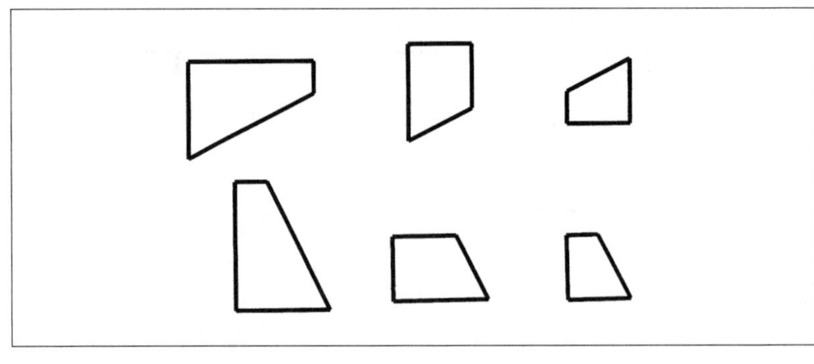

FIGURE 3.10

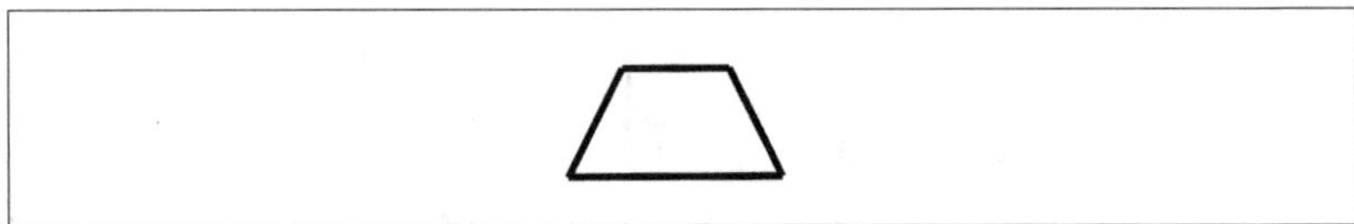

FIGURE 3.11

contrast the three shapes that constitute square H, shapes **f**, **o**, **q**. She might rotate them in a number of ways to make this visual task more difficult or easier. See Figure 3.10.

All three are trapezoids. At first, kids whose entire experience with trapezoids was with the red trapezoid of the pattern blocks (Figure 3.11) do not believe that these are trapezoids. In order to develop true understanding of the concept of trapezoid, the kids need to understand the concept of "parallel" and realize that the defining attribute of the shapes in Figure 3.10 is that each contains a pair of opposite sides that are parallel.

We will encounter the two different types of logical thinking processes continually in mathematics just as we did in this two-part activity. I don't want to pose these as being dichotomous or conflicting. They are different, to be sure, but they can be mutually supportive. It is also worth noting that these processes are not confined to spatial thinking or geometry. They permeate all of mathematics.

Answers to the fractions are: (**d**, **e**, **f**, **g**, **n** are 1/2); (**h**, **j**, **k**, **p** are 1/4); (**r**, **s** are 1/8); (**b**, **c** are 7/16); (**m** is 3/8); (**q** is 3/16); (**o** is 5/16); and (**a** is 3/4).

CREATING SENSORY IMAGES/VISUALIZING THE SITUATION

Students should be creating sensory images or using mental imagery whenever they read math textbooks, biographies of mathematicians, or story problems. Teachers should prepare beforehand specific passages, sentences, expressions, or words that are likely to prompt students to visualize the ideas in the text or problem. The teacher may do a whole-class KWC with each sentence separately shown on an overhead protector or written on poster board. As the students read each sentence the teacher can suggest that they imagine what is going on. Along with visualizing in the KWC are the questions about making connections from Chapter 2. These strategies (asking questions, making connections, and visualizing or imagining the situation) flow together easily and naturally as teachers develop their own way of orchestrating problem solving.

When most students read a story problem or hear someone describe a situation, mental images are generated. The words are catalysts for images and retain their imagery content. The PEBC folks mention that it is a good idea to picture story problems like a movie in the mind to help understand the problem. They should visualize concepts in their head (e.g., parallel lines, fractions). In fact, the more elaborate the images children have for mathematical concepts, the greater ease with which they can use them in problem solving even with what is probably the most hideous of all story problems. Let's see.

The Rendezvous of the Two Spies

Two spies decide to meet to exchange documents. One spy is in New York City (NYC); the other is in Indianapolis 700 miles away by train. They want to be together for only a few minutes at the train station. They consult the train schedules and find that there is one stop that will meet their needs. The Midwest Flyer leaves Indianapolis at midnight and arrives at NYC at 2:00 P.M. (14 hours later), covering the 700 miles at an average speed of 50 miles per hour. The Silver Streak leaves NYC at 2:00 A.M. and arrives at Indianapolis at noon (10 hours later), covering the 700 miles at an average speed of 70 miles per hour. How far from each city do the spies rendezvous and at what time?

It involves two trains going at different rates (different elapsed time to cover the same distance) and leaving at different times. One reason that it is a difficult problem is that there are multiple patterns. Each train has its own pattern of movement, essentially an average rate for covering a distance in a certain length of time. Added to these two are the patterns of the distances from each city and the distance they are apart, which narrows over time. It is inevitable that they will meet at some time (when the distance apart is zero). There is an overabundance of information.

For years I have used the expression and question, "Can you get your mind around it?" I think for this and other train problems, people cannot get their minds around this situation. They need help breaking it down. I almost always start with some version of a KWC. We carefully walk through "What do I know for sure?" I usually write down on the chalkboard abbreviated responses. Then "What do you Want to find out?" Most kids just say, "*Where will they meet.*" Other times someone will say that we also need to know what time. When no one does I try to get them to pick it up in the C question, "Are there any special Conditions?" If no one has focused attention on the passage, they might miss the need to know when—at what time.

This problem is ripe for visualization and for the math problem-solving strategy of *Act It Out* because there is a sequence of actions in the story. Using this strategy requires some creativity and a lot of common sense. I don't recommend it early in the year when you don't know the kids really well; some might take advantage of the opportunity to clown around. Also at the beginning of the year, some kids may be testing the teachers' limits, boundaries, and rules. An absurd example of how *not* to do this strategy would be to put the kids in pairs or triads and say, "Okay, go act it out."

I prefer the fishbowl, where the class is arranged roughly in a U shape and the actors are at the top of the U so everyone has a good vantage point. The teacher should be on one side near the front, so she can observe the actors, whom she will be choreographing, and the rest of the class, to whom she will address questions to keep them involved.

Because acting it out is a time- and energy-consuming approach, I use it sparingly. And since they cannot use Act It Out in a testing situation, I want them to use this bodily kinesthetic strategy to help them visualize the situation; I want to build their ability to visualize and wean them away from bodily actions.

So I choose two volunteers who go to the front of the room, one on the far left, the other on the far right, chalkboard between them. If the classroom has a U.S. map in the center of the chalkboard, I pull it down. I ask the class, "Which trains are each of our volunteers?" You may wonder why I don't have the two actors be the spies. In the past that has engendered some silly behavior. The class usually agrees that the kid on the right is the New York train and the left, the Indianapolis train. Why? Because on the map New York City (NYC) is east and on the right; Indiana (IND) is west and to the left.

How much choreographing or structuring of their behavior should you do? I try to ask questions of the actors and the class to keep the trains rolling. Some teachers put masking tape on the floor and put the two cities as far apart as they can in the room. Then they mark off the distance of 700 miles in increments of 100 miles, making a little scale model. I usually do not do that. I simply say, "It is now midnight. What is happening with them?" Many look puzzled. I ask, "Where are they? Have they left the station?" No, but the IND train is warming up. I ask the kid playing the train, "Aren't you going to work to warm up?" I make a chuga-chuga sound and move my arms like pistons. The kids chuckle.

"Okay. Now it is 1:00 A.M. Where are they now?" The NYC train is still doing nothing, but now the IND train has to move. I ask the class, "Where is the IND train now?" They say that the train is 50 miles away from Indianapolis. I turn to the kid playing that train and ask him/her to go forward what would look like about 50 miles. It really does not matter if the distance is exactly 50 miles of the 700 miles scaled by our masking tape at the beginning and end of the journey. They can just do a reasonable estimate. I ask the class, "How far away is the IND train from its destination?" (650 miles.) They need to visualize that the total distance of 700 is now partitioned into 50 and 650. As simple as this sounds, they need practice thinking this way.

"Okay, kids; it is now 2:00 A.M. What is happening?" They tell me the train from IND is now 100 miles along. The kid playing the IND train moves forward another couple of paces. "What is going on in NYC?" I ask. Invariably the kid playing the NYC train goes, "Chuga, chuga, I am warming up," and moves his arms like pistons. This time, I chuckle. I ask again, "How far has the IND train gone? How far away from NYC is it?" The class replies 100 and 600 miles. So far, so good.

When we go to 3:00 A.M., new things start happening. The IND train moves another estimated 50 miles and now the NYC train moves forward a few paces that the kid estimates to be about 70 miles. Sometimes the kid looks at the two pieces of tape and tries to figure out what one-tenth of the distance is. I reassure them all that the actors do not have to be exact, we just have to visualize what is going on—and that is the relationship between the two trains. I ask, "How far from Indianapolis is the IND train? How far from NYC? (150, 550.) "How far from New York City is the NYC train? How far is he from IND?" (70 and 630.) Now I ask the key question. "*How far are apart are the trains from one another?*" This time they need to really think and some kids in the audience grab paper and pencil. It is just so cool when they can visualize that the 700 miles can be partitioned into 150 miles away from Indianapolis and 70 miles away from NYC, which means that 220 miles out of the 700 miles have been covered, which leaves 480 miles between them.

Now the choreographer has to make a decision. Do the students all see all the elements in the problem? Do they truly understand what is happening? If so, then the Act It Out strategy has served its purpose. They can shift over to a more abstract strategy, such as drawing a picture or making a table to find a solution. How does the teacher/choreographer know? By listening to and observing everyone. If I think some are ready to solve with a more abstract strategy on their own, I ask them, "Do you feel like you understand the problem well enough now for you and your partner to use a different strategy to find the solution [pause] or would you like to continue acting it out a bit more?"

If they continue acting it out, then when they get to 4:00 A.M., I ask them these questions: "How far from where they started are they, and how far does each have to go to get to his destination?" (200, 500 and 140, 560.) "And how far apart are they?" (700 – 340 = 360). Also about this time one of the kids usually spots a key piece of the puzzle. After 2:00 A.M. the distance apart will shrink by 120 miles every hour (70 from one train and 50 from the other).

Once again I can ask if they want to keep on acting it out or just figure it out for themselves. Often I will get a mixture of responses. I have tried a variety of ways to continue this choreography. I have continued to act it out with the whole class; some students were annoyed and, in a somewhat clandestine spy–like manner, figured it out for themselves. Other times I have bowed to their requests to stop the action and let them in pairs work out the solution. On these occasions, some kids got lost because they had not fully grasped all the pieces to the relationship. Consequently, they did not get as much out of this as they could have. The middle ground has proven best for students. It is a form of *differentiation*. I have prearranged some tables at the far back end of the room for those who want to quietly go back and work out the solution. The rest, which may be more than half of the class or may be only a handful (like five), get up closer to the chalkboard and we quietly continue the action.

I have a standing routine with students of all ages. If they figure out the answer way before others in the class, they tell me privately. They do not yell out the answer. I want the rest of the class to keep working on it. This is part of being respectful to others. And then I have an extension problem ready to go for them.

Revisiting the Two Spies with a Different Representation

The next section, written by Mona Tauber of Lincoln Elementary School in Wheaton, Illinois, describes how her high-track fifth graders took on the two spies on the trains problem.

My students and I have discussed that problem solving is an essential math (life) skill. The students know they are expected to solve problems "KWC" style. This means after we read the problem, they are to first identify (by highlighting) what they Know that will help them solve the problem. Then, they are to underline what they Want to find out (the question). After that, they are to choose a strategy that would be most effective in helping them solve the problem.

Early in the fall, my 5th grade high track students tried a problem that addressed a concept that was still fairly new to them: rate (miles per hour). They have had some experience with ratios and proportions. We began by reading the title, "The Rendezvous of the Two Spies." I asked them what they predicted this problem to be about. They immediately told me they expected this problem to be about two spies and that it would involve a meeting, as they understood what a rendezvous was.

Then we began to read the problem together. I asked the students to highlight what they "Knew." This problem is challenging in this aspect alone, because mirroring real life, it shares more information than necessary to solve the problem. Some students stated that they highlighted that the Midwest Flyer arrived at NYC at 2 pm and that the Silver Streak arrives in Indianapolis at noon. A couple of others quickly stated that this was not important, because they were going to meet somewhere along the way. They made an inference while reading that aided their understanding of the problem. I asked one child to explain how he knew this. He said it was because one only leaves two hours later and travels at a higher speed. All agreed that they understood because the problem already told us the speed for each train and when they left their respective stations. I was most impressed.

They had no trouble identifying what they needed to find out, but I was glad to hear that one child emphasized that there were actually two questions in one. We didn't just need to know at what time the spies met, but also how far each spy was from the original stations.

I asked them to think about whether what they knew and what they needed to find made them think of a strategy that might help them solve the problem. It was at that point one student suggested a table. The others all agreed, but I want students to share their reasoning, so I asked the first student to explain how he decided on this strategy. He told us that he knew that we could keep track of the time and distance for both trains in one table, which would be important to knowing when they met, and that a pattern would emerge since every hour they would cover 50 or 70 miles. When I asked how they knew this meant a table would be the best strategy so quickly, another student said that we had done enough problem solving for which tables were best. It was music to my ears!

The students were essentially telling me that they had made a *math-to-math connection*. They knew that tables are effective when we want to keep track of information in an organized fashion and for which we expect to use a pattern to complete it. [See Figure 3.12.]

I quickly went around to check their tables. All were correct. I asked the kids to share how they knew the answer. One said that he also tracked the total mileage and when the total reached 700, he reached the goal, since the two cities were 700 miles apart.

I concluded the day's discussion by discussing rate and its algebraic formula. My students already know some algebra, so I knew they could comprehend. I wrote D = r * t, while explaining along the way what each meant and referred back to the problem

A: The spies will meet 350 miles from each city at 7:00 A.M.

Time	miles covered Midwest	Silver
1:00	50	0
2:00	100	0
3:00	150	70
4:00	200	140
5:00	250	210
6:00	300	280
7:00	350	350
8:00	400	420

FIGURE 3.12

to apply the formula. I then asked them to share when they might use this strategy and knowledge in the real world. They saw the real world connections, like meeting someone else at a given location, just trip planning, etc. Their homework was to write an extension problem, so that the spies would meet at a different time and/or different distance from each city.

This lesson proved to be more than I could have asked for. I know the benefits of taking more time through the problem solving process and requiring students to use the same strategies they use in reading to benefit them in mathematics.

VISUALIZING AND TRANSLATING BETWEEN REPRESENTATIONS

Another problem that profits greatly from visualization and kids acting it out recalls those great six years of Michael Jordan and the Chicago Bulls basketball team. Six championships in eight years was a fabulous time for the High Five problem. The lights at the United Center dim to total darkness. The familiar theme music comes on, blasting at eighty decibels. The announcer's deep bellowing voice bounces off the rafters, "And now, your Chicago Bulls." The crowd goes berserk. He calls out the names of the starting lineup for the game. They jog out to center court and . . . Well, what do most basketball teams do? In the math class we simply say that they give one another a high five. I model this with one student. We both raise our arms and slap our two hands against each other's two hands. Shouldn't this be a high 20 or a high 10, some kids ask. We just agree that we'll call this "high fives" and we will not do any gymnastic moves like jumping up and bumping chests.

The math problem is: "When the Chicago Bulls come out onto the court at the beginning of a game, the starting five are announced. Each player slaps a high five to each other player. What is the total number of high fives slapped by the starting five players on the Bulls? You count one high five when two players slap high fives with each other."

The class does a relatively fast KWC. In prior years the rabid Bulls fans among the kids (pretty much all of them) thought we should name the starting five in order. It varied a bit from game to game and year to year, but for example, it was Harper, Pippen, Jordan, Rodman, and Longley. Most of the kids knew for sure the names of the Bulls. Most had no trouble visualizing the ritual that introduced the Bulls. Those who had never seen this opening ceremony were treated to various descriptions of it by classmates.

Every now and then when I did this problem with kids in grades three through five, there would be some who had been to live games, but many more had seen the opening ceremonies on television. The K was easy: there are five players. They come out one at a time and slap a high five to each of the other players once. The W was pretty clear also. What is the total high fives or how many high fives get slapped altogether? The C for conditions is always the most difficult because it is not obvious. When it is obvious, they catch it under the W. Sometimes in this problem, they could not think of anything. On other occasions someone might spot that when two players slap high fives, it should count as two because there are two people and they are both doing it. I always let them talk it out to try to reach a consensus. Sometimes that just will never happen. In this case most realized quickly without needing to be convinced that two players hitting one high five was the only way for it to make sense.

I select five students to be the players and send them up to the front of the room into one corner. I then require the five actors to get in a line and come out when I call their names (or the name of the Chicago Bull they are role playing). I call them out from the corner one at a time amid wild applause from the audience. About half the times I have done this with kids they are so into the action that no one remembers to count the high fives. I could build someone who counts into the structure, but I like for them to realize this for themselves and then act it out again with someone keeping count. I do not want to dampen their enthusiasm for a math problem, and I don't want to spend twenty minutes giving directions. I want the minimum amount of directions to achieve the success that allows them to get into the problem. The KWC slows the action, but that step is necessary.

I call another group of five up to the front (the first five go back to their seats), and we do it again. When they count they get 10 for an answer. I ask straight-faced, "Are you sure? Does anyone see a pattern that will help us be sure we have the correct answer?" Almost never at this stage does anyone see a pattern. I bring another set of five kids up to the front I ask them to "Act it out again and see if you can detect a pattern." Of the two times they counted 1, 2, 3, 4, 5 . . . 10, many will not see what is going on. But some do and I'd like them to explain to the class what the pattern is. They always do some version of the following:

- The first player comes out and has nobody to slap. That is zero.
- The second player comes out and he hits a high five with the first player. That is 1.
- The third player comes out and he hits high fives with the first two players. That is 2, 3.
- The fourth player comes out and he hits high fives with the three players. That is 4, 5, 6.
- The fifth player comes out and he hits high fives with the four players. That is 7, 8, 9, 10.

I then ask the student who said this, "Then what is the pattern? How would you explain this pattern to your parents?" In this case the kid usually repeats what he says, "You know 0, 1, 2-3, 4-5-6, 7-8-9-10. They get more slaps each time." But that last statement could mean so many different things. So I seize this opportunity for a sermon, *Carpe sermonatum*. "You know, kids, math is the science of patterns and the patterns that you see belong to you; they are all yours. People often look at the same thing, and each person sees a somewhat different pattern. *Or* sometimes they will both see the same pattern, but they will talk about it differently. They'll use different words to describe the picture that they see in their minds. Now, P.J. gave us a good description. Can anyone tell us about different patterns or use another way to describe it?" Often someone (like P.J.) will say something like, "*You add one bigger each time.*" To illustrate what this kid was describing, we usually act it out again with another five. By now just about everyone has had a chance to come up and act.

When they act it out this time I tell them to count how many players get high fives each time somebody comes out. So the count becomes 0, 1, 1-2, 1-2-3, 1-2-3-4. I ask P.J. if this is what she meant. She says, "*Yes, 0 + 1 + 2 + 3 + 4 = 10.*" At this point a rumble from the peanut gallery can be heard and H.L. pipes up, "*But the fifth player to come out was the only one who slapped high fives with all four of the other players. The problem said [I am waiting for the kid to say "and I quote"], 'Each player slaps a high five to each other player.'*" "And your point is?" "*The other players did not hit four other people when they came out onto the court.*" About half the class tries to tell H.L. that the others did slap high fives with all the players, because they came out on the court and hit high fives with anyone who was there before them and then they waited for somebody new to come out and hit them. Their proof is that the first person out hit nobody; does that mean that he never slapped any high fives? No. He got a high five from each of the other four when they came out.

But some kids are now whining, "I'm confused. I thought the answer was ten. You mean it's not?" I suggest that we act it out one more time, which makes five times, so just about everybody has been up front to act it out. This time I tell the actors to keep track for us of which people they had a high five with. They verify that each of the five players hit four other players once. Now I ask, "If five players each hit four players, why wouldn't that be twenty high fives?" Most catch on that if I did it that way, I'd be double counting.

A simple T-table can help students keep track of what is going on. See Figure 3.13.

Player	**High Fives**
One	0
Two	1
Three	2
Four	3
Five	4
Total	10

FIGURE 3.13

An interesting question is what does the column label on the right mean? Compare this table to the table in Figure 3.14, which labels the column on the right as "Total hi 5s, which could also be a running total or cumulative total. It is very valuable for kids to seriously think about the difference, especially so that they develop the habit of asking themselves, what do these numbers mean?

Player	Total Hi 5s
One	0
Two	1
Three	3
Four	6
Five	10

FIGURE 3.14

One of the most important messages in this book is this: for every symbol that students write, there must be a concrete referent in their heads of what that symbol refers back to. They must be able to conjure up a mental picture, an image of some sort, that this symbol is a symbol of something specific, or we might say that this symbol represents something specific. I routinely will stop a lesson and do a spot check. I will point to a symbol and ask the class about what it represents. It would be a good idea to keep the columns simple until the kids have the hang of it. Some textbooks are a little too quick to show the kids how to make a double T-table. See Figure 3.15.

Player	High Fives	Total Hi 5s
One	0	0
Two	1	1
Three	2	3
Four	3	6
Five	4	10

FIGURE 3.15

Why am I spending so much time on one activity? If they have to act it out at all, why not just one time? Do they all need so many examples? I am a strong believer in, "If you do it thoroughly and well the first time, all who have the prerequisite, prior knowledge can get it, and you'll do far less reteaching in subsequent weeks."

CREATING REPRESENTATIONS

The third major way children and adults use visualization in mathematics is to create representations of what they perceive in their minds, their mental images. Probably in every chapter of this book I will talk about the importance of children creating their own representations. And the flip side is interpreting representations created by others.

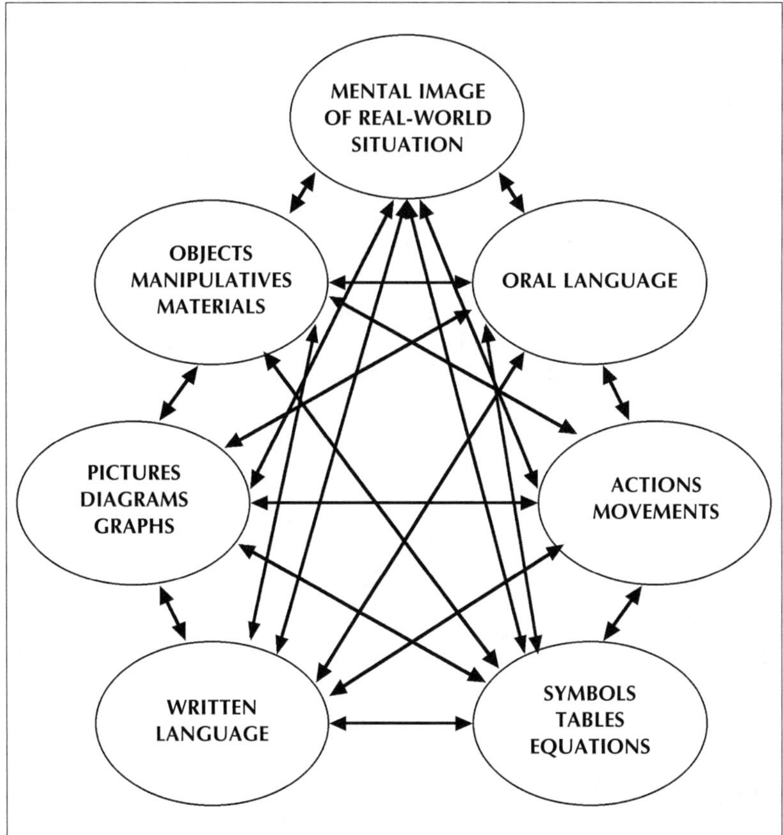

FIGURE 3.16

Of course, I feel strongly about the representational strategies being used in problem solving. Once students have a good "feel" for the problem from visualizing the situation, they should use one of the other representational strategies to work on it. In other words, they should try to represent the problem in a way that will help them to either understand it better, to understand it in another way, or to lead them to a good solution path. Zawojewski and Lesh (2003, 325–27) suggest that when students do math problem solving in small groups and work on rich problems they are using their representations to communicate their mental images to others. When students create and share multiple representations of the same problem or situation, they are continuing to keep their thinking alive. Multiple representations also may provide deeper, more elaborate understandings of the underlying mathematics, and fresh, new insights into the problem.

In the examples of different contexts in the previous chapter you probably noticed that with every new context we asked the kids to

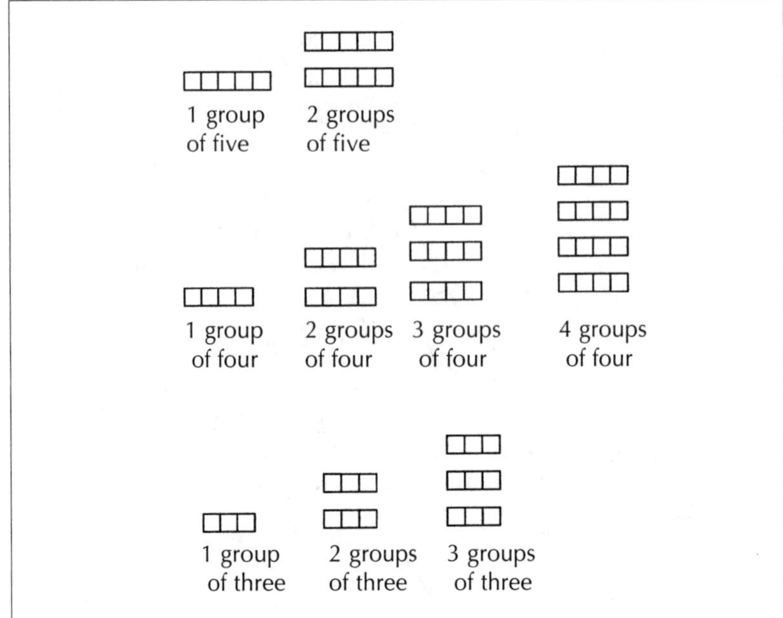

FIGURE 3.17

explore, we began fairly concretely and moved to more abstract representations. The teachers used situations that were discussed with a KWC enhanced by M-S, M-W, and M-M. They worked with objects (and language about the objects). Next, the students usually drew some pictorial representation (e.g., graph, picture, diagram) that I like to think of as a color-picture record. They often labeled the picture with symbols. Finally, they represented the data symbolically, first in the T-table, then some used an equation.

Figure 3.16 shows six major ways of representing the mental images in our heads. To build conceptual understanding to create multiple representations of a situation, and to be able to flexibly move back and forth across them, is critical. Teachers should ask students, "What does each representation reveal that the others don't, and what does each obscure?"

Our goal for mathematics teaching must be real conceptual understanding, and that means that at least some of the time, if not most of the time, students must work on complex, real-world problems, building mathematical models.

Models are mental maps, representations of relationships. They are ideas, constructs, schemata that have been generalized across a number of contexts. Perhaps this means that the problems students work on should be authentic to them in some way. But it definitely means they cannot thrive on a diet that consists only of the pablum of word problems. Students need experience with viable contexts to *mathematize* (a wonderful little word that signifies developing a way to conceive of or interpret a situation mathematically). To do so, they will need to be fluent in creating representations that capture the relationships in the situations.

Some excellent examples of this kind of "mathematizing" using multiple representations can be seen in the way one teacher builds an understanding of multiplication and division. Pam Regan, a third-grade teacher in River Forest, Illinois, had her students do a variety of problems and activities with equal groups. The kids used multilink cubes to create a physical model of all the multiplicative relationships they studied. For instance, when a story problem required them to think of a number of weeks, she would have them make chunks of seven multilink cubes to show the number of days (e.g., four weeks was represented by four chunks of seven cubes). They snapped the cubes together, threading strong nylon string through the holes in the hollow multilink cubes, and mounting it on a pegboard by passing the string through the pegboard's holes. See Figure 3.17.

Pam also worked with arrays much like Beverly did. Then she began a major unit on *area* during the first marking period. She used three major models (equal groups, arrays, and area) with activities designed to promote generalization of the concept of multiplication. For area, she started with a large number of real ceramic square tiles obtained from odd lots at a tile outlet. Ceramic tiles rarely come in whole number of inches for their side lengths. Therefore each size tile was a different nonstandard unit for measuring two-dimensional size (area). She gave each pair of children a box with about a dozen tiles. The dozen tiles in each box were identical in size, but colors did vary. There were three different sizes of square tiles across the pairs of kids in the classroom, 1¾, 2 5/16, and 4¼ inches. The students did not know these measurements. They decided to refer to these as small, medium, and large tiles.

Pam asked if they had ever seen tiles like this before. A few recognized them as being similar to what was in their bathrooms. Pam asked, "Where were they in the bathroom? Were they on floors, walls, counter tops?" Answers varied. She asked, "Does anyone have these in their kitchen?" One stated emphatically, *"Yes, but they are much bigger."* " How big?" The child put two hands up and separated them by about six inches. Pam pulled out of a large manila envelope a light blue square tile that was 7.75 inches on each side. Some of the kids said, "Wow!"

Each kid had an identical desk with a flat rectangular surface on top. Pam asked them, "How many tiles would it take to completely cover your desktop? You'd have to make a rectangle out of your square tiles. How many would you need?" She taped a sheet of newsprint to the wall that had those questions on it for all to see. Although her students did not know it, the desktops were 16 inches by 25 inches (but they had rounded edges so the table top was a little less on each side).

True to form, many of the pairs within a few minutes complained that they did not have enough to completely cover the desktop. The teacher asked, "Did you go through our KWC?" Some kids looked a little sheepish. "OK, let's do it. What do I know for sure?" *"I have a bunch of tiles."* Long pause. She asked, "What can you know about the tiles?" *"They are ceramic." "They come in different colors." "Ours are all the same color." "Ours are not."" Ours are all the same size."*

"What is the next question?" *"What do you want to figure out?"* "Okay. What *do* you want to figure out?

"How many tiles we'd need to completely cover our desktop."

Some again complained that they didn't have enough tiles. Others said to them, *"You don't need to cover it to figure out how many you'd need."* Some thought about that for a minute and retorted, *"But it would be much easier."* The teacher asked, "Okay. What is the third question?" *"Are there any special conditions, or is there something weird about this problem?"* The teacher and the kids together had modified the third question, because she often used weird problems.

The kids thought about the question and finally one said, *"I don't think ours will fit right."* "Please explain what you mean." *"Well, we made a whole row of our tiles across the desk and they don't go all the way to the other side. If we put one more on it would fall off. So we can't completely cover the top."* The teacher made sure that everyone understood and then asked, "How would we *interpret* the problem in light of this information?" This question is a deliberate link to the modeling perspective. The kids thought about this for a while. One asked, *"Can we use parts of a tile?"* The teacher said, "In real life, when professional tile artisans are doing this, they may cut the tile to make it fit." They discussed what an artisan is. They talked a little more, but the teacher ended up suggesting that they rethink the problem to be "how many tiles will completely fit on the desktop." To help them agree to this wording, she brought out a small number of cross-like "spacers" and showed them how they would fit next to the corners of each tile. Each spacer only took up a little space, but when a dozen or so were used, one could not pack the tiles tightly together, and the tiles would come closer to the edge of the desktop.

The students proceeded to place as many tiles as they could in rows and columns, then added up the equal-sized rows (or columns) needed. The desktops were all the same size, but the students found quite different answers according to the size of tiles they used. Some groups found that it would take 104 of the small tiles. They determined that it would take 8 tiles on one side and 13 tiles on the other. But that left a lot of border around the edges that they could not cover. The medium tiles would have to be in a 6 by 10 arrangement and the kids with these tiles easily counted by tens to find they'd need 60 tiles. The large tiles could fit only 15 in a 3 by 5 arrangement.

As the teacher debriefed the class, her major question was, "Why was there such a big difference in the numbers of tiles needed: from 15 to 60 to 104?" The students realized that fewer large tiles could cover the desktop. The larger the tile, the fewer one would need. The focus of the debriefing was twofold: (1) on the basic principle of measurement and division: the smaller the unit, the more you need (and its converse); and (2) when measuring area one must think in terms of squares. This second point is a critical one because many textbooks and teachers deal with area only as l x w = A. "Look at the picture of the rectangle. Take the two numbers and multiply them and then say square something afterward."

In contrast, Pam arranged this and several other activities to encourage them to think with squares when examining two-dimensional size. Over the next week Pam gave kids the opportunity to measure a wide variety of rectangular surfaces with these three ceramic tile squares. She cut out large rectangles of cardboard from appliance boxes. Like the desktop, they had to determine how many tiles of each size could fit.

They were "thinking in squares" with nonstandard squares. She then helped them see the value of working with standard square units. A key point is that with nonstandard tiles, you may know that the large tile is bigger than the small tile, but how much bigger?

Over the following weeks Pam had them working with one-inch square tiles as Beverly had her students do: making all the rectangles possible with 24, recording them on graph paper, making tables and writing the equations. Figure 3.18 shows three tables that each started with all rectangles or rectangular arrays that can be made from 24 square-inch tiles (rectangles of area 24 square inches.) It was a simple matter to transform those tables into equations. Teachers add the additional symbols in a different color to keep the integrity of the table, while emphasizing the inherent relationships of multiplication and division. There are many examples in the K–8 curriculum where one can help students understand mathematical relationships by first expressing them in a table and then allowing the patterns in the table to help them see the equation or formula (most abstract representations) that is readily created. After 24, they repeated the process with 20, 28, 32, and so forth.

horizontal	vertical
1	24
2	12
3	8
4	6
6	4
8	3
12	2
24	1

rows	columns
1	x 24 =
2	x 12 =
3	x 8 =
4	x 6 =
6	x 4 =
8	x 3 =
12	x 2 =
24	x 1 =

length	width
24 ÷ 1 =	24
24 ÷ 2 =	12
24 ÷ 3 =	8
24 ÷ 4 =	6
24 ÷ 6 =	4
24 ÷ 8 =	3
24 ÷ 12 =	2
24 ÷ 24 =	1

FIGURE 3.18

Both of these teachers' students spent lots of time working in one context with multiple representations: language, objects, pictures, lists, tables, equations. Then they had the students work in other contexts, again using multiple representations. In each context or situation, the children learned to move flexibly from one representation to another with full understanding and appreciation of what each representation shows.

USING MULTIPLE REPRESENTATIONS TO CONNECT CONCEPTS AND PROCEDURES

Some of the most difficult of the math-to-math connections are between concepts and procedures, made even more difficult because many people don't see the need to connect them. In the "how to teach mathematics" debate (or "war"), one of the battlegrounds concerns procedures or algorithms, ways people have developed to conduct efficiently some kind of operations or set of operations. Procedures tend to be general and therefore can be applied to a wide range of contexts. So when dividing a number by a fraction or mixed number, if you invert the divisor and then multiply, you will always get the right answer. This procedure will work for any divisor that is a fraction (any fraction) and any number, whole number, integer, fraction. It even works for decimals and mixed numbers (although you are supposed to turn them into an improper fraction or an immoral fraction, but it will never rise to the level of an indictable fraction).

But why does this work? Being able to memorize *how to do* the procedure to get the right answer and understanding *why* are two very different kinds of knowledge. (To my way of thinking, knowing why includes knowing how, even though you may not have practiced it a thousand times.) Many parents in the United States have given up on ever knowing *why* things work in mathematics. So when their kids can get the right answer by using a procedure, regardless of conceptual understanding, they are satisfied. One problem is that for most of us, this lack of conceptual understanding is cumulative and it all eventually catches up with us.

A second reason to be wary of memorized procedures can be seen when a student invokes a procedure in the wrong situation. Part of conceptual understanding is knowing *when* to use a particular procedure. For instance, ask a class of fourth or fifth graders, What is the mean? They will likely say something approximating, "It's when you add up all the numbers and divide by how many numbers you added up." But that is not what the mean is; that is the procedure for calculating the mean. Sometimes to illustrate this point I will ask all the students at one table or on one side of the room to one at a time tell me their phone numbers (seven digits). On my calculator I add up the phone numbers, divide by the number of people, and recite to them what is their *average* phone number. I take out my cell phone and tell them I am calling the average person who is just like them. They get a kick out of that, but it gets them thinking about the differences between numbers that are on an equal interval scale and numbers that are just markers for something else.

Psychologists are now seeing that people who have conceptual understanding and organized knowledge are able to "conditionalize" what they know. They understand the conditions (contexts or situations) under which it is appropriate to use it, when to apply it, or where it works. Conditionalized knowledge does not come from memorizing things you don't understand. It comes from generalizing from a variety of similar contexts, representing one's conceptions, creating mental models, communicating with others, and consciously reflecting on what you are doing.

A third reason for being cautious about procedures comes from research with young children first learning mathematics. Connie Kamii and others' research (Kamii and Dominick 1998; Kamii 1994; Mack 1990) shows that the premature imposition of standard, traditional, efficient, general procedures and algorithms actually is harmful. Why? How could that be? Children come to school with some fairly good ways to figure out what they need to do in many real-life situations involving mathematics. Their home-grown ways make sense to them. However, in school we tell them to forget about the way they did it on the street and "learn the right way" to compute. This may be harmful in two respects: (1) they stop relying on their own reasoning and sense-making and (2) most of the procedures for multidigit computation taught in school require that the child ignore the base ten, place-value structure of our number system. Just at the time when they are building this crucial knowledge, they are required to abandon it. "Write down the 2, carry the 1." See Figure 3.19.

```
   1
   1 4
 x 1 3
 -----
   4 2
 1 4
 -----
 1 8 2
```

FIGURE 3.19

This action is incomprehensible to most kids. However, it can be understood by using multiple representations of the partial products and the rectangle/area model. Situations abound in students' lives where they encounter rectangles and need to find the areas.

I was in two fourth-grade classrooms helping the teachers try a different approach to multidigit multiplication. I gave each kid a zip bag of base ten blocks with 1 one-hundred flat, 10 ten-sticks, and 20 little unit cubes. By exchanging ten-sticks between two base ten sets, one yellow and one blue, I was able to give each kid blue ten-sticks while the other two sizes were yellow. The bag also contained yellow and blue crayons, one of each. The teachers in third grade and these two teachers in fourth had done a great job of helping the kids understand area. In fact, one of them had made up the language device of referring to the "Area Sod Company" and the "Perimeter Fence Company." In this suburb of Chicago, Glen Ellyn, the kids are very familiar with large rectangles of sod.

I told the kids that I was planning to convert a room at home to a home office. I asked them to help me figure out the area of the room in square feet because I wanted to cover the floor with one-foot-square tiles. I held up a one-foot square of cardboard. I gave them each a piece of centimeter-square graph paper. "The room is a rectangle, exactly 14 feet by 13 feet. Please draw the perimeter of this rectangle on your graph paper. Remember the scale is one centimeter equals one foot and one square centimeter equals one square foot." They did.

"We are going to use our base ten blocks to help us figure out the area of this 13 by 14 rectangle in square centimeters and then we'll know how many square feet of tiles I'll need. Please fill this 13 by 14 border with your base ten blocks." From previous work, the kids knew that the base ten blocks were made of cubic centimeters so that when one lays them flat on a table or paper the surface of the blocks can be measured in square centimeters. When everyone had filled their rectangles, I showed them a way to group all the ones together in one corner opposite the hundred. I told them that this way will make it easier to see what is going on. See Figure 3.20.

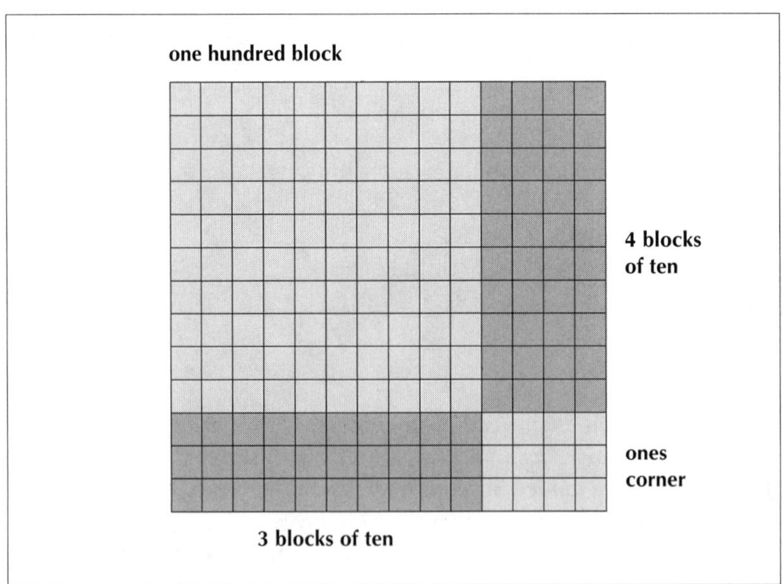

FIGURE 3.20

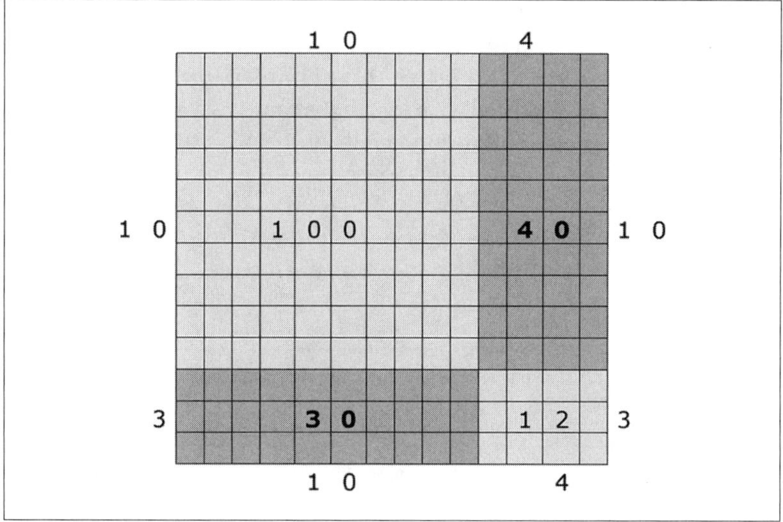

FIGURE 3.21

Then I asked the kids to remove the base ten blocks and use the appropriate color crayon to color in where the blocks were. Next I asked them think about how one big rectangle had been cut into four smaller ones and then write down how long the sides of these rectangles were. See Figure 3.21.

I asked, "How can we figure out the area of the big rectangle?" A dozen kids chimed in, *"Figure out the areas of the four smaller ones and add them up."* And so they added 100 + 40 + 30 + 12 = 182. I wrote on the board and said, "3 times 4 is 12. Do you see a 3 by 4 rectangle? Write down the 12 square centimeters of its area." Next, I pointed to the 1 in the 14 and asked them what that number meant. Several volunteered that it meant one ten. Another said it comes from 14 being 10 + 4. See Figure 3.22.

I told them the next thing we'd do was to multiply the 3 times 10. "Do you see a 3 by 10 rectangle?" They did. "What is its area?" They said, *"30."* I showed them where to write it down.

14		14	
x 13		x 13	
12	3 x 4 = 12	12	3 x 4 = 12
		30	3 x 10 = 30

FIGURE 3.22

I have a confession to make. My usual way to introduce these partial products is starting with one digit times two digits. But in this case, the two teachers said the kids had done that in third grade and they had reviewed it already. So I started with two digits times two digits to see what would happen. The kids did quite well. If you look at the two partial products in Figure 3.23, so far all we've done is the one digit by two (that is 3 times 14) that we'd started with. And if they did not remember doing this in the previous year, I would have stayed with the two partial products of 3 times 14, cutting them into two smaller rectangles and adding their area. See Figure 3.23.

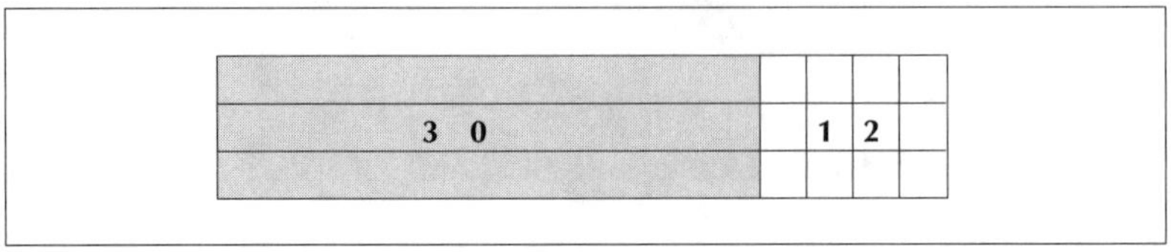

30	12

```
   1 4
x    3
------
   1 2
   3 0
------
   4 2
```

FIGURE 3.23

Let's go back to the original problem of 13 by 14. The four rectangles would give us four partial products. The tricky maneuver is the 10 times 4. It is much easier to "see" why it is 10 times 4 by looking at the four rectangles. I asked, "Do you see a 10 by 4 rectangle? What color is it?" The 10 by 10 is of course the hundred flat, which is easy for them to see. Then they added the four partial products to find the overall product of 182. See Figure 3.24.

```
    1 4
x   1 3
-------
    1 2        3 x  4 = 12
    3 0        3 x 10 = 30
    4 0       10 x  4 = 40
  1 0 0       10 x 10 = 100
-------
  1 8 2
```

FIGURE 3.24

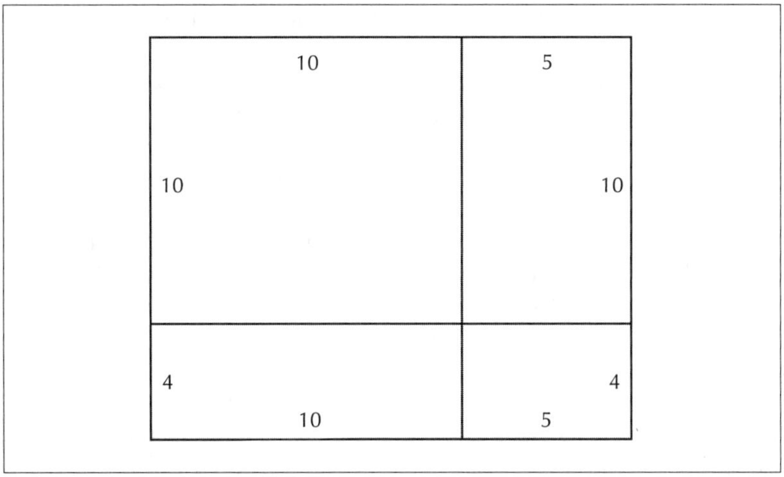

```
      1 5
x     1 4
   ------
      2 0        4 x  5 = 20
      4 0        4 x 10 = 40
      5 0       10 x  5 = 50
    1 0 0       10 x 10 = 100
   ------
    2 1 0
```

FIGURE 3.25

We did another example in that math period in the same way. The two teachers followed up in the next few days with a sequence I showed them that I have done many times. Here it is. The next day, I usually come in and act very surprised to find there are no base ten blocks. I tell them that I'll bet they learned it so well yesterday that we can use graph paper without the blocks. "I am thinking of a rectangle that is 14 centimeters by 15 centimeters. What is its area?" I walk them through (1) drawing the perimeter on the graph paper, then (2) drawing a vertical line and a horizontal line separating the two dimensions at their place value. We have our four rectangles. Finally, (3) they merely find the areas of the four to find the total area. See Figure 3.25.

I usually have them do two or three more of these and on the next day, I tell them in mock horror, "I forgot the graph paper! What will we do? I have an idea. You have seen your teacher and me just quickly draw rectangles on the board. It doesn't have to be to scale. Let's try it. Take out a clean sheet of paper. I am thinking of a rectangle that has dimensions 19 feet by 28 feet. What is the area? Draw the perimeter.

Just make one side longer than the other. Lable the lengths of the sides. Now put in the cross bars. Where do they go? Break the sides between the tens and the ones." See Figure 3.26.

Even with an ugly drawing like this one, the kids can conceive of what is going on. And they say the area is 532 square feet. When I ask them how they calculated it, some say they added 200 + 80 + 180 + 72. Others added these same four numbers (the partial products), but in a different order. Some kids become incredibly adept at the mental math of doing this in their heads. I have yet to find a kid who, if taught the partial products in this "multi-rep" way, fails to understand what is going on in multidigit multiplication. Everyone gains immensely from this combination of representations.

Some teachers basically stop here because the understanding is so good and just use calculators from this point on. Others, including me, use this base of conceptual understanding to help them see why the traditional algorithm works. It takes about twenty minutes for them to make that connection. Essentially, the four partial products that are made explicit by the rectangle model are folded into two partial products in the traditional algorithm. I have found that it is worth having the kids connect the procedure to the concept and not just use calculators. First, someone is going to show it to them anyway, and they won't try to make it as sensible as we can. Second, it helps students believe that math is understandable.

Each of these representations is building understanding, building part of the snowman; they should not be skipped. Some textbooks show the four partial products without the rectangles. To my way of thinking that defeats the power of the approach. Some skip the step when the kids make the rectangle with base ten blocks. They assume that this step is unnecessary. They think the kids can get the idea from just looking at pictures, like those in this book. I can assure you that anyone and everyone profits from making the representations of the physical model and

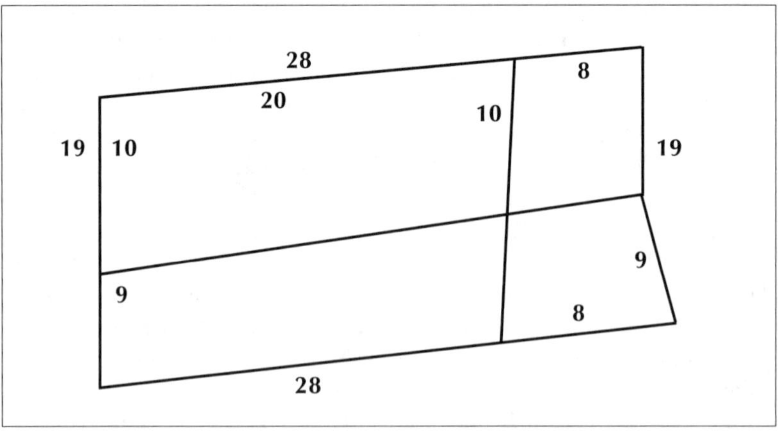

FIGURE 3.26

the drawings. Some kids are in desperate need of those sensory modalities to spark initial understanding. Others who are less in need of them will appear to be able to move to more abstract representations or even the mental computation, but they may be rehearsing something they have memorized.

I know many people who believe they understand some aspect of mathematics, but actually have only procedural knowledge. I also know many people who were taught only procedures, but by their own interest or persistence kept trying to make sense of what was going on and, in effect, they inductively derived a fairly good conceptual understanding on their own. Now they think that it is fine to teach only procedures because the kids "will pick it up later. It will make sense later." This is a dangerous assumption. Even more dangerous are those who believe that the optimal order is to use algorithms first because one cannot understand concepts until they've done a lot of work with algorithms. Working a bunch of similar problems with an algorithm is *not* the same as working with examples of concepts in a context. The former avoids the concept, the latter provides good examples of the concept.

CONSIDERATIONS IN PLANNING FOR PROBLEM SOLVING

Language Representations

How do I talk about the concept or ask questions to reveal connections or promote reflection?

How can I model thought processes, strategies, practices to encourage both cognitive and metacognitive processes?

How can I incorporate reading, writing, speaking, and listening into the activities?

How can I help the students use journals to document, reflect upon, and refine their thinking?

How can I help them explain their representations (orally/in writing)?

Other Representations

How do I scaffold experiences to move from concrete to abstract?

What manipulatives or physical objects can help students see what is going on?

Should they draw a picture of objects or of the situation/problem as they imagine it?

Does the situation contain a sequence of actions that students might act out?

Should they record information in a list and later organize it into a table?

What symbols are essential for them to understand?

How does each symbol specifically relate to the situation, objects, or pictures?

The Braid Model of Problem Solving
New entries from Chapter 3 are in italics.

Understanding the problem/Reading the story
Visualization
Do I see pictures in my mind? How do they help me understand the situation?
Imagine the SITUATION
Asking Questions (and Discussing the problem in small groups)
K: What do I know for sure?
W: What do I want to know, figure out, find out, or do?
C: Are there any special conditions, rules, or tricks I have to watch out for?
Making Connections
Math to Self
What does this situation remind me of?
Have I ever been in any situation like this?
Math to World
Is this related to anything I've seen in social studies or science, the arts?
Or related to things I've seen anywhere?
Math to Math
What is the main idea from mathematics that is happening here?
Where have I seen that idea before?
What are some other math ideas that are related to this one?
Can I use them to help me with this problem?

Planning how to solve the problem
What REPRESENTATIONS can I use to help me solve the problem?
Which problem-solving strategy will help me the most in this situation?

Make a model	*Draw a picture*	*Make an organized list*
Act it out	*Make a table*	*Write an equation*
Find a pattern	*Use logical reasoning*	*Draw a diagram*
Work backward	*Solve a simpler problem*	*Predict and test*

Carrying out the plan/Solving the problem
Work on the problem using a strategy.
Do I see any PATTERNS?

Looking back/Checking

Does my answer make sense for the problem?
Is there a pattern that makes the answer reasonable?
What CONNECTIONS link this problem and answer to the big ideas of mathematics?

4 INFERRING AND PREDICTING

INFERRING, AN ESSENTIAL PROCESS IN UNDERSTANDING

With language we communicate and we obfuscate. The prose and poetry of Shakespeare can be written on a subway wall next to the graffiti du jour. Much of the true meaning of what is spoken or written is embedded in the figures of speech, allusions, and implications provided by our language. Inferring the deeper meaning of what was written or said is absolutely essential to understanding; staying at the surface level of the literal risks misunderstanding. However, inference should be done with awareness and it ought not be haphazard.

Inferring and predicting are considered related because both require that readers go beyond the information set before them in the text. An inference depends on readers (or listeners) seeing things that are not there in print. They take in the words that are actually written, determine what they mean literally, and simultaneously, instantaneously, effortlessly combine them with things they already know so that even more meaning can be derived.

A prediction is an inference with *attitude*! I think I know what is going to happen. Inferring, drawing inferences, or (grimace!) inferencing is an inductive process in which the reader blends the words in the text with the schemata in her head and derives some kind of pattern. And in this pattern 2 + 2 may equal 5 because there are more things going on beneath the surface than is immediately apparent in the literal meaning of the words.

Keene and Zimmermann state, "Inference is a mosaic, a dazzling constellation of thinking processes. . . . There must be a fusion of words on the page . . . and the experience and knowledge of the reader." They tell children, "Inferences are like lifting ideas out of a book and adding your own ideas to them" (1997, 154).

Miller (2002) has her second graders fully engaged in the process of inferring to discern the meaning of words that are new to them. She reads aloud a story to them that contains many exotic words (e.g., veld, kloofs, koppies). She models by thinking aloud how she goes about using what she knows (e.g., her knowledge of syntax, her schemata for Zimbabwe, where the story is set). Then she asks the kids what they noticed about how she inferred the meaning of words she did not understand. They mentioned that she:

- reread the passage
- paid close attention to the words
- looked at the pictures for clues
- used her schemata
- took her time
- thought really hard

Working together the teacher and students made a big three-column chart with headings: *Word. What we infer it means. What helped us?*

After they finished the story they went back and checked to see which of their inferences were confirmed and which were not. They coded C (confirm) or X (not) on each entry in their chart. Note how the third column is a gentle reflective question, essentially metacognitive. In second grade they are able to reflect (Miller 2002, 107–9).

Many educators believe students have to be taught how to read for literal meaning first. When they demonstrate that they can comprehend literal meaning, then they may be able to handle inferences. Many question whether young children are able to think as abstractly as inferring requires. In contrast, the Public Education and Business Coalition (PEBC) folks use the literal as a base to launch children to interpret, infer, predict, and conclude. They believe that young children can: (1) create their own meaning by imaginatively expanding a story in their minds, (2) argue with literal information, (3) question the conclusions drawn by other readers.

Kieran Egan has written extensively about imagination and creativity. He declares that children are quite capable of abstract thought. Egan questions the belief that young children are concrete thinkers and must be kept at that level (essentially concrete and literal) until they are ready to think more deeply. As Egan points out, how is it that they can grasp the meaning of symbols which are inherently abstract ". . . and are arbitrarily connected to what they symbolize. By age four, children who are exposed to symbols do not confuse writing, numbers, and drawings, for instance. They have no apparent difficulty grasping that symbols refer to things" (2002, 81). Egan notes that young children "eagerly engage with characters and settings that were previously unfamiliar, that their language and thought is suffused with abstractions" (2002, 62).

Students must know when and how to infer answers to unanswered questions. They must draw conclusions about their reading by connecting the text with their schemata. They must make judgments and create generalizations about what they read. All these ideas lead to the belief that students should form unique *interpretations* to deepen and personalize their reading experiences.

"To infer is to manipulate, to sculpt, to shape, to argue with themes, concepts, or characters. To infer in a pure sense, is to build meaning . . . by doing something with the text" (Keene and Zimmermann 1997, 161). Sometimes we consciously realize we have inferred, but other times a more subtle, perhaps subconscious knowing occurs.

Teachers use a number of devices, most of which now should be familiar. Teachers explicitly explain what they mean by inferring and use think alouds that model what to do. Then the students practice inferring. For instance, they read, place sticky notes with "I" on the page and jot down their inferences.

Teachers do individual lessons in which the students compare and contrast the somewhat abstract ideas they are wrestling with. For instance, it is important to distinguish between theme and plot. Teachers may give a good initial explanation of the two concepts, but we know that students will need tons of examples to really understand the differences. They may use a two-column chart for kids while reading a story to jot down their thoughts about the plot versus the theme(s). One column can help them see how the plot develops, the other how and where in the story or plot the writer tosses out tidbits about the themes. The two-column chart is an *analytical device*. It not only records information, it is a tool in the representation of the information.

Themes are inferred and not directly given by authors. Teachers create "theme boards" where students list themes they are inferring from a particular story as they read. By reviewing the theme board they can see recurring themes across different stories, some by the same author, some by several different authors.

Miller effuses, "Children love to use a two-column format to help them organize their thinking as they practice inferring" (2002, 113). Other two-column charts are:

Facts (something we can see and observe)	Inference (interpretation)
Questions	Inferences
Quotes	Inferences

They also use three-column charts to help record and analyze:

Quote	Inference	Personal Response
Facts	Questions	Inferences

Just as an inference requires that you bring your schemata to the table, so does a *prediction*. Both give you information and you have to add your own knowledge. Predictions have the special connotation that what you put together will come to fruition in the future; you'll find out later if you are accurate (e.g., predicting tomorrow's weather). Miller specifically chooses books to read aloud to her children that have "opportunities for clear-cut predictions that can be confirmed or contradicted in the text" (p. 109). She also uses DR–TA (directed reading–thinking activity), a well-researched and proven-effective approach to comprehension. The key feature of a DR–TA is the teacher reading a lengthy passage and stopping at propitious moments to ask, "What do you predict will happen next?" While reading, students are expected to highlight or code with P when they read something that makes them have a prediction, something that is going to happen.

Kieran Egan minces no words when it comes to children predicting or imaginatively creating meaning.

> Relatively little effort has gone toward disclosing the areas of children's cognition that seem superior to adults'. Yet in terms of simple intellectual energy and imaginative productivity, the average five-year-old leaves the average adult limp with exhaustion. . . . One area of children's cognition that seems clearly superior to adults' has been investigated. Metaphor . . . is important in all flexibility in thinking . . . (2002, 91)

> Metaphor is clearly one of the foundations of all mental activity, a foundation upon which our systematic logic of rational inquiry also rests. . . . Perhaps surprisingly, it has been shown that the capacity to generate and recognize appropriate metaphors seems to peak in humans at about age four. (Gardner & Winner, 1979; Winner, 1988) . . . In many of us, as our cognitive tools develop, that metaphoric capacity . . . can become desiccated and conventionalized. (Egan 2005, 15)

Figures of speech such as metaphor, simile, euphemism, hyperbole, and irony depend on our human ability to make lightning-fast connections between what is written or said and our prior knowledge. We juxtapose those words against the awesome panoply of our schemata. We realize there is more here than meets the eye, ear, nose, and throat doctor. Jokes, puns, cartoons, or witty sayings require that we make a special kind of connection to something else not present, but nonetheless lurking in our minds. In these cases the writer or speaker intends for you to make that inference and depends on you to invoke the right schema. A political cartoonist draws a caricature of President Clinton, dressed in colonial garb complete with a wig, holding an axe and looking very sheepish next to a chopped down cherry tree, and says, "Al did it!" The cartoonist expects us to infer that Al is Vice President Gore and that, unlike President George Washington, who allegedly could not tell a lie, Clinton was never addicted to the truth.

Considering *assumptions*, we bring a different perspective to our compare and contrast exercise. Assumptions are taken for granted, often beneath our conscious awareness, and rarely examined unless we are provoked to do so by circumstances or other people. In fact it must be so, or we'd be paralyzed by the imaginable possibilities of life around us. You are driving your car down a two-lane street; you assume the cars coming in the other direction are going to stay on their side of the white line. You would not be able to function as a driver if you did not assume that all was well on the road and then *not think about your assumptions again.*

In Chapter 3, I described the problems of the basketball players hitting high fives. There's an extension to it in which the nine Supreme Court justices shake hands. Some texts refer to both as "handshake" problems. The mathematical structure of the problems is the same; each additional action causes the amount added to the total to be one more than was added before. This is a special pattern called the triangle numbers. The mathematics really has nothing to do with handshakes. But what do kids do when confronted with the following problem?

> At the end of the soccer match the opposing teams always shake hands. All 15 players from each team shake the hand of each opponent. What are the total number of handshakes?

Many kids read the word "handshake" and *assume* that they are dealing with just another triangle number problem. However, when they act it out with two lines of kids shaking hands with the other team, and not members of their own team, they realize that they have made an assumption that is incorrect.

Modes of Language

Our attempts to analyze our own thinking are determined by the concepts we use and the distinctions we make. The processes we've been discussing have somewhat different emphases. Some of the differences are subtle, some more easily stated. In addition, each of the terms used has several slightly different meanings according to context. Here is a list of the terms and a way to think about their similarities.

Infer: to reason from premises, circumstances, or evidence
Predict: to make known in advance, possibly from special knowledge, data, or evidence

Assume: to take for granted or accept as true without proof or evidence
Connect: to consider that two things are related
Conclude: to reach a decision or arrive at a logical end by reasoning based on evidence
Interpret: to explain the meaning or to conceive the significance of something

Australian educators Jennie Bickmore-Brand (1990) and Sue Gawned (1990) have looked at how specific language (words, terms, etc.) are used in the interaction of teachers and students during various parts and processes of doing mathematics. The language modeled by teachers for their students to use in problem solving includes five different modes of language, each with a different purpose. They would say that the six processes discussed in this chapter (infer, predict, assume, connect, conclude, and interpret) are in the same *mode* of language with the same purpose. It is the language of *reasoning*, which is probably the most difficult mode for kids to understand and use.

The modes of language that they ask teachers to explicitly model for their students include the following (I have listed some typical verbs and nouns that teachers would likely model for their students to use):

the language of reasoning (compare, contrast, infer, predict, interpret, conclude)
procedural language (plan, sequence, order, organize, follow rules, procedures, and conventions)
descriptive language (describe, select, notice, clarify, classify attributes, components, features)
reflective language (think, reflect, wonder, imagine, speculate, concepts, ideas, thoughts)
the language of explanation (explain, summarize, synthesize, justify, defend)

The Australians tell us that kids can deal with these five as being somewhat different and having different purposes when the teacher models the language she wants them to use and makes explicit to them *why* (i.e., the purpose). Primary teachers often start with descriptive and procedural language. Explanatory and reflective language usually come a bit later, with the language of reasoning flowing out of reflection. "Reflective language is a part of the language we use when thinking, either aloud or mentally. . . . There is a groundswell of evidence that where the language of reasoning and reflection are used explicitly by the classroom teacher, students are empowered to use the same language—indeed, the same processes—in their problem solving" (Gawned 1990, 35).

INFERRING, PREDICTING, AND REASONING IN MATHEMATICS

The notion of inferring operates on several levels in language and so it does in mathematics as well. On one level, when we read a story problem we should be watching out for our inferences. But to do this systematically is not easy. So we put kids into groups of three, and have them do a KWC and record all the parts of the problem that fall into categories of K or C. This can be done as a whole class, in small groups, or at home, individually. After all the ideas have been generated, we take them each one at a time and ask the kids, "Is this an inference? Or is this actually, literally written there in the story?" If it is not there, it is undoubtedly an inference; and that is fine! But it is very important to know that it is an inference, so that you can check for accuracy. This is somewhat different from reading comprehension, where teachers tend to be more interested in the richness, the new meanings, and interpretations of the inference than in its accuracy.

Mathematical situations are different from fiction and poetry, where the language is supposed to evoke images and emotions. It is certainly valuable to draw inferences in math problems, to broaden one's perspective on a situation. The issue is again *metacognitive awareness* of what you are doing. Some situations or problems call for estimates, others require accuracy to a specific degree. For example, if a nurse is to administer an injection of .6 cc of medication we don't want her estimating that it is about 1 cc. Furthermore we want her to know decimal concepts and symbols because we want exactly .6 cc; we don't want .06 cc or 6 cc! The difference could mean life or death!

When I am doing problems that involve rate (with sixth graders), during the KWC, I often hear kids making unrecognized inferences. The problem may be worded, "The car traveled the 90 miles from Philadelphia to Baltimore in two hours." During the K someone will say, "They went 45 miles per hour." After we have listed all the things they believe they know for sure and all the special conditions under C, I ask them to go back and inspect each one, deciding if it is a fact or an inference. This statement (45 mph) is a good one because it stirs a lot of discussion. Some think it is a fact, others say, "But that is not what the problem says." Others say, "Forty-five mph is an average; they may never have been going at that speed. They may have made a stop for lunch and driven 60 or 70 mph for most of the actual driving time."

With a good discussion like this, I can readily make the point that it is useful to infer and it is important to know when and why you are inferring. Then you can check to see if your inference is warranted or if it needs to be modified.

Earlier in this chapter I quoted Kieran Egan making some disparaging remarks about literal thinking. However, I do see the value of sticking to the literal, dissecting the story's words, terms, and their connotations. Of course, it is essential to infer as you read. I also enjoy imaginatively brainstorming problems with the kids to get at creative solutions. Inference and brainstorming are both valuable; kids just need to be clear on what they are doing and why.

Sometimes the inferences kids draw are wrong and they think their inferences are facts. Returning to our little rate situation, what if the problem was:

> A family made a round trip journey. The car traveled the 90 miles from Philadelphia to Baltimore in two hours. The return trip took three hours. What was their average speed for the entire trip?

Let's make it multiple choice.

a. 35 mph
b. 37.5 mph
c. 36 mph
d. 40 mph
e. I have lost the capacity for rational thought.

Most people would infer that the first part was at an average of 45 mph and the return trip was 90 miles in 3 hours or 30 mph. Both of these speeds are inferences. Next they would take the average of 45 and 30 (45 + 30 = 75 and 75/2 = 37.5) and thus mark b. And they would be wrong. They have made an inference or perhaps an assumption that it is appropriate to take the average of the averages. It isn't. The appropriate way to think about the problem is to *not* make any inferences about the averages on each leg of the trip. The family travels a total of 180 miles and they were on the road 5 hours. Then you would divide 180 by 5 and get 36 mph for the average rate (answer c).

Because assumptions keep popping up in unexpected places, we added a fourth question to the KWC a while ago. Some teachers with students in grades four through six use it effectively. When a group or person has completed a problem we may ask, "Is there a different way to do this problem?" This is asking, in effect, Did you make an assumption based on inferences you made?

Third Graders' Interpretations

Lisa Groves (a third-grade teacher in River Forest, Illinois) and I had been talking about a variety of language-related math issues. Lisa put her own spin on this activity that I had done for years. She'll tell her story now.

When third graders read, teachers often ask them to predict what will happen next. In our classroom, we talk about the difference between a prediction based on story evidence and a more random prediction based on mere whim. Children can eventually see that textual support is part of what grounds a prediction and makes it reasonable, but examining the story for both literal and inferential clues on which to base good predictions is a difficult task that requires year-long practice.

If children struggle to find the meaningful signals, both literal and inferred, within their "real" reading, how can we be sure that they're doing a solid job of it within their math reading? It seems obvious that students who truly comprehend a math story have a much better chance of successfully solving it, but their level of comprehension must move beyond simply noting the numbers that lie within it. They must grasp the inferred nature of the problem as well.

To assess whether or not my class was able to glean the implications within a number story, I gave them two prompts, complete with all the story details *except* the final question. I asked students to compose a question that reflected all the data within the story and also showed me their understanding of the *kind* of story this was (i.e., multiplication, division, perimeter, measuring, etc.). I also asked them to solve the problem they had created and to write about why their question made sense within the context of the story.

My grading rubric gave points for creating a question that used the stated information within the problem, was solvable, and reflected third-grade thinking (e.g., composing a multiplication problem, rather than an addition problem). I also awarded points for clearly explaining how the question arose from the story data, using a good strategy to solve the problem, and solving it correctly.

The first prompt was as follows:

Ms. Groves's son Brian is coming home from the University of Illinois tomorrow. Ms. Groves is so glad that she bursts into tears at the very thought of it! In the last complete week, she used up 6 little packets of tissues per day. Each packet had 12 tissues in it. (Create your question)

Students needed to draw inferences from several sources: "complete week" (inference: 7 days), "tissues per day" (inference: *for each day* suggests multiplication), "each packet had 12 tissues" (inference: *each packet* again suggests multiplication). These inferences would strongly suggest that there is a multiplication question embedded within the story.

6 pack egers
12 per pad

Read the following stories. Decide what problem-solving question YOU would come up with, based on the details within the story. Your question has to make sense and be solvable.

1. Ms. Groves's son Brian is coming home from the University of Illinois tomorrow. Ms. Groves is so glad that she bursts into tears at the very thought of it! In the last complete week, she used up 6 little packets of tissues per day. Each packet had 12 tissues in it.
(Create your question:) How many are theris in all?

Explain WHY you think this is a good question for this story. Because it said, "In the last week, she used up 6 little packets of tissues pur day. Each packet had 12 tissues in it." So I think you have to find out how many did she yous. So you need to multiplic 6x12=? And then that is the anser.

Solve your own problem: I think she yused 72 tissues.

Show your work here.

1 2 3 4 5 6 7 8 9 10 11 12
6 12 18 25 30 36 42 48 54 60 66 72
Anser

Number Modle: 6 x 12 = 72 tissues

I think 72 is the anser.

FIGURE 4.1

Sixteen of my 19 students were available to complete this assignment. Thirteen of those 16 used the above information to ask: *How many tissues did Ms. Groves use during that week?* Nine of those 13 students recognized it as a multiplication problem and used either an array, another kind of drawing, or a calculation to attempt to solve it. [See Figure 4.1.] Seven of them specifically referenced the words *per*, *multiplication*, or *factor* in their written explanation. The other 4 students used addition. Only 1 student out of those 13 students solved the problem correctly; however, I suspect that I overreached in using the number 12, a difficult factor for third graders to work with. The remaining 3 of my 16 students added their own information to the story to pose a different question, one of which related well to the story and made sense, although it was not solved correctly. The other two questions took up residence in left field.

I hoped the second prompt might be somewhat easier to work with:

Liz is hoping that Brian or Dan might drive her to the mall over Thanksgiving weekend so that she can get some of her holiday shopping done. She has saved up her allowance and has $120.00 to spend, but she needs to buy presents for her 4 family members, 3 grandparents, 3 aunts, 3 uncles, and 6 cousins. Then, of course, there's Max, who will most certainly be expecting his holiday bone underneath the Christmas tree! (Create your question here)

Students needed to recognize literal clues such as the $120.00 Liz had available and the various people for whom she had to buy presents, including the inference that Max, the faithful hound, counts too! Students at a more advanced level of math thinking could see a division story implied here; those at a less developed level might see an addition story.

Out of my 16 students who participated, 4 students posed the question: *How much money will Liz spend per person/dog?* Another 6 students created the simpler question: *How many gifts did Liz need to buy?* Of those 4 students who posed the division question, 3 were able to solve it correctly, though one lost touch with her reasoning at the end. [See Figure 4.2.] Of the 6 students who posed the addition question, 4 solved it correctly. The remaining students all added information to the story to pose other questions: 4 of these made sense and were solved correctly, 1 made sense but was not solved correctly, and 1 joined the left field contingent.

As I look over these results, it makes sense that more students were able to recognize the multiplication question inferred in the first prompt than were able to recognize the division question within the second prompt. Although few students feel competent about division right now, many classmates are fluent with multiplication facts, and this prior knowledge helped steer them. It is also interesting to see the connections between students' interpretive thinking within their reading work and within this interpretive math exercise. In general, my more able reading students, whose paragraphs usually reflect much extrapolation of the ideas in their reading text, were also more likely to extrapolate here by adding more information. One of my most intuitive readers posed the following question to the second prompt [see Figure 4.3]: *Liz buys a present for everyone but realizes that when she's buying her last present she is $55 over her budget! She has to return some gifts! (Each gift costs $11.00.) How many gifts do you* [sic] *have to return?* After several interesting calculations, he decided that the answer was 5 gifts, and triumphantly announced, *"So now Liz is back on budget!"*

Just as inferences exist within third-grade story reading, they exist within math reading. The more I can coach my students to find these clues, the more likely that they will seize upon a sensible strategy and find a solid answer.

How much will Liz spend for each preseant. 120 ÷ 28 = ?

Explain WHY you think this is a good question for this story.
You have to divide because theres 20 relatives and $120.00. You can't draw pictures, you cant multiply, and you cant make a chart. Now I need to know how much Liz should spend on each present (hopefully the same amount of dollars for each?)

Solve your own problem: Liz can spend 3 dollars on each person.

Show your work here.

120 ÷ 20 = 6

FIGURE 4.2

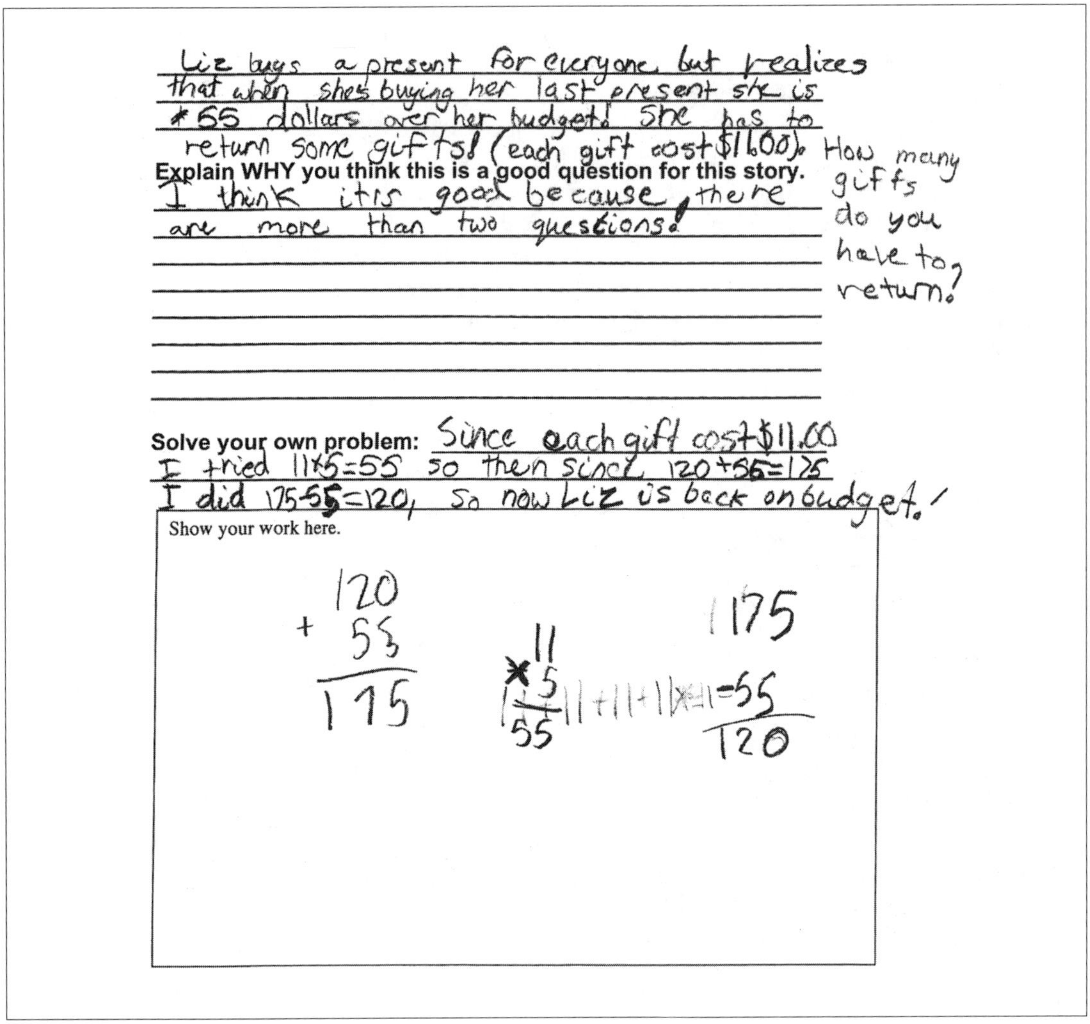

Liz buys a present for everyone but realizes that when she's buying her last present she is *55 dollars over her budget! She has to return some gifts! (each gift cost $11.00). How many gifts do you have to return?

Explain WHY you think this is a good question for this story.
I think it's good because, there are more than two questions!

Solve your own problem: Since each gift cost $11.00 I tried 11×5=55 so then since 120+55=175 I did 175-55=120, so now Liz is back on budget!

Show your work here.

$$\begin{array}{r} 120 \\ +\ 55 \\ \hline 175 \end{array} \qquad \begin{array}{r} 11 \\ \times\ 5 \\ \hline 55 \end{array} \quad 11+11+11+11+11=55 \qquad \begin{array}{r} 175 \\ -\ 55 \\ \hline 120 \end{array}$$

FIGURE 4.3

MATHEMATICS: THE SCIENCE OF PATTERNS

I can remember the thrill I felt the first time I heard mathematics described as the science of patterns (or patterns, order, and relations) by Lynn Arthur Steen (1990). I thought, "This makes so much sense!" One of the greatest gifts we can give our students is to help them develop their innate capability to *infer patterns and then use these inferences to predict.* The first part, inferring, is an inductive process that reaches a point at which the child thinks he or she has *inferred* a pattern. Then the child makes a subtle shift and, in a somewhat deductive process, tests the hunch by *predicting* subsequent manifestations of the pattern. Helping children become more sophisticated in their inferences and their predictions is a major job for the teacher. Whether the patterns are numerical, visual, auditory, or otherwise, the cognitive processes are very similar and they are greatly facilitated by language.

Presenting mathematics as the science of patterns can bring coherence to a bouillabaisse of disconnected ideas. Every branch of mathematics has its own characteristic patterns. Mathematical concepts describe these patterns and relationships. In geometry one can find patterns in the properties of polygons, in the tessellations that tile a plane, or in the way cubes fill a box. Working with data, children can see patterns that describe the shape of how the data are distributed. There are amazing patterns to be discerned in experiments with probabilities, if one can be patient in the long run. Many people think of algebra as a course or maybe two that one takes in high school. But algebra is really a way of looking at and representing patterns a bit more abstractly than the way numbers do. Through algebra we represent information in tables, graphs, and equations and we look for patterns in each of these representations.

In Chapter 2 I talked about how a concept is an abstract idea that explains and organizes information (or data) of some kind. I believe that every math concept in the elementary school mathematics curriculum is a pattern or relationship of some kind. When kids are having a very difficult time with a particular problem or bunch of similar problems, we try to the help them see and use patterns. A good way to enrich almost any chapter in the math text is to rethink it in terms of patterns. How would I use patterns to do it? What kind of patterns do I want them to see?

Basic Skills

I have never run into anyone who has said that basic skills are not important (except for cartoon ne'er-do-well urchins, like Calvin and Bart Simpson). Why, you might ask, do so many children have so much trouble memorizing them? Number 1: Most kids are required to memorize "facts" that they do not fully understand. They are trying to use brute-force memory that connects to nothing. If you took a course in foreign language and had to "learn" their counting numbers, you probably memorized them in a particular order (and maybe with a little sing-song rhyme to help you). But if someone were to ask you, how do you say 35? Could you do it quickly? If you are fluent in the language you can draw on a whole raft of experiences that have given meaning to "trianta u chianca." If not, you may have to recite what you memorized starting at "unta."

Number 2: They have skipped some steps. When children experience the fundamental processes needed to construct rich, deep knowledge of numbers and operations, they have no problem remembering or memorizing single-digit operations. I mentioned these pieces of the puzzle in Chapter 1. They are:

Counting: building one-to-one correspondence and number sense. A serious problem with traditional basic skills is going directly from counting to memorizing computation facts.

Number relations: decomposing and recomposing quantities to see relationships among the numbers (e.g., 10 objects is one less than 11 and one more than 9. Ten objects can be separated into two piles many ways, such as 7 and 3; 10 can be five groups of two). They are developing models of number and a generalized concept of equivalence. Skipped by traditionalists, yet it is absolutely essential for students to invest great amounts of time investigating and playing with these relationships. If done well, it facilitates other processes immensely.

Place value: On the basis of number relations, students create sets of ten with objects and begin to understand the base ten, positional notation (e.g., "1" in 15 means 1 group of 10 and the 5 means a group of 5 more). Traditionalists briefly explain place value and do not see how all these processes are related.

The meaning of the operations: creating models (mental maps) of different situations and realizing that operations have multiple meanings (e.g., subtraction does not always mean "take away"; it could mean the "difference" in comparing two quantities). This step is skipped by traditionalists.

Fact strategies: thinking strategies for learning the facts for the operations. If students have done extensive work on number relations they can group the fact into patterns for meaningful understanding, derivation, and recall. This is very different from the rote memorization advocated by traditionalists.

Numbers and Computation in Asian Languages

It is critical that American children explore number relationships combined with rich language. We often hear how Asian students outperform us in mathematics. I discovered in 1987 in *Science News* that psychologist Irene T. Miura had compared the "conceptualization of numbers across languages" in first-grade students from upper-middle-class families in the United States, China, and Korea (and Japan in a second study). "In Asian languages, number names follow a base-10 number system. Place value is inherent in the number language." When counting, English speakers will say ten, eleven, twelve . . . twenty. In contrast, Asian speakers will count, ten, ten-one, ten-two . . . two-tens. Asian languages introduce and support base ten, place-value concepts, and symbolism. This language feature greatly facilitates regrouping and renaming in computation. In Miura's research, Asian language-speaking students showed "greater flexibility for mental number manipulation." (See also Miura 2001.)

Chinese teachers build on this base ten language by using specific thinking strategies for students to learn the basic facts. The thinking strategies U.S. teachers typically use are counting up, learning doubles, double plus one, and fact families (e.g., all the sums of 12). In contrast, Chinese teachers use "make 10" as their major strategy and introduce basic facts in units, such as the 6+ unit. "When Chinese children learn the basic facts, their task involves not only memorizing but also using logical thinking and reasoning based on relationships among the numbers. . . . [Teachers encourage students to] . . . look for patterns and relationships" (Sun and Zhang 2001, 31).

And the base ten advantage is not the only gift from Asian languages. The concept of fractional parts is inherent in the words used—"one-third" in English would be spoken in Japanese as *san bun no ichi*, literally "of three parts, one" (Miura 2001). These language differences probably give Asian children a two- to three-year advantage over English-speaking students in computation and a much stronger foundation in number sense, number relations, place value, and fractions. U.S. elementary teachers need to provide their young students with a wealth of experiences that Asian students have had before entering school. The Americans especially need those experiences that involve the kind of sense-making and building of understanding that only language can provide.

Repeat Business

To anyone who has young prereading children to whom you read aloud regularly, it is an understatement that the children want you to read to them the same stories day after day, night after night, until you are begging them to let you read something new or just something *else*. I love Dr. Seuss too, but how many times can you hear yourself rhyming with the same nonsense words . . . or real words? (A couple of years ago I taught a math class of twenty-five female students, including Dina, Gina, Tina, Nina, Lina, and Rina. It drove me crazy because I continually mixed up the six of them.)

Why do children want to hear the same stories *again and again*? It is an emotional high point in the daily life of a child to curl up in the lap of a parent who reads aloud. It is a warm, safe, abundantly nurturing, intellectually stimulating period of time and place. They are enthralled not only by the content of the stories, but repeated readings allow the kids to predict what is coming next in the story. Before you turn the page many are spontaneously reciting the words on the next page. They begin to think of themselves as readers.

Over the years many teachers have come up to me and said, "I have done the things that you suggested, but the kids don't get it and they seem to want to do the same thing over and over." I tell them about the snowman and how understanding doesn't come from one or two exposures. It comes from many examples and kids perceiving the patterns. They need to see, hear, and touch the patterns to fully understand them. Then they can use the patterns to predict and that makes them feel confident and even powerful. And they believe in themselves. This is so obviously true in reading. Why should it be any different in mathematics?

Inferring the Meaning of Operations

There have been several truly excellent books that help teachers to create meaningful experiences with computation. At the top of my list are the works of Catherine Fosnot and Maarten Dolk. Rather than attempt a comprehensive review, I will try to shed some light on some issues. The Cognitively Guided Instruction (CGI) research and development program has helped us to see the true cognitive nature of the arithmetic operations. Of course, Lewis Carroll, in *Alice in Wonderland*, referred to them as "Ambition, Distraction, Uglification, and Derision." His real name was Charles Dodgson, professor of mathematics at Oxford.

In addition (no pun there) to the cognitive nature of the operations, we should help students develop their meanings for these operations *in contexts*, or real-life situations. We get a fascinating picture from CGI of what addition and subtraction are in terms of the relationships involved. John Van de Walle (2006) has an excellent overview of eleven different situations for addition and subtraction. Kids can model all of these situations with good language and actions on objects. I favor Unifix cubes because kids can stick them together and they come in multiple colors, allowing color-coding of the different addends.

If kids have in their heads that addition always "means" combine things and subtraction always "means" take away, they will be in deep linguini before too long in school. Yet, doesn't the very word *subtract* itself have strong connotations for extracting something out of something else? By the wonderful conceptual power of language we also refer to *comparison* as subtraction. We may want to figure out: If Bobby has 15 baseball cards and Billy 9, how many more does Bobby have than Billy? This problem would be called "compare: difference unknown." Note that the problem does not use the word "difference" in it; nor "comparison" for that matter. These realities must be *inferred* from the *context*!

Therefore, my colleagues and I simply frame these problems as *situations* and address them with our KWC and language. Our students don't memorize key words. They don't try to guess the operation. They use language, objects, and actions to help them *think, imagine, and infer*. Here are six story problems that are considered the most difficult for kids in first and second grade.

1. Kathy has 17 juicy jelly beans and Lenny has 8.
   How many more juicy jelly beans does Kathy have than Lenny?
2. Sally has 12 cookies and Kevin has 9.
   How many fewer does Kevin have than Sally?
3. Mary has 6 Britney Spears CDs.
   Alice has 3 more than Mary does.
   How many CDs does Alice have?
4. Henry has 4 Rambo DVDs.
   He has 2 fewer than Alan does.
   How many Rambo DVDs does Alan have?

5. Dale has 7 florescent gel-pens.
   He has 3 more than Laura does.
   How many florescent gel-pens does Laura have?
6. Danny has 8 markers.
   Larry has 4 fewer than Danny does.
   How many markers does Larry have?

Let's attack number 1 head on. I tell the kids to get out their Unifix cubes. Okay, kids, let's read the first part, Kathy has 17 juicy jelly beans. Pull out 17 cubes that are the same color. Stack them together. Each cube represents one jelly bean. What is next? Lenny has 8. Get 8 Unifix cubes of the same color, but pick a different color than Kathy has. Stack up the 8 and put the two stacks side by side. Now I want everybody to answer my question out loud and don't be shy.

How many does Kathy have? *(17)*	How many does Lenny have ? *(8)*
Do they have the same amount? *(NO!)*	Do they have different amounts? *(YES!)*
Are they the same? *(NO!!)*	Are they different? *(YES!!)*
Are they equal? *(NO!!)*	Are they unequal? *(YES!!)*
Who has more? *(Kathy!!)*	Who has less? *(Lenny!!)*
Who has the smaller amount? *(Lenny!!!)*	Who has the greater amount? *(Kathy!!)*
Who has fewer? *(Lenny!!!)*	[They're getting excited now.]

How MANY MORE does Kathy have?

At this point I push the two stacks together next to each other and I ask the question again. I break off the top cubes of Kathy's stack so that the two stacks are the same height and I have in my hand "the difference." I say to them, "Here is the difference. Here is how many more she has. Now you do the same to your stacks and tell me how many more Kathy has." After they've done that, I tell them to give Kathy back hers and I ask them, "How many fewer does Lenny have?" We repeat this process of putting the two stacks next to one another and breaking off a bunch at the top to make the two stacks the same height. Then we count the cubes in our hands to make sure.

We continue with problem 2 in the same fashion. All the questions I asked will work, if you change the names and the final question. Of course, you can make up dozens of comparable questions by changing the names, the objects, and the numbers.

Problems 3 through 6 have a small twist to the questions. In each of these cases, you are told what one person has and what the difference between the two is. You simply set up a stack of one color for the person you know and then in problems 3 and 5, you model the difference in four ways. You should still run through the list questions to which they respond because that helps make the connections.

By using the more concrete representations initially, we set up a good foundation for the students to be able to make those inferences suggested by the words of the problems. We also help them *visualize* the situation so that they will be able to move away from the concrete as soon as possible.

INFERENCE AND PREDICTION IN PROBABILITY

A final example illustrates how patterns in data may be inferred and used to predict. With minor modifications this activity has worked wonderfully for grades two through six. Although you'll find many similar activities in books, our version has some unusual twists and turns not found elsewhere.

I divide the class into eight groups of three or four students and assign each a task role of supplier, grabber, recorder, and reporter. Each group is designated by a letter S–Z and a large index card with their letter is taped to their table. I hold up a brown paper bag with which I demonstrate and explain the task. "The suppliers will come to me and get a bag with the letter of their group. They are responsible for making sure no one looks inside their bag. Inside your bags are 10 cubes, some red, some blue, some yellow." (I pull out one of each color and drop it back in the bag.) "You are *not* to look in the bag. Instead, you must take out 1 cube, record its color, and drop (replace) it back in the bag. This is called a sample of 1, with replacement. Do this sampling 25 times. Then analyze your data and predict how many of each color are in the bag. The supplier will shake the bag, hold it up, above eye level, and open it so that the grabber can reach in and grab one without looking. Recorders should use the sheet to write down the color of each sample of 1." (The sheets have numbers 1 to 25 down the left margin so there will be no miscounts.) "The group analyzes the data together and must agree on a prediction for the 10 cubes: how many of each color are in the bag? The reporter of each group will explain their reasoning to the class. Each student will write an individual report about the group's reasoning from data to prediction."

Suppliers get the bags and the groups begin sampling. When a group has finished, I take their bags, which are labeled so I can give them back later. I usually let them do any analysis they want to make the prediction; on other occasions I require them to use a particular procedure, such as represent the number of each color as a fractional part of the total of 25. When they have their prediction, the recorder goes up to the chalkboard or a poster that I have prepared and enters that group's data and prediction (see Figure 4.4). When all have entered their information, we have some debriefing.

We debrief on how they made their predictions. Each group explains its reasoning for going from data to prediction. There are always two approaches. In the first, using their number sense and the data, the students

	DATA				PREDICTION		
GROUP	R	Y	B		R	Y	B
Z	6	4	15	>>	2	2	6
Y	7	2	16	>>	3	1	6
X	8	5	12	>>	3	2	5
W	6	6	13	>>	2	2	6
V	7	5	13	>>	3	2	5
U	7	4	14	>>	3	1	6
T	5	6	14	>>	2	2	6
S	9	5	11	>>	4	2	4

FIGURE 4.4

play with possibilities, much in the same way that in reading they juxtapose schemata with text. Both are interpretive, inferential processes. For instance, group W reasons: "*We got 13 blue which is a little more than half, so we should say 5 or 6 blues. Red and yellow were both 6 so they should be the same, like 2, 2 or 3, 3. If we do 3, 3 then that leaves only 4 for blue, which does not seem right. So, we went with 2, 2, 6.*"

The second approach is to use some kind of procedure that will always work regardless of the actual data one has. This approach must be accompanied by thinking to make sure you are using a good procedure and using it accurately. For example, group Z reasons that "*There were 15 blue (which is 15/25 or 3/5 or 60 percent). Red was 6/25 so 6 divided by 25 is .24 or 24 percent and 4/25 is 4 divided by 25 or .16 or 16 percent. Then we took 60 percent of 10 and got 6 for blue, 24 percent of 10 is 2.4 red, which we rounded down to 2 red. AND we took 16 percent of 10 for yellow, which is 1.6 yellow. We rounded that up to 2. So our prediction is 2 red, 2 yellow, and 6 blue.*" Note that even with a good procedure, they still must use number sense and round.

Somewhere during this debriefing, a student will ask, "*Can we collect more data?*" or "*Can we do it over again to see if we get the same thing?*" I seize the opportunity to engage them in two conversations: (1) the law of large numbers, where increasing the samples will give us more stable statistics and (2) a little workout with proportional reasoning. I ask them, "If your data today gave you 14 out of 25 blue, how many blues would you expect to get if you did it again 75 times so that you had a sample of 100?" A couple of students blurt out, "*56!*" "What reasoning brought you that insight?" They fumble around trying to explain that "*Everything is four times bigger.*" I may have to summarize it for them that if we can assume that in general, the balance or ratio of blue to the total will remain the same 14 out 25, then the three additional samples of 25 (to get 75 more) will each have 14 blues (maybe).

Another way to see this would be a proportional equation:

$$\frac{14}{25} = \frac{X}{100}$$

Many textbooks tell the kids, just cross-multiply to solve for *x*. I'd much rather they think about what is going on here. The new sample is 4 times bigger (100 vs. 25). Wouldn't we expect that the number of blue would also be 4 times bigger (4 x 14 = 56)? Some texts show

$$\frac{4}{4} \times \frac{14}{25} = \frac{X}{100} = \frac{56}{100}$$

which is justified as multiplying by $\frac{4}{4}$ (which is 1). I use

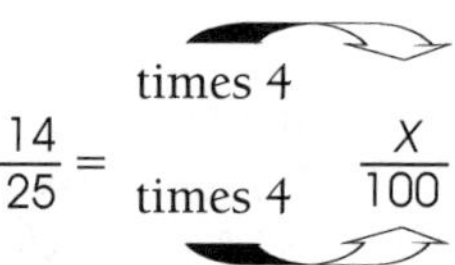

a little diagram to try to capture the language of *4 times bigger* for the sample and for the blue. Each group reports on how its students came up with their prediction.

Another question that comes up along the way, I hold off until the debriefing. I will always get the question, "Are the contents of the eight bags all the same?" Up until now I've been saying, "Let's wait and see." Now look back at the table in Figure 4.4. The class invariably divides into three camps: the largest group thinks the bags are all the same; the smallest group says some are different; in between are those who say, "*We can't tell. There is no way to tell. You are playing a trick on us.*" So I ask them to look at the data for each color. "How spread-out is it?" They tell me that the red goes from 5 to 9, yellow from 2 to 6, blue from 11 to 16. "If the bags are all the same, why are there differences among data?" They say things like, chance, random, they cheated. I ask, "If one of the bags was different, but the other 7 the same, which would you think is the different one?" They nominate group S and group Y. I ask them to explain their reasoning. They tell me that Group S had the lowest blue (11) and the highest red (9). Group Y had the lowest yellow.

For those who are not sure what can be said, I ask, "How different would the data in one bag have to be before you were fairly certain that the contents of the bag were really different and that the data could not reasonably have happened by chance?" Pause. "How about 1 red, 1 yellow, and 23 blue? Do you think that could happen by chance?" Yes, but it is *very* unlikely.

Then I tell them the truth. "*All the bags are the same!* These differences in the data happened by chance. S and Z are just random fluctuations that are to be expected. Now what do you think about the data? Do

DATA			
GROUP	R	Y	B
Z	6	4	15
Y	7	2	16
X	8	5	12
W	6	6	13
V	7	5	13
U	7	4	14
T	5	6	14
S	9	5	11
TOTAL	**55**	**37**	**108**
percent	**27.5**	**18.5**	**54.0**
decimal	**0.275**	**0.185**	**0.540**

FIGURE 4.5

you want more data?" Some think of another possibility: If the bags are all the same, the 8 groups give us 200 samples of 1. More often than not, I have to suggest this idea of summing the data for each color. See Figure 4.5. I assigned 8 groups of 25 in order to have a base of 200, which allows the students to easily calculate percents; just divide by 2. Therefore, 55, 37, and 108 become 27.5 percent, 18.5 percent, and 54 percent. I ask the students if they want to change their predictions. "Let's think of some possibilities. Is 2, 2, 6 *possible?* Is 3, 1, 6 *possible?*" They have not caught on yet to what I am asking. I ask, "Is 1, 0, 9 possible?" Finally, they get it. They tell me that 1, 0, 9 is *impossible* because there must be some yellow. I ask, "Did you do a KWC?" Some did; some didn't.

"Let me change the question. Is 2, 2, 6 *probable*? Which is more probable: 1, 1, 8 or 2, 2, 6? Another way to ask this question is, which is the more *likely*." Finally, I ask them to nominate the three *most likely* combinations. This generates a lively discussion. They decide to go with 2, 2, 6; 3, 2, 5; and 3, 1, 6. Recall that the total data showed 27.5 percent, 18.5 percent, and 54 percent. Each student is asked to "individually vote for your personal prediction of the most likely combination." With this data, about 19 students (2/3 of the class) went with 3 red, 2 yellow, and 5 blue; 4 students went with 2 red, 2 yellow, and 6 blue; and 5 students went with 3 red, 1 yellow, and 6 blue. I hand back the bags to the team with the corresponding letter. They fairly tear their bags open to reveal 3 red, 2 yellow, and 5 blue.

There are many variations of this activity and I think I've tried them all. I like it this way because:

1. It is very potent in small groups; it contains sufficient action, decisions to be made, and so forth.

2. Using 10 as a total and 3, 2, 5 in the bags provides a good balance. In contrast, having only 1 of a color (e.g., 3, 1, 6) in the bag will occasionally give you data like 8, 0, 17, which is more annoying than intellectually provocative. Having a separation of 5 and 3 means that about 9 out of 10 times, blue will be the biggest number in the data. That is good. We don't want to trick the kids. We want them to see patterns in the data.
3. I like 25 for the number of samples because it can be readily converted to decimals, multiplying by four as we did. For second graders I use 20 samples. One would think that 20 would make it too simple because they could just take half of each data point. But at least half of the data are odd numbers, so the little kids would have to use their number sense, rounding, or other strategies.

Some teachers will have one or more bags different, but I have found that is unnecessary. There is enough random variation so at least one group is a little divergent. You can get to what is perhaps the most important point in the activity, the basis of inferential statistics and a cornerstone of probability theory. *How different does the data have to be between groups for us to think that there is something other than chance operating to create these differences?* There are only two possibilities: the differences are random, chance variations *or* something is causing a difference (in this case, could the contents be different?). This simple activity illustrates this big idea based on patterns in the data in a fabulous way.

CONSIDERATIONS IN PLANNING FOR PROBLEM SOLVING

Patterns

What patterns (visual, spatial, or numerical) do I want them to see?
What questions do I ask to help them see patterns?
What questions do I ask to build bridges, helping them make connections?
How do I talk about the other mathematical concepts that are related?
What terms or language could I use? What metaphors or analogies could I make?
What connections are important for them to make as we debrief the activity?
How do I help them move from natural language to more precise mathematical terms?
How do I help them communicate (orally and in writing) their solutions and understandings?

The Braid Model of Problem Solving
New entries from Chapter 4 are in italics.

Understanding the problem/Reading the story

Visualization

Do I see pictures in my mind? How do they help me understand the situation?

Imagine the SITUATION

What is going on here?

Asking Questions (and Discussing the problem in small groups)

K: What do I know for sure?

W: What do I want to know, try to figure out, find out, or do?

C: Are there any special conditions, rules, or tricks I have to watch out for?

Making Connections

This reminds me of . . . Math to Self; Math to World; Math to Math

Infer

What inferences have I made? For each connection, what is its significance?

Look back at notes on K and C. Which are facts and which are inferences?

Are my inferences accurate?

Planning how to solve the problem

What REPRESENTATIONS can I use to help me solve the problem?

Which problem-solving strategy will help me the most in this situation?

Make a model	Draw a picture	Make an organized list
Act it out	Make a table	Write an equation
Find a pattern	Use logical reasoning	Draw a diagram
Work backward	Solve a simpler problem	Predict and test

Carrying out the plan/Solving the problem

Work on the problem using a strategy.

Does this strategy show me something I didn't see before now?

Should I try another strategy?

Am I able to ***infer*** *any* ***PATTERNS****?*

Am I able to ***predict*** *based on this inferred pattern?*

Looking back/Checking

Does my answer make sense for the problem?

Is there a pattern that makes the answer reasonable?

What **CONNECTIONS** link this problem and answer to the big ideas of mathematics?

Is there another way to do this? Have I made an assumption?

5 DETERMINING IMPORTANCE

ANALYZING TEXT

When I first encountered reading comprehension strategies, I recall being a bit surprised that the different strategies were not as distinct as I thought they would be. The more I read the more I realized that they were not prescriptions, but vehicles to help us find our way through the maze of possibilities. I love how Keene and Zimmermann (1997) talk about determining importance as the "antithesis of denial" (p. 93). Finding the essence of a text means uncovering what may be important "denied or ignored" (p. 93) ideas hiding beneath the surface and may escape notice if we don't dig for them. Harvey and Goudvis (2000, 118) likewise speak to "distilling the essence of text" that is far more than picking out the so-called main idea from a contrived paragraph on a reading test.

When proficient readers tackle authentic texts (e.g., newspaper editorials, books, poetry), they have to decide what is important on several different levels: the text as a whole, each sentence, and even each word. These decisions are greatly influenced by their purposes, which may be to

- understand new concepts or information
- determine what is important and what is interesting
- uncover a theme, opinion, or perspective
- answer questions
- decide if the author is trying to inform, persuade, or entertain

Decisions about importance are based not only on one's purposes, but also on

- the reader's prior knowledge and schemata concerning this content
- the reader's beliefs and opinions concerning this content and this author
- the reader's schema for the text format
- the concepts and opinions of others

How do we help young children learn how to distinguish *important* from *interesting*? Debbie Miller (2002) helps second graders to distinguish fiction from nonfiction by arranging the attributes of these two genres into a Venn diagram. They use sticky notes to code when they come upon something new and interesting that they want to remember. They create special notebooks of the conventions typically found in nonfiction books, such as the kinds of labels, captions, types of print, and so on.

When addressing a nonfiction text our concern is more about getting information and acquiring knowledge than discerning themes (as in fiction). Nonfiction texts are full of structures, features, and text cues that signal what is important and scaffold readers' understanding. Students need to be taught how to glean possible importance from these structures, features, and cues. For instance, in *overviewing*, students are explicitly taught a form of skimming and scanning a text before reading. They're instructed to look at headings and subheadings, noting the length of sections, and so on.

Students need to know different expository text structures to determine what is important. These structures are part of our cultural heritage, reflected in expository texts. They include:

- cause and effect
- problem and solution
- question and answer
- comparison and contrast
- description and sequence (Harvey and Goudvis 2000, 121)

In this strategy the Public Education and Business Coalition (PEBC) staff developers suggest a very similar process to what we've seen in other chapters. The teacher models with think alouds about her own process for determining importance during reading. She should focus not just on her own conclusions of what is important, but specifically on how and why she drew such conclusions. There may be minilessons for small and large groups in which students are invited to share their thinking about text-level ideas. In small groups or pairs the students can compare their ideas about what was important and why. In addition, they could discuss how thinking about big themes enhances their comprehension (Keene and Zimmermann 1997, 95).

Two other familiar processes are advocated. The first is to affix sticky notes to the book with text codes while reading (codes such as: I, important; L, learned something new; S, surprise; etc.). Harvey and Goudvis are trying to help kids move away from looking for the one main idea by giving them three sticky notes on which they draw big asterisks for the big ideas. "Sound a little hokey? We thought so too until we saw how well it worked" (Harvey and Goudvis 2000, 131).

The other is note-taking on two- or three-column charts. These *analytical devices* help the students organize their thinking and make distinctions. Two-column charts might ask students to distinguish between

- Topic/Details
- Words from the Text/Important Information
- Words from the Text/Important Ideas
- What Is Interesting/What Is Important
- Opinion/Proof from the Text
- Theme/Evidence for the Theme
- Important Events/Evidence from the Text
- Character's Motivation/Evidence from the Text

In similar fashion, three-column charts help students discriminate among such ideas as

- Facts/Questions/Response (the reader's personal response)
- Topic/Details/Response (the reader's personal response)
- Evidence For/Evidence Against/Personal Opinion

These ideas, processes, and practices can be readily applied to mathematics textbooks.

MATH STORY PROBLEMS AS A GENRE

Are math story problems a genre? I was quite intrigued to discover a book that came out in 2004 addressing that question. The book is entitled *A Man Left Albuquerque Heading East*, by Susan Gerofsky. She embarks on a fascinating journey in which she considers mathematical word problems or story problems to be a linguistic and literary genre thoroughly embedded in the mathematics curriculum and pedagogy. Her work is especially pertinent for this chapter because the reading folks emphasize the value of understanding text structure of different genres when deriving meaning and determining importance. If story problems are a special genre, then understanding their fundamental structure is important in meaning making.

Gerofsky uses pragmatics, a branch of linguistics thought of as *language in use*, to assert that story problems have "certain oddities or particularities" such as "unusual forms of reference, an anomalous use of verb tense, and a particular discourse structure" (pp. 4–5). People in these problems have no background or reality other than the hypothetical or imaginary world of the particular story problem. The verbs are often conditional or subjunctive and even arbitrary, lacking the logical consistency of standard expository English prose.

Gerofsky credits Aristotle for the first notions of genre as he tried to establish a comprehensive set of categories for all types of poetry (e.g., tragic, epic, lyric, etc.). According to Gerofsky, our current conceptions of genre are more directly derived from Russian literary critic Mikhail Bakhtin. In his formulation of *speech genres*, he stressed that all oral and written language is a dialogue in which the one who creates the "utterance" is addressing a known or imagined other who is *not* a passive listener or reader, but rather is a "force" influencing the writer or speaker who anticipates certain responses. To Bakhtin, genres are relatively stable forms with appropriate contexts, styles, formats.

Contemporary notions of genre are not especially concerned with establishing criteria for what constitutes a particular genre, but rather see a genre as a cultural convention including the intention and expectation of the writer. All of these elements combine to make a genre recognizable and understandable to the reader, listener, or viewer (of films or stage plays). Gerofsky outlines a "constellation of features" that co-occur in story problems. For instance, they have a three-component, ordered structure consisting of (1) a set-up component that establishes the setting, the context, the situation, the characters, and so on. This component is usually not essential to the mathematical solution to the problem; (2) an information component that gives information needed to solve the problem as well as irrelevant information to lead the unsophisticated astray; and (3) a question. She notes the parallel to Wickelgren's classic work (1974) in which he sees story problems as having three types of information: (1) the givens, and (2) the operations, which together transform the givens into (3) a goal state.

A truly remarkable fact in considering the math story problem as a genre is the longevity and stability of the structure for over four thousand years. Quite a few scholars have discovered a wealth of story problems on Babylonian clay tablets circa 2000 B.C., on the Rhind Papyrus of ancient Egypt circa 1560 B.C., and the writings of the Ch'in Dynasty in China circa 300 B.C. Similar story problems have been found in ancient and medieval India, medieval Europe, and the Islamic world. A continuous record of story problems exists that stretches from early Renaissance Europe right through to the present. How similar? See if these sound a bit familiar.

> I found a stone, but did not weigh it; after I subtracted one-sixth and added one-third of one-eighth, I weighed it: one ma-na. What was the original weight of the stone?

> A man had to take a wolf, a goat, and cabbage across the river. The only boat he could find could only take two of them at a time. But he had been ordered to transfer all of those to the other side in good condition. How could this be done?

> You have 100 drachmas and you are told to buy 100 birds. Of the birds, Ducks are sold at 2 drachmas each, Hens at 1 drachma, Doves at 2 for 1 drachma, Ringdoves at 3 for 1 drachma, and Larks at 4 for 1 drachma. How many of each type of bird was purchased?

I trust you had a déjà vu moment. The first is from a Babylonian tablet. Did you stop to think, how did "he" know he was taking one-sixth of the weight, let alone a third of one-eighth, if he had not weighed the stone? The crossing the river problem is truly a classic with dozens of versions. This example is from Alcuin of York, advisor to Charlemagne circa 780 A.D. Among the Swahili, it is a leopard, a goat, and some medicinal leaves. In Zambia it is a leopard, a goat, a rat, and a basket of corn. The 100 birds and 100 drachmas problem was from 900 A.D. by Abu Kamil. Alcuin of York has a version with 100 animals and 100 shillings; the animals are camels, asses, and sheep.

I love the following one from Renaissance Italy:

> The Holy Father sent a courier from Rome to Venice, commanding him that he should reach Venice in 7 days. And the Signoria of Venice sent another courier to Rome, who should reach Rome in 9 days. And from Rome to Venice is 250 miles. The couriers left at the same time. In how many days will they meet and how many miles will each have traveled?

Sound familiar? It is the two trains problem without the trains! But stop for a minute and think. How did you make the connection to the trains? You perceived the mathematical structure of the problem. As far as the math is concerned it does not matter if it is trains or donkeys moving. What is similar is that two things are moving toward each other (instead of away from each other or one trying to catch the other). We know the distance between the two and the rates at which each is moving (just like the trains). However, there is one key difference: the couriers leave at the same time, whereas the trains in the problem in Chapters 3 and 4 left at different times, which does make that problem more difficult.

Gerofsky makes the conjecture that story problems thousands of years ago were a fairly sensible method of teaching the next generation of merchants, traders, and builders of their societies the mathematics they needed to know. Some, but by no means all, of the story problems were practical applications of math to real-life settings. On the other hand, many were fanciful, whimsical, and unrealistic, and versions of them are with us today in recreational math puzzles and problems.

Gerofsky speculates that since the first component of the three (the context) was virtually irrelevant mathematically, it could be changed readily to make the problem amusing, unusual, or interesting and hence more memorable. Certainly the student of the day would have to imagine the situation and perhaps some of the nuances would rub off. Students completed dozens of these problems deriving or practicing a standard algorithm, a method that worked.

But even going beyond the motivation of amusing settings and memorable contexts (way too many camels in these stories; such disproportionality has suggested to scholars that the problems were passed along the Silk Route), there was a sound mathematical reason for the longevity of these problems. There was no algebra—no way to show the generalized method for doing the calculations of the various problems confronting the merchants of Babylon or Zanzibar.

Without generalizable formulas they had to explain each step in language and give many numerical examples. The graduates of Nebuchadnezzar High School, class of 2000 (B.C.) had worked through hundreds of examples of "Ashpenaz wanted to buy 100 creatures and he had 100 pieces of silver" with varying costs for the different animals (lions, horses, and of course, camels). It was very practical for students to be able to do such calculations efficiently. They came to understand the method and had the procedure down cold by the time they graduated. (Ashpenaz was the master of the king's eunuchs. King James Bible, Daniel 1:3.)

Gerofsky makes the conjecture that the pedagogical purposes of the story problems changed when algebra had become a prominent tool in Europe by the 1400s, the early Renaissance. Students no longer needed to have the general method expressed through numerous examples of similar problems. The rationale for story problems "had to be shored up by a sometimes spurious emphasis on their practicality and applicability" (Gerofsky 2000, 131). She points out that story problems are justified by their "usefulness" even today despite numerous research studies that have shown that the "practical, applied mathematics in work situations today are often quite different from the word-problem forms and solution methods taught in schools" (p. 131). "The pretext of practicality and usefulness has justified the use of word problems . . . since most school students are either pre-algebraic or novices at algebra, word problems may continue to serve the purpose of expressing generality through repeated exemplification for them" (p. 137). "Educators involved in elementary schooling valued practical, contextualized, open-ended problems over abstractly mathematical ones" (p. 135).

Applying the KWC to This Genre

In its simplest form these traditional story problems have a three-part format: context, information, question. For most of these problems, the context is window dressing. However, I believe this does not have to be the case. The contexts that can be created are not only motivating but provide avenues for activating relevant schemata, surfacing the prior knowledge that students must use in problem solving, and helping them make connections between the new concepts and their known concepts. I will return to this idea shortly. For now, students have to deal with contrived situations and questionable contexts in story problems that are not practical, useful, or conceptual. The KWC and all its enhancements can be their best friend.

In designing the KWC based on Donna Ogle's KWL (Blachowicz and Ogle 2001), I attempted to address the three components of the traditional story problems. Although I had not read Gerofsky's book, I was very familiar with Wickelgren (1974). The KWC breaks down the three parts of the problem so the kids can see which is what. In this sense it is *analyzing* the meaning of each part of the problem. When students brainstorm the K—What do I Know for sure—they are laying out the context and the mathematical information. When they identify the W (What do I Want to find out?), they are explicitly identifying the third component of the genre (the question).

Although less prevalent in textbooks today than five years ago, the problem-solving strategy of Look for Relevant and Irrelevant Information sounds quite similar to Determining Important Information in reading. However, a student working on a story problem cannot possibly determine the importance of various pieces of information until she/he has read the question (done the W) and has thought about the nature of the problem. In Chapters 1 and 4, we examined how students can make up their own questions to go along with a fairly long narrative. If they are doing the KWC thoroughly, as shown in the previous chapter, they will have some listing of what they know for sure. They will have thought about which of these are facts and which are inferences. They will have thought about the question being asked, What do I Want to find out? They will have thought about special conditions or constraints. For most of the K–6 problems at this point, they would be able to assess information to determine if it was important, relevant to the task at hand, or if it were extra, or irrelevant to the mathematical task.

For more complex problems and tasks that do not follow the story problem genre's structure, students may have to try one or more of the representational strategies in order to get a deeper understanding of the problem before making a judgment about extra versus missing, irrelevant versus relevant. Before we examine more complex story problems, let's take a look at what a third-grade teacher, Colleen Moore, found early in the school year. Her students had never done anything like a KWC with problem solving, but were familiar with KWL in reading. She started slowly with the K and the W and then had them look for extra information.

> For three weeks I have been using the KWC model, but without the C, which I thought I'd wait a bit on. We did: What do I Know for sure? What do Want to find out? And then I added: Is there any extra information? They also were looking for Connections. The results have been interesting. My more literate students are making some deeper connections to the problems, and it has seemed to increase their interest level in finding answers. (I had several get so excited because I was letting them work with big numbers that they begged me not to tell them the answer to the challenge until after lunch, so they could finish it at recess. Oh, my Math Nerd heart beat proud!) Several students

drew pictures and visualized elements of the story problem in the margins. It provided an interesting glimpse into how they were seeing the problem unfold. They may have been unable to verbalize their connections but somewhere they had seen an image, stored it, and recalled it for this situation.

The situation that stood out the most has evolved with my struggling readers. I have a group that has just conquered decoding and has yet to mold their comprehension and connecting skills. Asking them to connect to the problem throws them for a loop because it seems like a completely new concept for them, reading or otherwise. They have seen it before, but they weren't in a place to fully understand it. Now they are trying to do it in math, and it is an even bigger struggle than the math problems. Third grade is traditionally the year where making deeper connections to their reading really takes shape for the majority of students. I think as the year progresses and they have some more experience with this skill it will become easier for them to think about.

They also have a hard time putting ideas on paper. My struggling readers seem to get caught up in rewriting the information and labor to move into the actual problem solving. However, they are able to verbally assign information to a correct column when prompted. At times I let them dictate their answers to me to help them move beyond it, but this is an area where problems will crop up as we begin writing about our problem solving.

In terms of solving the actual problem, several struggling readers have been able to get a better grasp of what is important and what is being asked through the K, the W and the extra. It will be interesting to see how this will translate into their paragraph writing. We are working on setting up parallel templates for our writing in response to reading and our math written responses.

See Figures 5.1 and 5.2 for some examples of how Colleen's students approach these problems.

ANALYZING MATHEMATICAL ATTRIBUTES

Although the PEBC folks are not explicit about the analytical nature of many of their techniques, they are definitely using such things as the two- and three-column charts to analyze specific features or attributes of texts. An important part of any area of knowledge is knowing what features, attributes, or units on which to focus attention. Determining importance often hinges on breaking ideas or information down to essential elements and knowing what to look for.

There are about half a dozen publishers of textbook series for the elementary school grades. There are also three major "reform" mathematics

On Friday, Ozzie's mom bought him a guinea pig. This was a magical guinea pig. Each night while Ozzie sleeps, the total number of guinea pigs doubles. By Saturday, he has a total of 2 guinea pigs. On Sunday, he has four. His mom is beginning to worry and wants to know how many there will be on Thursday. Tell her how many pigs there will be and how you figured it out. (Try using a chart to explain.)

K	W	E
That everday the guinea pig dobbles each day.	That how many guinea pigs there are on Thurday.	His mom is begning to worry about this.

Find a connection:
That my firend had a guineapigs but they got stolen.

Show your work here.

unit
dobble

	in	out
Sat →	1	2
Sun →	2	4
Mon →	4	8
Tues →	8	16
Weds →	16	32
Thurs →	32	64 guineapigs

64 guinea pigs

You have 64 guinea pigs.

FIGURE 5.1

curricula for grades K–5 developed in the last ten years through funding by the National Science Foundation. They do not include traditional textbooks, but instead make extensive use of activities, handouts, supplementary resource booklets for kids, and children's literature. Reform curricula often involve more reading than in traditional texts. Consequently, many teachers complain about the reading. Nevertheless, the practices endorsed by the PEBC folks could readily be used with these nonfiction materials.

The traditional textbooks are 650 to 700 pages long and each page is a full-color collage of images and print. Each page has a tremendous amount of information. About every other page includes a full-color picture that is perhaps thematically related to a story problem somewhere on the page. I say *thematically* meaning the *context* of the problem, not the

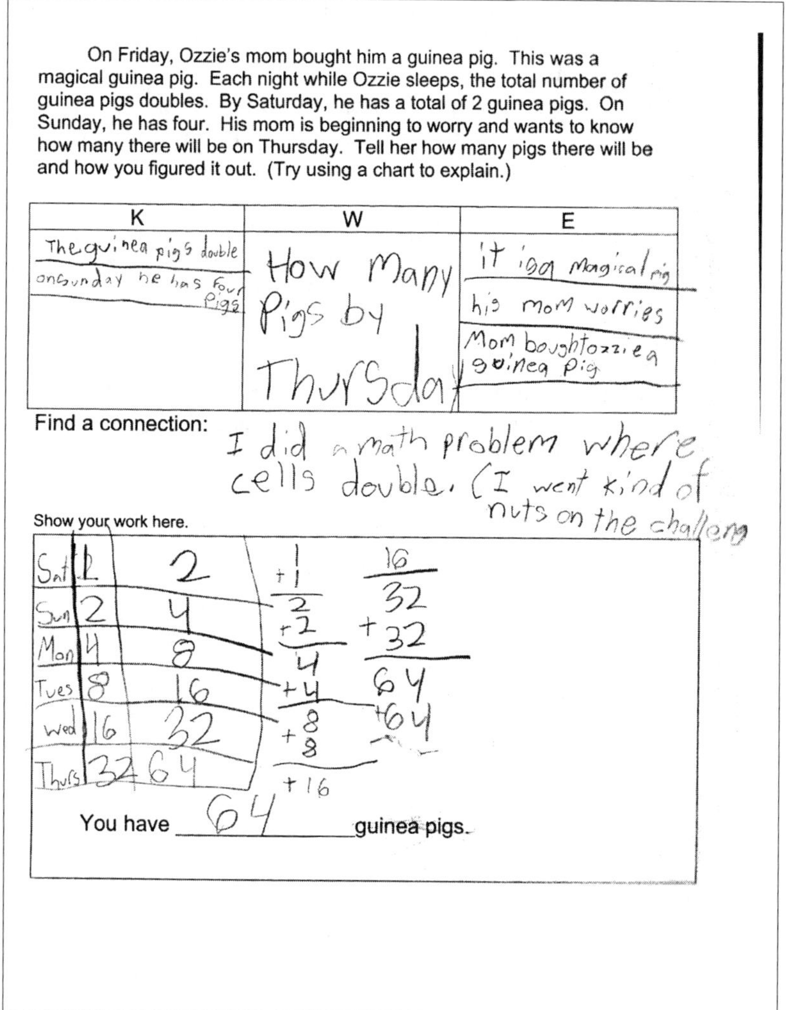

On Friday, Ozzie's mom bought him a guinea pig. This was a magical guinea pig. Each night while Ozzie sleeps, the total number of guinea pigs doubles. By Saturday, he has a total of 2 guinea pigs. On Sunday, he has four. His mom is beginning to worry and wants to know how many there will be on Thursday. Tell her how many pigs there will be and how you figured it out. (Try using a chart to explain.)

K	W	E
The guinea pigs double on Sunday he has four pigs	How Many Pigs by Thursday	it is a Magical pig his mom worries Mom bought ozzie a guinea pig

Find a connection: I did a math problem where cells double. (I went kind of nuts on the challeng

Show your work here.

Sat	1	2
Sun	2	4
Mon	4	8
Tues	8	16
Wed	16	32
Thurs	32	64

You have 64 guinea pigs.

FIGURE 5.2

concept. You may have noticed in the textbooks you're using that some pictures don't really do anything to illustrate a concept. Look for opportunities to use these pictures to your advantage, to get the students thinking and talking about what they're doing.

These textbooks have maps, graphs, charts, or tables, at least one on every page. PEBC staff developers are right on target about helping kids carefully attend to headings, captions, labels, and legends. These structures may contain information that will enable the children to understand and make connections among concepts. Analytical charts of two or three columns can help make critical distinctions (e.g., between concepts, between concepts and procedures, between data and predictions, between representations). These charts are essentially graphic organizers that not only organize information, but also may greatly facilitate its analysis.

For example, I often ask students to describe the properties of a geometric figure or to compare and contrast several figures. This analysis may be part of the K (What do I Know for sure?). Analysis of attributes, properties, and features is essential in areas of the math curriculum (e.g., geometry) where there is a tendency for students to approach it as a big vocabulary game, memorizing definitions without really thinking about what they could possibly mean. Years ago my wife had her third graders develop their own glossary of Latin and Greek prefixes and suffixes which she helped them connect to anatomy, physiology, mathematics, and everyday life.

Frequently this renaissance of the classical world manifests itself as comparing and contrasting geometric shapes. Here is an example that we've used in a geometry unit. Compare and contrast the two shapes in Figure 5.3. Let's use the two columns listing similarities and differences that typify what kids have said (Figure 5.4).

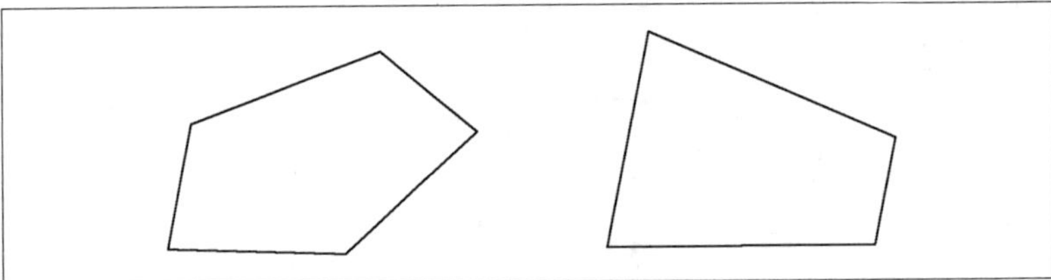

FIGURE 5.3

Similarities	**Differences**
They are both polygons.	One has five sides; the other four.
Neither one is a regular polygon.	One is a pentagon, the other a quadrilateral.
They have line segments for all their sides.	The pentagon may have some congruent sides (we can't tell until we measure). The quadrilateral does not appear to have any congruent sides.
They are both convex.	The pentagon has five vertices; the quadrilateral has four.
Both shapes have some acute and some obtuse angles, but no right angles.	The pentagon has two obtuse angles adjacent and the two acute angles are separated by the third obtuse angle. The quadrilateral has adjacent obtuse and adjacent acute angles.

FIGURE 5.4

The table shows a lot of sound information, written in complete sentences. It also shows an informed use of vocabulary with fairly precise mathematical terms. From this two-column chart some kids may infer the key concepts in this activity. The same information may be translated into the following three-column chart. Note how the attributes are easily derived from the two-column chart. It is fascinating to me that kids who have enormous difficulty analyzing attributes or properties can get a lot of success if the teacher provides them with a simple set of tools (Figure 5.5).

We often add some kind of prompt at the end to see if things come together at all. The Inference prompt didn't show any surprises for the pentagon, but the continued thinking about the attributes of the quadrilateral did launch a good discussion about what it means if opposite sides are parallel. What shapes do we know that have that attribute? As you may have realized, both shapes have been rotated from their conventional orientation. Would you have "felt better" if they looked like Figure 5.6? These are the identical shapes to those in Figure 5.1, just rotated.

ATTRIBUTE	PENTAGON	QUADRILATERAL
Number of sides?	Five.	Four.
All sides line segments?	Yes; it is a polygon.	Yes; it is a polygon.
Any side lengths equal?	Maybe two pairs.	No.
All side lengths equal?	No; not a regular polygon.	No; not a regular polygon.
Is it a convex polygon?	Yes.	Yes.
Angles: obtuse, acute, or right? How many of each?	Two adjacent obtuse angles; two nonadjacent acute angles with another obtuse in between; no right angles.	Two adjacent obtuse; two adjacent acute; no right angles; adjacent angles may be supplementary. If so, then opposite sides are parallel.
Inferences	If sides are equal, opposite angles are equal.	If opposite sides are parallel, the quadrilateral is a trapezoid.

FIGURE 5.5

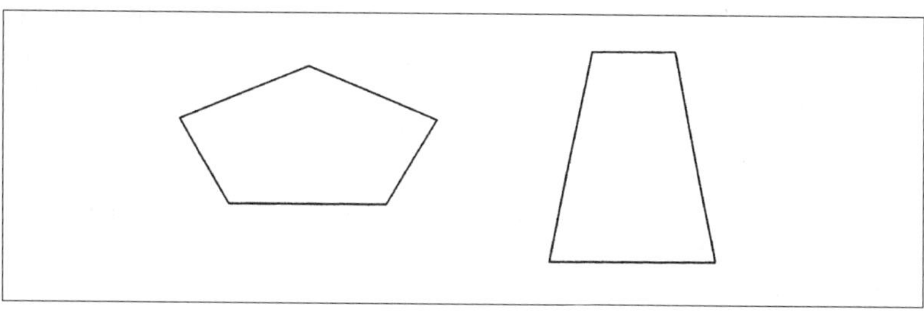

FIGURE 5.6

Are you surprised that Figures 5.3 and 5.6 are the same and merely involve a rotation? Textbooks have enabled us to develop an unfortunate mental habit of fully perceiving certain shapes only when they are in a conventional orientation.

ARE THERE ALTERNATIVES TO THE TRADITIONAL GENRE?

Gerofsky's ideas about the genre of story problems should provoke us to think about how we can make story problems more powerful and conceptual. Here is a typical problem from a fourth-grade math textbook.

> On Saturdays, Billy earns $16 for mowing his neighbor's lawn and $10 for gardening. On Sundays, he earns twice as much. How much will he he earn in five weekends?

What is your reaction to this problem? (Besides wanting to know what union this kid is in.) There was a color photograph of a young lad mowing a lawn. However, the context of mowing lawns is totally irrelevant. It might as well be:

> Ahkmed cleans out the stables for 5 dinari and feeds the goats for 3 dinari on the night of a full moon and he gets paid double when there is a waxing gibbous. Once a month there is a full moon and once also a waxing gibbous. How much money will Ahkmed earn in five months?

You might say that fourth graders can relate to mowing lawns. Are there kids in the United States who would not relate to mowing lawns? Who don't have a lawn or a lawn mower? Who've never seen a lawn except on television? Maybe more kids could relate to cleaning stables and feeding animals. We have plenty of farms and ranches. But in neither case does the context provide any bridge, any insight, any entree into the mathematical structure of the problem.

What is the mathematics in the problem? Why would this problem be included in the curriculum? The context offers no answer. How would students approach this? They'd probably see a multistep arithmetic exercise using the distributive property of multiplication over addition such as: Saturday $16 + $10 plus Sunday 2($16 + $10) becomes 16 + 10 + 2 * 16 + 2 * 10 = 26 + 32 + 20 = $78.00. And then over five weekends is 5 * 78 = $390.

Or maybe each weekend is: Saturday $16 + $10 plus Sunday 2($16 + $10), which becomes 3(16 + 10). But what is next? 3 * 16 + 3 *10 = 48 + 30 = 78. *Or* is it 3 * 26 = 78? Then for five weekends regardless of how you do the arithmetic, the mathematics of the situation are pretty much the same.

Let's play with a different context for the same mathematics.

> I have to fence in five identical rectangular plots, 16 feet on one side and 10 feet on the other. How much fencing do I need?

You know it is a rectangle and you know that you want the perimeter because your fence is going around the plot of land. See Figure 5.7. Do you think of the formula: P = 2(W + L) or P = 2W + 2L? Without algebra you'd work out the perimeter somehow and then multiply by 5.

Notice how the context of perimeter makes sensible the idea of adding the two numbers together and multiplying by 2. First you get the semiperimeter by adding 10 + 16 = 26, then multiply by 2 to get the perimeter: 2 * 26 = 52. Because you need five of them, you'll mutltiply 5 * 52 = 360 feet of fencing. The context is pertinent, not irrelevant as it is in so many story problems. I imagine Ahkmed calculated dozens of rectangular plots by using only a numerical method and not algebra.

You may be wondering why Ahkmed was multiplying everything by 3 at one point [3(16 + 10)] and the perimeter problem multiplied by 2 [2(16 + 10)]. Ahkmed needed 3 because he was adding Saturday plus Double Sunday, which would mean the weekend salary would be three times the Saturday salary.

The perimeter problem with a rectangle is a wonderfully easy way *to begin* this kind of thinking *and* have the context help. To make the perimeter problem fully comparable, we should look at fencing the perimeter of five hexagonal shapes that alternate 10 feet and 16 feet on each side. See Figure 5.8. This perimeter can be written the same way as Ahkmed.

I have not seen a textbook use the formulas for the perimeter of a rectangle to teach the distributive property. Someone really should.

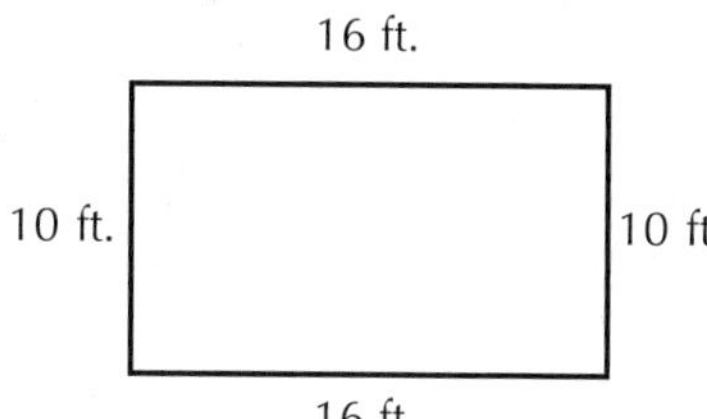

FIGURE 5.7

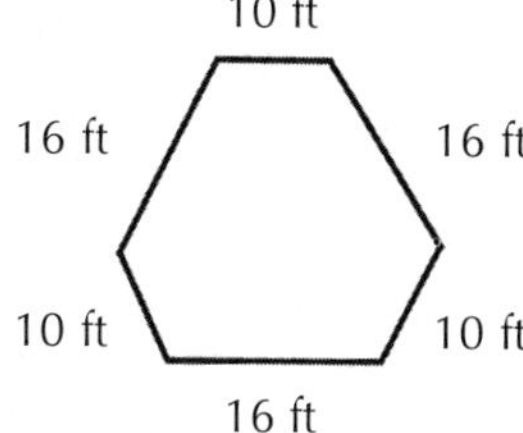

FIGURE 5.8

The point is that the traditional textbook programs have not departed from the genre. I could go through all the textbook series and catalogue all their problems and there will be a handful that have a context that facilitates understanding the concepts. We would find most of these in the chapters dealing with money, making change, or understanding two-place decimals.

Have the reform curricula made some movement toward authentic, real-world, practical, useful problems? In general they do provide more real-world situational problems. And in teacher resource books, you'd be able to find more story problems with meaningful contexts. Then there are a few books with "open-ended problems," which have multiple answers depending upon assumptions. There are resource books with wonderfully complex mathematical tasks, like the Gingerbread Village (Burk, Snider, and Symonds 1991), by Excursions. Assessment devices such as Exemplars and Balanced Assessment have many excellent problems. Alternatives exist, but you have to dig a little.

Mathematical Model

Several dozen mathematics and science educators argue for problem solving to be seen as the creation of a mathematical *model*. This perspective has been under development for about fifteen years (or even twenty-five, depending on what you count). Referred to as a *models* or *modeling perspective*, it stands a chance of significantly broadening the nature of problem solving. However, as of now there is no fully developed and field-tested program.

These educators' definition of problem solving is based on the meaning of mathematical modeling, where problem solvers are required to create mathematical ways of thinking about a new situation for some purpose (e.g., to make decisions or predictions). It is as much about *interpreting* a situation mathematically as it is about solving a particular problem. It emphasizes situations in which the problem solver is expected to *create*, *refine*, or *adapt* mathematical interpretations, ways of thinking, and procedures.

This approach assumes that the learning of mathematics takes place *through* creating and refining one's model. Students *begin* their learning experience by solving "real-life" applied problems that require them to create, revise, or adapt a mathematical way of thinking (i.e., a mathematical model). Students are expected to bring their own personal meaning, prior knowledge, and schemata to bear on a problem, and to test and revise their interpretation as they work. Students are assumed to simultaneously increase their understanding of the problem, the mathematical concepts they are using, and their mathematical model over a series of modeling cycles.

Modeling tasks can be carefully designed to ensure that the product (artifact, tool, or procedure) students create *embodies* the mathematical process or procedure they constructed for the situation. Here is one example from Zawojewski and Lesh (2003, 322).

> John is constructing a recreation room in his basement. He has put up the walls and put down a floor. He needs to buy a baseboard to put along the walls. The room is 21 feet by 28 feet. The baseboards come in 10-foot and 16-foot lengths. How many of each kind should he buy? He has several options.
>
> If John wants to have as few seams as possible, how many of each size baseboards should he buy?
>
> If John wants to have as little waste as possible, how many of each size should he buy?
>
> If the 16-foot boards cost $1.25 per foot and the 10-foot baseboards cost $1.10 per foot, how many of each kind should he buy if he wants to spend the least amount of money?

Transcripts of middle school students working on this problem in groups of three or four illustrate how the thinking processes of individuals and small groups change as they revise their interpretations of the problem and the concepts that they use. There is no obviously correct answer. Multiple answers are possible depending upon one's assumptions, preferences, and mathematical sophistication. Nonetheless, one can see gradual, incremental growth in understanding of concepts during the problem-solving sessions.

Understanding is not thought of as being an all-or-nothing situation. We are building our snowman again. Mathematical ideas and problem-solving capabilities codevelop during the problem-solving process. The constructs, processes, and abilities that are needed to solve real-life problems are assumed to be at intermediate stages of development, rather than mastered prior to engaging in problem solving.

In the optimal learning of mathematics, students go through cycles of reconceptualization, mathematizing a given real-world situation as a mathematical model. Students engage in a series of modeling cycles: interpreting the problem, developing trial solutions, testing the trial solutions on the real situation, and reinterpreting the problem situation. The cycles continue until the students' solution evolves to the point that one's mathematical representation (especially symbols and procedures) of the real world reasonably meets the constraints and specifications set in the real world.

Lehrer and Schauble have conducted classroom-based studies in which elementary students constructed mathematical models, especially modeling with data they had collected. An overview of this work is in the first chapter of a book they edited in which elementary school teachers describe eight different classrooms of children doing data modeling activities (Lehrer and Schauble 2002). They found that even first and second graders were indeed able to develop and represent mathematical models of data they collected on such diverse phenomena as fruit fly dispersion, traffic patterns, recycling, and changes in shadows during a day. These elementary school students created their own notation systems, diagrams, experience-based analogies, and other media to express their thoughts. These examples show that it is quite possible for young students to create and represent mathematical models.

Usually, the most problematic aspect of solving a real problem is developing useful ways to *think about* (describe, explain, interpret) relevant relationships in the situation; in other words, "see" the problem mathematically. Once a way of thinking about patterns, regularities, and major concepts has been considered, relevant mathematical tools can be adapted to the situation. Let me offer an example from my own work with students in third through sixth grade with a particular problem.

AN EXPERIMENTAL PROBABILITY GAME AS AN EXAMPLE OF MODEL BUILDING

Dozens of my classes have worked on this problem/game. Montana Red Dog (or Red Dog) is an example of experimental probability that relies on data collection rather than on theoretical probability formulas. It should not be the only experimental probability activity the students do. Probability concepts and the interpretation of probabilistic situations is one of the notoriously tricky areas of mathematics. Over the years I have refined it several times. It exemplifies the cycles of rethinking, reinterpreting, and reconceptualizing that students go through, individually and in small groups. Note how their thinking changes with each successive data-gathering experience.

The card game of Montana Red Dog originated in the Old West and is rarely played today, but is in *Hoyle's Book of Games*. A standard deck of 52 cards, 4 suits, Ace high is used. I arrange the kids into 10 groups (2 or 3 per group). I am the dealer and I will give each group 4 cards, leaving 12 cards for me. I will turn over the top card of the 12 in my hand and each group will try to beat me. A group wins if one of their 4 cards is higher in number than mine, but it must be in the same suit (or color). The question that kids must answer: Is this a fair game?

Getting Familiar with the Game

Many children of today are not familiar with cards, so I display an overhead transparency as in Figure 5.9.

SPADES♠	HEARTS♥	CLUBS♣	DIAMONDS♦
A	A	A	A
K	K	K	K
Q	Q	Q	Q
J	J	J	J
10	10	10	10
9	9	9	9
8	8	8	8
7	7	7	7
6	6	6	6
5	5	5	5
4	4	4	4
3	3	3	3
2	2	2	2

FIGURE 5.9

I explain how we play the game and my desire to know if it is fair. I demonstrate how we will play. When I am fairly sure the kids understand, I shuffle the cards and walk around the room giving 2 cards at a time to each group. I do this twice until all 10 groups have a 4-card hand. I remind them of the rules and note that I have dealt out 40 cards and I have 12 in my hand. They will play against each one of my 12 cards using and *reusing* their 4 cards. I ask again, "Is this a fair game? Talk about it in your group and then tell me what you think." Sometimes I have them write in their journals what they think.

Note their initial conceptions, which are very similar from third to sixth grade. They say things such as:

"It is fair because it is just dumb luck what cards you get."

"It is not fair because you have 12 cards and we have only 4. You are going to win."

"It is fair because you shuffled and everybody got random cards."

"We will win more because we have four cards against your one card."

I ask them, what does *fair* mean? How would I know? Older students pick that up quickly and say, it's fair if *"we win half the time"* or *"we both have an equally likely chance of winning."* Younger kids might say *"50/50."* I ask them what that means and some do not know.

Playing the First Game

We play one game. I show them my top card and ask, "Can you beat this? Show me *one* card in your hand that can beat me; hold it up." I want to actually see their winning cards. On the chalkboard I have made a two-column T-table with headings Dealer Wins/Dealer Loses. I play my top card against all 10 groups at once, which generates a lot of data quickly.

I count the winning cards as the kids hold them up. Only 1 card per group may be held up. I write that number under Dealer Loses. It is the number of groups who beat me. And then I write the difference between that number and 10 under Dealer Wins. With older students (fifth, sixth, and up), we go through the 12 cards I am holding and have 120 trials/data points (12 cards times 10 groups). With the younger kids I usually will play my top 10 cards and ignore the bottom 2. That way the data on the chalkboard will be based on 100 trials of my cards against their hands. By simply summing my losses and my wins out of 100 trials, percentages are easy to see.

Figure 5.10 illustrates what happens in a typical game. It is the actual data from the most recent game I did. If you were observing this activity, what you would see live is given in Figure 5.10. The dealer reveals 1 card from the top of his pile of 10 (e.g., my first card was the Ace of Diamonds [A♦], the highest diamond and thus unbeatable). No one in the 10 groups of students held up a winning card. Therefore, in the T-table on the far right, I entered the data 10 0 in the top row. The next card I turned over was the 6 of Spades (6♠). Students from three groups (V, T, S) held up winning cards (7♠, J♠, A♠ as shown). These three groups beat the dealer (dealer loses 3), but that means dealer won 7. The data 7 and 3 were entered into the Dealer Wins/Dealer Loses table.

Dealer's	**Groups with winning cards**										**Dealer**	
Cards	**Z**	**Y**	**X**	**W**	**V**	**U**	**T**	**S**	**R**	**Q**	**Wins**	**Loses**
A♦											10	0
6♠					7♠		J♠	A♠			7	3
9♥	Q♥		J♥						A♥		7	3
Q♠								A♠			9	1
9♣			Q♣		A♣		10♣		J♣		6	4
8♣			Q♣		A♣		10♣		J♣		6	4
4♦	5♦		6♦	K♦		J♦		Q♦		10♦	4	6
9♠							J♠	A♠			8	2
7♦				K♦		J♦		Q♦		10♦	6	4
6♣			Q♣		A♣		10♣		J♣		6	4
Number of wins	2	0	5	2	4	2	5	5	4	2	69	31

FIGURE 5.10

As I turned over each of my 10 "dealer cards" one at a time, each group that had a winning card held it up. You can see the information in Figure 5.10. The dealer won 69 percent of the time. Only groups X, T, and S won 5 times (i.e., beat 5 of the dealer's 10 cards). Once again I ask, "Do you think the game is fair?"

More Games, More Data

We play two or three games in which each group gets a new hand. I ask them to look for patterns in the data. Even in a single game of 100 (as in Figure 5.10), one often sees the dealer wins 60 percent or more of the time. The dealer does not necessarily have an abundance of high cards (A, K, Q, J, 10). In Figure 5.10 the dealer had only 2 of these high cards, yet won 69 percent of the time. Of the 10 competitions of the dealer's 1 card against each group, on only one occasion did the dealer lose more than win (with his lowest card, the 4 of Diamonds [4♦]). With every other card (even 6s), the dealer beat 6 or more of the 10 groups. Even his 4 of Diamonds (4♦) beat 4 groups. This is strange!

I ask the kids again, "Is the game fair or does someone have an advantage? What would fair look like as data?" Now the meaning of 50/50 becomes very clear to the third and fourth graders. Just about everybody says, if these data were close to 50 for each, the game is probably fair. However, there are always other students who cling to the phrases dumb luck, chance, and random and say it's always fair.

I pose some hypothetical data to the class. "If the dealer won 90 percent of the time on every game of 100 we did, week after week, what would you think?" Some quickly respond, *"I'd think he was cheating."* I reply, "So you would think it was not pure luck, but rather something is going on?" Some of them agree. Then I ask, "What if he were definitely *not* cheating?" Some say, *"He had a lucky streak."* I counter, "What if this happened all year long? Is there something in the game of Red Dog that makes it more likely for the dealer to win?"

Compare to a Different Probability Situation

Some are still thinking that it is just chance or a lucky streak. I show them a spinner with two colors, about three-fourths red and one-fourth blue. I tell them, "Two people play a game with the spinner. Each has one of the colors. Which color would you rather be? Which color will win more often if we play many times? What percent of the time will the red win? Would you think this game is fair?" Everybody agrees that red would win more times. But some are not sure how that applies to Montana Red Dog. Others try to explain the connection as they see it. One time a kid said, *"The spinner is rigged so that if you played a lot of times, the dealer would win most of them. Like at some of those carnival games, they look so easy, but the guy running the booth always has some angle. Sometimes people win, but mostly they lose. It is the same thing with this card game.*" Another kid wisecracked, "*Somehow the dealer has 65 percent of the spinner marked for him, but we don't see the spinner.*"

Analyzing a Hand

On the third or fourth deal, I ask them, "Who has a good hand now? Show us your cards." One group thinks it does. They show the class and I ask, "Is this a good hand? Why or why not? What makes a good hand?" This is a key question. Many initially say "*High cards.*" I ask, "If I turned up a 2 of clubs, who could beat me?" Typically 6 of the 10 groups could, to which I respond, "Do you mean 4 of your 10 groups cannot beat even the smallest club?" The kids all begin to see that this can definitely happen when the dealer's card is from a suit they do not have. I try to crystallize their understanding by explaining that no matter how high the cards are, if they are missing a suit, right off the bat, they will not beat one-fourth of the cards I could have. They realize a really good hand has high cards in all 4 suits.

Protests return from the proponents of dumb luck. "*But you don't know how many of your 12 cards are from that suit; maybe none, maybe all 12.*" Misconception: they are focusing on individual hands, trials, and not thinking about what happens in the long run. They need to appreciate concepts such as the law of large numbers, sample size, and *in the long run*. I ask them about the spinner where three-fourths of the face is red. "If I spun this 4 times, will it definitely land on the red 3 of the 4 times?" Some say, *yes*. Some say, *maybe*. Some say, *not necessarily*. You can see the movement across these three responses and a steady dwindling of the "yes" response across grades three through six.

I go back to a version of the handout that gave them an overview of the entire deck. See Figure 5.11. All that has been added here are some little boxes to help them analyze their hands. I tell them to go to the table and circle the 4 cards in their hands. Then count how many cards are above the highest card they have in a suit. Enter that number in the box under the suit name in "Cannot beat" row.

In Figure 5.11 we have the example of the analysis of the 4-card hand from Group S in Figure 5.10. The group had the Ace of Spades (A♠), the 5 of Spades (5♠), the 6 of Hearts (6♥), and the Queen of Diamonds (Q♦). The students in this group circled these 4 cards. They see 4 cards in their hand. That leaves 48 cards they don't see: 12 are with the dealer and the remaining 36 cards are with the other nine groups. Then they filled in the boxes by counting how many of the 48 cards are higher than the cards they have. Figure 5.11 shows no Spade cards above the Ace of Spades, so (0) zero goes in the Cannot beat box on top of the Spades. There are 8 Hearts higher than six, so 8 goes in the Cannot beat box on top of the Hearts. This hand has no Clubs and therefore cannot beat any of the 13 Clubs. Only the Ace and King of Diamonds can beat the Queen that they have, so 2 goes in the box. Add those numbers across and you'll get a total

	SPADES♠	HEARTS♥	CLUBS♣	DIAMONDS♦	
Cannot beat	[0]	[8]	[13]	[2]	**Total cannot beat [23]**
	(A)	A	A	A	
	K	K	K	K	
	Q	Q	Q	**(Q)**	
	J	J	J	J	
	10	10	10	10	
	9	9	9	9	
	8	8	8	8	
	7	7	7	7	
	6	**(6)**	6	6	
	(5)	5	5	5	
	4	4	4	4	
	3	3	3	3	
	2	2	2	2	
Can beat	[**11**]	[**4**]	[**0**]	[**10**]	Total can beat [25]

FIGURE 5.11

of 23 cards that this hand cannot beat. The good news is that this means out of the 48 that cannot be seen, this hand can beat 25.

A really important idea now is how do the students *interpret* the number of cards in the "Total can beat." What does the 25 in the Total can beat box in Figure 5.11 mean to the kids? Third graders initially think about this "statistic" as a whole number indicator. The bigger the number, the better your hand. Why? Because there are more cards you can beat. This idea is more empirical and more powerful than the way they had been thinking—high cards mean good hands. They definitely could see that if one had Ace, King, Ace, King in only two suits (e.g., A♠ K♠ A♥ K♥) that would not win with half the cards in the deck (Clubs and Diamonds). In fact, they would actually only be able to beat *less than half* of the 48 cards out there. How can this be true? They'd lose to that half of the deck that are Clubs and Diamonds, but they'd beat that half of the deck that were Spades and Hearts. Right? Not quite. They would lose to the 26 Clubs and Diamonds and their 2 Spades and 2 Hearts would beat the 11 Spades and 11 Hearts still out there. They can beat only 22 cards.

Calculating the Probability

If one group has 24 cards that can beat and 24 cards that cannot beat, it is easy to help the kids see that means beating 24 of the 48 or the fraction 24/48 or half the cards out there. Then all groups can represent their hands as fractions with 48 as the denominator, allowing students to get good experience with equivalent fractions. There is logical reasoning aplenty about part/whole relationships that form the basis for fractions, decimals, and percents. The teacher can use the game as a vehicle for investigating any of these representations and their interrelations.

How do these representations influence the students' conceptions of probability? Most of the fifth and sixth graders can see 16/48 as equivalent to 1/3 and to .33 or 33.33 percent, but only some of them see that these statistics could mean this hand should beat the dealer's card 33 percent of the time in the long run or has a probability of winning equal to .33. Every time I play this game with older kids, a discussion ensues in which some kids argue with that statement and say, "*You can't say that. It is just random, just chance.*" Or, "*It depends on what cards the dealer gets and that is just chance.*" This is essentially the same conception that we saw earlier. Even some kids who were able to see how the dealer appears to have an advantage built into the game *in the long run* do not conceive of this statistic in the long run.

The kids learn quite a bit from analyzing their hands and looking at who has good hands in the class. Figure 5.12 supplements what we saw previously in Figure 5.10. At the top of the table in Figure 5.12 we can see the 4 cards that each group had. The major portion of the table in the middle is exactly what was in the table in Figure 5.10: the dealer's 10 cards, the winning cards that were held up, the wins and losses and directly under the 10 group columns are the number of times out of 10 that a particular group won. The bottom two rows in Figure 5.12 give the number that each group can beat, this number as the numerator of a fraction with denominator of 48, this value as a decimal (you could readily use percent instead of decimal). These statistics are the probability of winning that each group has.

The kids who have an initial, reasonable interpretation of these percents are quite surprised. I'd even say some are stunned. Their "threshold" understanding of the fraction and the decimal told them: In the long run, regardless of which particular cards the dealer has in any one game (or many games), if they decided to keep this hand, that is the fraction or decimal part of the times that they would win.

Only one of the 10 groups had more than a .500 probability of winning (Group S). Nine of the 10 hands have less than .500 chance of winning. Furthermore, even in one game (the short run), the probability of winning is close to what actually happened. Each group compared the number of wins they actually had as a decimal (wins divided by 10) to their probability of winning. For instance, Group S had a probability of .521 and actually beat 5 out of 10 (or .500) of the dealer's cards. The next highest probability was Group X with .458 and they also won .500. Only group T did much better than would have been predicted from analyzing their hand (probability .313 versus actually won .500).

The first game when they analyze their hands in this way, they are surprised. When they get similar probabilities upon analyzing the hands in three other games, most decide that the game is not fair. Some have even been known to say, "*We have found the spinner!*"

But have they? What "causes" the probabilities of the hands to be relatively low?

GROUPS (hands and winning cards)

	Z	Y	X	W	V	U	T	S	R	Q	Dealer	
Dealer	Q♥ 10♥ 7♥ 5♦	2♠ 5♥ 3♦ 2♣	J♥ 3♥ 6♦ Q♣	K♦ 9♦ 3♣ 8♦	A♣ K♣ 2♦ 7♠	8♥ J♦ 4♣ 4♠	10♣ J♠ 10♠ 8♠	A♠ 5♠ Q♦ 6♥	A♥ 4♥ J♣ 7♣	5♣ 3♠ 2♥ 10♦	W	L
A♦											10	0
6♠					7♠		J♠	A♠			7	3
9♥	Q♥		J♥						A♥		7	3
Q♠								A♠			9	1
9♣			Q♣		A♣		10♣		J♣		6	4
8♣			Q♣		A♣		10♣		J♣		6	4
4♦	5♦		6♦	K♦		J♦		Q♦		10♦	4	6
9♠							J♠	A♠			8	2
7♦				K♦		J♦		Q♦		10♦	6	4
6♣			Q♣		A♣		10♣		J♣		6	4
Number of wins	2	0	5	2	4	2	5	5	4	2	69	31
decimal	.200	.000	.500	.200	.400	.200	.500	.500	.400	.200		
Number can beat	11	4	22	10	16	19	15	25	19	12		
Prob. of winning	$\frac{11}{48}$	$\frac{4}{48}$	$\frac{22}{48}$	$\frac{10}{48}$	$\frac{16}{48}$	$\frac{19}{48}$	$\frac{15}{48}$	$\frac{25}{48}$	$\frac{19}{48}$	$\frac{12}{48}$		
	.229	.083	.458	.208	.333	.396	.313	.521	.396	.250		

FIGURE 5.12

Do I Have a Suit for You

Most of the time, somewhere along the way, one or more of the kids will go back to the idea that good hands are not just high cards, they are also suits. When they look at the 10 hands in any game, they are surprised. From Figure 5.12 they see that only 3 hands had a card from each of the 4 suits (groups Y, U, and Q).Together they only won 4 trials. What happened? They only had 2 high cards: the Jack of Diamonds and the 10 of Diamonds.

How many groups had 3 suits covered? Only 3 groups. And they generated 14 wins.

Two suits? Four groups. And they generated 13 wins. That's it. No 1-suit hands. I ask them, "Why is having all 4 suits advantageous?" Eventually, kids say things like: *"The dealer does not have to worry about suits." "The dealer determines the suit. He's got it and you'd better have one."*

Although it is too difficult for sixth graders to follow an analysis of the theoretical probabilities of the game, I do tell them that dealer will win about 62 percent of the time. The groups will have cards in all 4 suits only 10 percent of the time. The kids can figure out that when having 2 suits, which is fairly frequent, even the best hand (2 Aces) only gets you a .458 probability of winning.

The students are convinced that Montana Red Dog favors the dealer.

What a Fair Game Would Look Like

I end Montana Red Dog with a twist. I have a new game for them to play, Illinois Blue Dog. The kids get into their 10 groups again. I have prepared a deck of cards with the 4 suits separated. I ask 4 kids to shuffle them and I put them into 4 piles. Then I deal out 1 pile (1 suit, 1 card to each group). I repeat this with each pile so that each group has 1 card from each of the 4 suits. The 12 cards I have left must be 3 cards from each suit. I shuffle my 12, then turn them over one at a time, like in Red Dog, asking each time whether they can beat this card with a higher card in its suit. I ask, "Is this a fair game?" The students think about it and most say, "*It is fair because in the long run it will be my spade and your spade so it is really only the numbers that matter. That is like the card game of War and that is fair. Except in this game there would be no ties.*" If they wrote that in their math journals, I'd be happy.

6 | SYNTHESIZING

THE CHALLENGE

In the movie *The Hustler*, Paul Newman plays pool shark Fast Eddie Felson (a role he reprised forty years later in *The Color of Money*). In the earlier film, he challenges the reigning champion, Minnesota Fats, to a marathon pool game. Well into the game the dapper Fats asks for his favorite brand of bourbon along with a glass, some branch water, and ice. In a typical display of bravado, Eddie orders "Old J.T.S. Brown, no ice, no glass." After seeing the movie, I tried some Old J.T.S. Brown. It is definitely the hard stuff; nothing smooth and easy there. And so it is with synthesis.

In synthesis one combines new information with existing information to create something new. Analysis traditionally has meant breaking down things or ideas into component parts. Synthesis has been seen as putting together these separate parts into a new, coherent whole. It would seem at best paradoxical to break down synthesizing into component parts. It seems like what we ought to do is '"catch" kids synthesizing and tell them that was great; do it some more. Reading is not a set of isolated subskills and neither is synthesis.

Keene and Zimmermann (1997) and Harvey and Goudvis (2000) all seem to agree that synthesizing is the most challenging of the comprehension strategies. Not always certain how to bring about synthesizing in children, they broke it down into more think-aloud modeling by the teachers and more one-to-one conferences to help the kids synthesize via thinking aloud. Seeing synthesis on "a continuum of evolving thinking . . . A true synthesis is an Aha! of sorts . . . light bulb occurrences when we read, but they don't come around every day" (Harvey and Goudvis 2000, 144). One end is taking stock of meaning while reading (stopping to "digest" the parts to construct meaning). Move up the continuum a bit and you'll find summarizing, retelling, and recreating. At the other end is a "true" synthesis when a "new perspective or thought is born out of the reading" (p. 144). The notion of a "true" synthesis at one end of a continuum is very appealing.

"Synthesis is the mind's mosaic artistry" (Keene and Zimmermann 1997, 169). Through synthesis we selectively perceive the millions of pieces information, sensory stimuli, and impressions bombarding us and extract those to be connected to an idea we deem important (perhaps only subconsciously). We organize these pieces to create a tapestry, a magnificent portrayal of our schemata. As we look at some things teachers can do to nourish, support, or foster synthesis, we need to keep our eyes on the prize, the true synthesis at the high end of the continuum.

As we have seen in the other reading comprehension strategies, synthesizing involves think alouds, making notes on sticky paper, in margins, on two-column charts. These devices help students make distinctions and are fairly analytical in nature (and analysis, if not the opposite of synthesis, is at least significantly different).

The Public Education and Business Coalition (PEBC) folks introduce synthesizing by teaching children to stop during their reading every so often and think about what they have just read. They encourage readers to "interact personally with the text" (Harvey and Goudvis 2002, 145). Other synthesis-provoking devices used for reading comprehension include retelling, summarizing, writing from a first-person perspective (personal response) and synthesizing information to answer a difficult question. To help students learn how to summarize, the teacher models retelling a story that she has read to them (or they have read themselves). She models using guidelines such as:

- remember to tell what is important
- tell it in a way that makes sense
- try not to tell too much

The teacher makes sticky notes, or writes ideas briefly on a chart, or sometimes just talks. And of course, the kids have to practice. The process of pulling together good ways to get children oriented toward the kind of "true" synthesis that makes for a new powerful whole is begun by retelling and summarizing. However, merely to retell and summarize is not enough. If we want to help students have "aha!" experiences or the true synthesis of deep personal meaning, we will have to push the envelope for personal response and try to answer difficult questions.

Another device contrasts summarizing with personal responding. A piece of paper divided in half is used with the top half for writing a summary of the text and the bottom half for the student to write a personal response. This device helps integrate their thinking about the meaning of the text with their own personal response.

When reading expository text, the teacher shows kids how to enter some synthesized information into brackets in the margins, or onto sticky notes marked "S," or onto two-column charts with headings of What's Interesting/What's Important. Teachers help them practice how to keep it brief, get the most important information, and use their own words.

The PEBC folks have said that the major insight/true synthesis does not happen every day. The teacher cannot force it. (You can't tell someone to have an epiphany!) The teacher can set the stage, create a conducive environment, encourage particular experiences, and be an adult mediator. Throughout their books the PEBC writers describe interpersonal relationships and classroom structures that support and enhance the reading comprehension strategies. I believe these relationships and supports are especially necessary for the high end of the continuum of synthesis to occur.

When the reading folks talk about taking stock of meaning while reading, stopping to digest the parts, thinking evolving slowly over time, or how each piece of new information enhances understanding, I think of my snowman. Conceptual understanding is built up slowly from many connections. Therefore, I raise the question, are the cognitive processes of making connections and synthesizing essentially the same?

When reading folks talk about a continuum, I see one end being very much like the connections discussed earlier in Chapter 2. However, the other end of the continuum, the true synthesis, the Aha insight, the deep personal meaning in mathematics, is what I call a *breakthrough* experience. This powerful moment occurs when a student, regardless of age, truly grasps a mathematical concept, perhaps for the first time. Although it may appear as if it were a light bulb and an instantaneous insight, it really is *not* like someone flipping a light switch. There has been a process of accretion until the substance of the concept crystallizes. When a string, hung in a pot of formerly boiling, liquefied sugar, slowly cools, it gathers to itself tiny, imperceptible crystals. Then, in a moment of rapid acceleration, it suddenly seems to instantly form crystals all over itself. When we have had a supersaturation of wonderful experiences, all that need happen is someone strategically placing that piece of string at the right moment. These descriptions and metaphors are trying to convey something probably more profound, more significant, and more meaningful than simple connections.

What happens when we encounter new ideas, concepts, information, words, sights, sounds, and myriad sensory input? Some theories focus on sensory perception, some on the brain and neural processes, others on the nature of the information, and yet others on the responses humans emit with different kinds of stimulation. As I said in Chapter 2, I don't feel a need to define and explain all the different theories about how humans "connect" or "synthesize" information. There are many and to tease out the nuances of each or differences between them (e.g., encapsulation vs. reification) would drive anyone to drink . . . Old J.T.S. Brown.

When we encounter new information, we try to relate the new ideas to our existing schemata (in fact, we wouldn't know it was "new" unless we did). If we perceive the new information as a variation of what we already know, then by a process that developmental psychologist Jean Piaget called *assimilation,* the new is incorporated into the existing schemata. It is a further elaboration with a bunch of new connections between and among concepts, without significantly changing our schema for that concept. Of course, these processes occur almost entirely below our level of conscious thought. I would venture that the connections we described in Chapter 2 and also part of the synthesis continuum can be explained by assimilation.

Most likely what we are calling "true synthesis," at the more profound end of the continuum, occurs when the new information cannot be assimilated and a person's schemata or cognitive structure experiences significant change, establishing new branches, closing avenues here, demolishing walls and making new pathways. Piaget referred to this process as *accommodation*.

The mind with its marvelous pattern-seeking propensity is always trying to make things fit together into familiar patterns. Perhaps it is wired into the neurons in our brains to let information flow through our existing synaptic patterns. When something does fit our existing patterns, perhaps we ignore it or forget it. But if the conditions are right, we are motivated to keep trying to find a way it could fit *if* we thought about it a little differently.

I am very fond of conceptual metaphors, but I have a real love for oxymorons. My favorite is "recreational mathematics." Oxymorons force us to pay attention to the juxtaposition of two very different things, to synthesize them, to integrate them, to blend them. When our minds are ready or able to blend into a pattern things that may have been in distinctly different patterns, then I think we may experience true synthesis.

SYNTHESIS IN MATHEMATICS

In the arena of school mathematics, what happens when a child is initially confronted with:

- Subtraction is not always "take away."
- One-fourth is smaller than one-third, despite the fact that 4 is larger than 3.
- They find out that multiplication does not always make things bigger; if the multiplier is less than one, the product will be smaller than the multiplicand.

In each of these cases and dozens of others, the children are confronted with information that cannot be assimilated into their existing schemata. In order to actually understand the new conception at all, one has to change one's way of thinking or dramatically, fundamentally change one's schemata or cognitive structure. This is true because if you don't change your old way of thinking, then you will not be able to fully understand nor appreciate the main ideas. If you cannot assimilate the new idea, you will not understand it *unless* you accommodate it by changing yourself.

What follows next are several different processes and activities that each in their own way illustrate the synthesis in mathematics that we can use to help kids learn.

WHAT'S THE NUMBER?

Children love to play games. With young children we can start slowly by giving them some information about a particular whole number. They have to figure out what number is being described. In my version of the game, the information must be cleverly worded so that no one piece of information will be sufficient to conclude that they have determined the secret identity of the number. The simplest way to do that is for each clue, hint, or piece of information to apply to more than one solution. The kids must synthesize a bunch of disparate data—I have found that three, four, or five new pieces of data are about all kids can handle. Remember, they are not comparing and contrasting. They are also not simply looking analytically for what these bits of data have in common. They are juxtaposing these data to pull them together into one entity. At the end of the continuum, their synthesis should be an "imagined conception," a coherent portrait or representation of the fundamental relationships present. A new way of seeing, a new way of organizing the world, a deep conceptual understanding.

With one number, we might give the children information A, B, C, and D. We would expect them to make something like the inferences listed. They see all the information and are able to combine and synthesize at will.

Information	**Expected Inferences**
A. It is less than 100.	(1 . . . 99)
B. It is one more than an odd number.	(An even number)
C. It can be divided evenly by exactly four different numbers (including 1).	(6: 1, 2, 3, 6); (8: 1, 2, 4, 8) (10: 1, 2, 5,10) . . . (38: 1, 2, 19, 38) . . . and many others
D. The Romans liked it so much, they gave it its own numeral.	I, V, X, L, C, M

We make some explicit suggestions early on, such as "Read Everything Before You Do Anything." For instance, in this problem I mention that it is *not* a good idea to immediately write down every number that is one more than an odd number. It would take too long and it is unnecessary because you will be combining or synthesizing information. Look what happens when you synthesize A and B (A says it is less than 100 and B tells you it is even [by inference]). Together they signify that the number is an even number less than 100. This is about 50 numbers.

If they have heeded my suggestion, they will read C, but not act on it until they have read D, the final piece of information. Without D, this problem will have a great many answers and it would be quite laborious to check the number of factors (as it says in C) of the even numbers less than 100. When you incorporate D into the synthesis, you cut down the possibilities to six and four of them do not fit with the clues A and B; only X and L are left. Therefore you only need to check the factors of X and L (10 and 50).

When the children get each piece separately with a pause in between, they try to solve by guessing any number the two most recent clues had in common. My modus operandi is to try to get all the information out to them as quickly as possible so that the kids can seriously consider all clues as simultaneously as their minds can process. We usually do problems like this as a whole class so we can provide some guidance and illustrate how we think about what we are doing (essentially, think alouds). After several examples, we have the kids work in pairs. In either case, they do a KWC with all the additional reflections on connections, inferences, patterns, and so forth.

FIGURING OUT NUMBERS AND NUMBER RELATIONSHIPS

More than a dozen years ago I had the good fortune to meet Mary Fencl, a wonderful primary grades teacher who had great experience teaching kids with learning disabilities. She now has a 1–2 loop, which means she starts a group of first graders one year and then continues with them the subsequent year. Mary has a knack for taking an abstract mathematical idea and coming up with a concrete representation of that idea to help kids get started on the right track. She often juxtaposes two very different things that urge her kids to synthesize.

For example, when working with arrays she had kids pick up Styrofoam cups that were littering the playground. They then inserted the cups into the gaps in the wire fence to make parallelogram arrays. They then counted the groups of cups by rows. The equal groups method of thinking about multiplication is a good one and this activity provided good foundation.

In the following example, when Mary told me what she was doing, I nearly blurted out that it was too difficult a concept for second graders. Mary uses many different activities to develop place-value and base ten concepts. In this one, she gives each student a lunch tray and then scoops out a cup of Raisin Bran Flakes, and pours it onto each tray. She asks the students to count all the individual flakes and all the raisins. They count out ten flakes and then drop them in a small plastic cup. When they complete ten flakes in ten small cups, they then dump them all into a medium size "hundreds cup." They have done this kind of counting before and they know that they could dump ten medium hundreds cups into a large thousand cup. But not today. Mary has something else in mind.

A slight digression: an interesting question is "What do we count as a flake?" In any data-based study one must know what the unit of measurement is. And so it is also with flakes. The kids found small pieces that they did not want to throw away. The class discussed how to count them. The entire class had to agree to count them the same way.

This activity went very well and then she asked them how many raisins each of them had found. Then she asked them to do something they had not done before. She asked them to spread the raisins out across their desks and think about how tiny they look and how all alone. "They need some flakes to keep them company. Your job is to give all your flakes to your raisins so that each raisin will have the *same number* of flakes surrounding it. Pile them up on your desk next to each raisin."

The kids used a wide variety of strategies. I had originally thought that Mary was leading them into the concept of rate (flakes per raisin = 392 to 18 or about 22 to 1). Or that she was preparing them for long division (392 flakes are divided equally among 18 raisins. 392 ÷ 18 =). She was doing neither of these things directly; however, indirectly she was paving the way for both . She was helping them, guiding them to wrestle, to play with a relationship, a special kind of relationship in which you compare two quantities, though they are entirely different things.

Mary and Her Sisters

This is a problem that Mary does each year. Kids are almost always intensely interested in their teachers' personal lives. Mary takes advantage of this fact. She has each child take out one Unifix cube for their age in years. Depending upon the time of year or the month or where they are in the 1–2 loop, the kids will be 5, 6, or 7. She notes on the board how many of each number there are. She asks them, "How many years would that be all together?" True, that may seem like an odd question, but from the kids' vantage point, it is sensible. Working in pairs they pull out their objects and group them by tens for easy counting. They work with nearby groups to help one another make tens with any leftovers; the total comes out to 168.

The kids take the cubes apart and Mary puts them all in a pile. She tells them that they have figured out how old they are altogether, but what about her? Then she quickly dumps a bunch of Unifix cubes into the pile and tells them that the number of cubes she added is her age. She asks them to figure out what that number is. She knows that she has quite a range of math knowledge in her students. Some attack the pile and make groups of ten again. They count 204. With that information, some are able to figure it out on paper. They ask, *"Are you 36?"* Most of the class wants proof, so they take 168 (their total) out of the pile and what is left must be from Mary. They count them and there are indeed 36 cubes.

The next day Mary tells them that she has two sisters, Carol and Julie. She tells the kids that if all three sisters put their three ages in the pile, there would be 96. What can you figure out from that information? Some kids start scribbling on paper. Others grab boxes of cubes. One says, *"If all together you add up to 96, if you take out your 36, how many will be left?"* Mary asks if anyone knows how to do that. Several raise their hands and Mary calls on one, who says, *"We are trying to subtract 36 from 96, right? First I can see to just take the six away, leaving 90. Then I can take ten away from ninety three times. That would leave me with 80, 70, 60. The two sisters' ages must add up to 60 years."* Mary asks the rest of the class if they have found a different answer. They have not, so she says, let's go ahead and assume that is fair to do.

"Now let me tell you exactly what the problem is. What are all the possible combinations of ages for my two sisters if they add up to 60?" She heard 20 and 40; 30 and 30. *"Are they twins?"* Mary asks, "What would be a good way to represent what we know about them?" After a brief brainstorming, she suggests that everyone take out 60 cubes and place them nearby. She gives each student a workmat with two halves; the left is labeled Carol and the right labeled Julie. She asks the students to put all 60 cubes on Carol's side. She asks, "How old are the sisters now?" She reminds the students that infants are not 1 year of age until their first birthday. Mary instructs the students to take one cube from Carol's side and put it on Julie's side of the mat. They have to say what this new combination is. Mary writes each combination as they say it on a big sheet of lined newsprint. As they continue moving one cube from Carol to Julie, they say aloud what the combination is and Mary writes it down. In future activities that follow this kind of structure, the children will make their own tables.

When they get to the end of making the combinations, she asks, "How many different combinations did we find?" They have found 61. She reminds them that these are possible ages, but we want to find their real ages. They tell her that they need more information. She provides a series of clues. After each clue she lets someone come up to the table and draw a line through combinations that have been eliminated. Mary provides several clues that narrow the possibilities if the students reason properly. Because this is the first problem of this kind that she has done with them, she provides more scaffolding assistance to the whole class.

Carol	Julie
21	39
22	38
23	37
24	36
25	35
26	34
27	33
28	32
29	31
~~30~~	~~30~~
31	29
32	28
33	27
34	26
35	25
36	24
37	23
38	22
39	21

FIGURE 6.1

Carol	Julie
~~21~~	~~39~~
~~22~~	~~38~~
~~23~~	~~37~~
~~24~~	~~36~~
25	35
26	34
27	33
28	32
29	31
~~30~~	~~30~~
31	29
32	28
33	27
34	26
35	25
~~36~~	~~24~~
~~37~~	~~23~~
~~38~~	~~22~~
~~39~~	~~21~~

FIGURE 6.2

Carol	Julie
~~21~~	~~39~~
~~22~~	~~38~~
~~23~~	~~37~~
~~24~~	~~36~~
25	35
26	34
27	33
28	32
29	31
~~30~~	~~30~~
~~31~~	~~29~~
~~32~~	~~28~~
~~33~~	~~27~~
~~34~~	~~26~~
~~35~~	~~25~~
~~36~~	~~24~~
~~37~~	~~23~~
~~38~~	~~22~~
~~39~~	~~21~~

FIGURE 6.3

Carol	Julie
~~21~~	~~39~~
~~22~~	~~38~~
~~23~~	~~37~~
~~24~~	~~36~~
~~25~~	~~35~~
26	**34**
~~27~~	~~33~~
28	**32**
~~29~~	~~31~~
~~30~~	~~30~~
~~31~~	~~29~~
~~32~~	~~28~~
~~33~~	~~27~~
~~34~~	~~26~~
~~35~~	~~25~~
~~36~~	~~24~~
~~37~~	~~23~~
~~38~~	~~22~~
~~39~~	~~21~~

FIGURE 6.4

The first clue is "Carol and Julie are not twins," and 30/30 is eliminated. The next clue is "All three sisters graduated from college and they went to college directly after high school." After extensive discussion about their own siblings, they settle on eliminating 0 to 20 on one sister, which meant eliminating 40 to 60 on the other. The remaining table looked like Figure 6.1.

The next clue was "Mary is the oldest of her sisters." The kids know that Mary is 36, so they reason that they can cross out at both ends of the table 36, 37, 38, and 39. See Figure 6.2. The clue "Julie is older than Carol" allows the kids to cross out half of the remaining combinations (see Figure 6.3). Two clues are left: Carol is an even number of years old, which knocks out three more and leaves only two possible combinations (26/34) and (28/32). See Figure 6.4. The final clue is "Each sister was born four years after the previous one." Since Mary is 36 then her sister Julie must be 32 and sister Carol 28.

Later in the school year these youngsters were capable of writing their own ideas and Mary did more problems of this kind with them. Figures 6.5, 6.6, and 6.7 show how one of her students worked on the problem of Mary's *nieces*. The problem was posed as before: "If you add the ages of Mrs. Fencl's two nieces, the sum is 30. How old are they? What are the possibilities?" Figure 6.5 is Mary's version of a KWC. Figure 6.6 shows how the kid wrote down the clues and then eliminated combinations. In Figure 6.7 the kid reflects.

Asking Math Questions

PROBLEM: How old are Grace and Kelly?

What Do I Know Already?	What's My Plan?
Their combined ages are 30. They are girls in Mrs. Fencl's family. they are younger than Mrs. Fencl.	☐ Draw A Picture ☒ Make A List ☐ Look For A Pattern ☐ Guess/Check ☐ Write A Number Sentence ☐ Other____

What Tools Could I Use?			
	☐ calculator	☒ counters	☐ number line/chart
	☐ coins	☐ ruler/tape	☐ cubes
	☐ tiles	☐ dominoes	☐ pattern blocks
	☐ other ____		

FIGURE 6.5

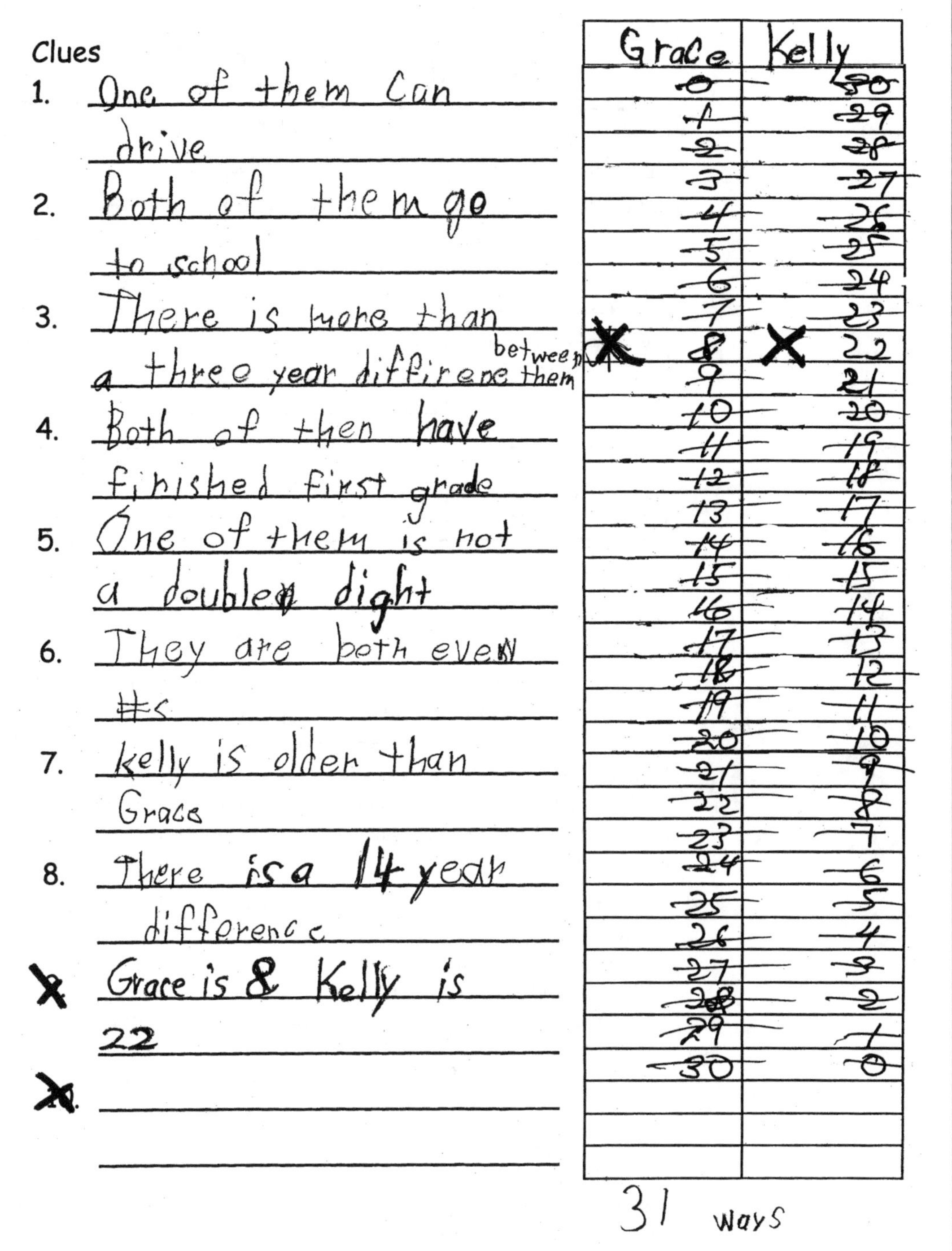
Clues
1. One of them Can drive
2. Both of them go to school
3. There is more than a three year diffirence between them
4. Both of then have finished first grade
5. One of them is not a double dight
6. They are both even #s
7. kelly is older than Grace
8. There is a 14 year difference
Grace is 8 Kelly is 22
Grace
Kelly
31 ways

FIGURE 6.6

SUM IT UP

WHAT DID I DO?	WHAT DID I LEARN?	HOW DID I FEEL?
We figured out how old Mrs. Fond's nieces are if total is 30. We found all the possibilities. We made an organized list and followed clues.	Strategies help us think. Math has patterns. We figured out how old are Grace and Kelly.	It was fun figureing it out.

FIGURE 6.7

WRITING FOR REASONING, REFLECTION, AND SYNTHESIS IN MATHEMATICS

There are many excellent ideas and practices in the National Council of Teachers of Mathematics (NCTM) 2000 Standards and Principles about using oral and written language. The Communication standard states that students can:

- organize and consolidate their mathematical thinking through communication;
- communicate their mathematical thinking coherently and clearly to peers, teachers, and others;
- analyze and evaluate the mathematical thinking and strategies of others;
- use the language of mathematics to express mathematical ideas precisely.

Communication requires both oral and written language and should be a dialogue between teacher and student as well as among students. Some psychologists and educators are now investigating the power of "a community of practice," in which the essential mechanism for significant change in thinking or knowing is the interaction with a variety of conceptual systems of others.

Throughout this book I have emphasized the importance of oral language in problem solving and mathematics in general. When students in groups of three or four are working on a challenging problem, especially if it is one that individuals working alone would be unlikely to solve, the potential is there for all students to get extensive "air time." They share their ideas and have to explain them or clarify them to other members of the group. They make conjectures and have to defend them. They must justify their reasoning and refine the processes of solving problems. Throughout this interaction, students are reflecting on how they are doing the mathematics and becoming more aware of the processes they use.

As valuable and necessary as discussion and dialogue are in enhancing mathematical thinking and problem solving, there are additional benefits to be accrued from writing. When students write about their mathematical concepts, conjectures, questions, and solutions they consolidate their thinking because it requires them to reflect on their work and clarify their thoughts about the ideas. While oral language is able to take advantage of the spontaneous, the immediate insight, the hunch, writing requires a special kind of intensity, analysis, thoughtfulness.

Of course, all this is potential that has to be fostered by the teacher. In Chapter 4 we discussed the different modes of thinking that teachers should *model* themselves so that students can get a feel for these different language vehicles for communicating ideas. The teacher should vary the questions (or prompts) that she gives the kids so they get practice writing in different modes. For instance, for many years Illinois state tests in writing required kids to demonstrate their proficiency in writing expository, narrative, and persuasive essays. A number of teachers purposely used the state's distinctions of these types in math and gave the kids three different kinds of writing prompts in math. An expository prompt would require students to explain a concept or explain the difference between two concepts (e.g., area and perimeter). A narrative prompt would make explicit the steps taken, the sequence of actions, and how these steps lead to the solution. A persuasive prompt would require the students to prove to the reader the correctness of their answer.

In the past ten years we have seen many forms of "show your work" in math such as extended-response questions on state tests, open-ended problems, and performance-based assessments (e.g., see Balanced Assessment or Exemplars, two commercially published materials whose websites are listed in the references). They are usually accompanied by a *rubric* used to give scores to the students' work on several dimensions. For instance, the Math portion of the Illinois State Assessment Test (ISAT) has included sixty multiple choice questions to be completed in an hour, but also two extended-response questions that students have thirty-five minutes to answer. A typical third-grade problem is given in Figure 6.8.

These questions are scored on a rubric with three scales: the first assesses knowledge of the math concepts in the problem, the second

Big sleds must hold 3 children, and small sleds must hold 2 children. If 17 children want to go sledding at the same time, how many of each type of sled is needed?

Show all your work. Explain in words <u>how</u> you got your answer and <u>why</u> you took the steps you did to solve the problem.

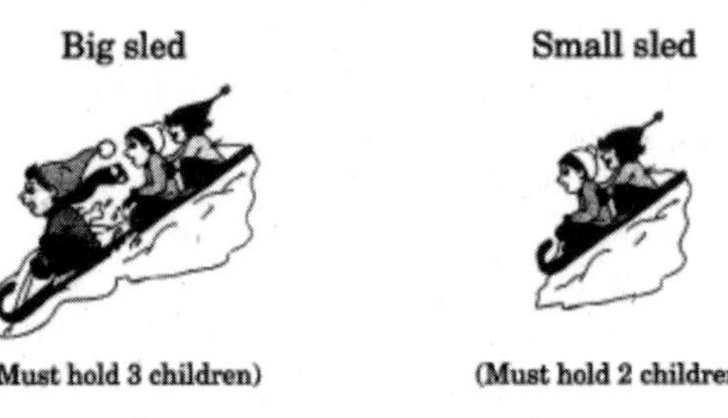

FIGURE 6.8 ISAT Math extended response item by Forness, Megan, et al. Copyright © 2003 by the Illinois State Board of Education. Reprinted with permission.

assesses the knowledge and use of an appropriate problem-solving strategy, the third assesses the quality of the explanation—both what was done and why. See Figure 6.9 for criteria for the maximum scores. People may debate the value of certain ISAT problems or the ratings on a 0 to 4 scale for each of the three. However, assessing the depth of conceptual understanding, the appropriateness of a strategy, and ones' ability to explain what and why are things I value.

These are certainly worthwhile, and yet some teachers are doing much more. Some teachers use a workshop and conference format to help students through the drafting and revision process of writing about their mathematical and problem-solving experiences.

Because drafting and revising have almost never been allowed in math, teachers must first assure students that rewriting is not only permitted, it is encouraged. It is a natural part of learning and doing. It is not just a "do over" because you made a mistake. The teacher can use conferences to give support, guidance, and one-to-one feedback on written work. If the teacher has set up the classroom to include peer review of one's writing, the teacher must build supportive and encouraging norms into the process, teaching the students how to critique their peers without engendering hurt feelings.

Perhaps the best mathematical writing kids do is when they feel a real need for a reader (an audience) to understand them, their point of view, their interpretation, or the correctness of their answer. Teachers of writing have long spoken of the value of kids writing for *authentic purposes*. Why not in math? For many years, Mary Fencl's second-grade classes have created a village. (See this wonderful simulation in *Excursions* [Burk et al. 1991].) Mary has added several twists to the project. Be-

Mathematics Scoring Rubic: A Guide to Scoring Extended-Response Items

	Mathematical Knowledge:	Strategic Knowledge:	Explanation:
	Knowledge of mathematical principles and concepts which result in a correct solution to a problem.	Identification and use of important elements of the problem that represent and integrate concepts which yield the solution (e.g., models, diagrams, symbols, and algorithms).	Written explanation of the rationales and steps of the solution process. A justification of each step is provided. Though important, the length of the response, grammar, and syntax are not the critical elements of this dimension.
Score Level 4	• shows complete understanding of the problem's mathematical concepts and principles • uses appropriate mathematical terminology and notations including labeling answer if appropriate • executes algorithms and computations completely and correctly	• identifies all important elements of the problem *and* shows complete understanding of the relationships among elements • shows complete evidence of an appropriate strategy that would correctly solve the problem	• gives a complete written explanation of the solution process, clearly explains *what* was done and *why* it was done • may include a diagram with a complete explanation of all its elements

FIGURE 6.9 ISAT Math extended response item by Forness, Megan, et al. Copyright © 2003 by the Illinois State Board of Education. Reprinted with permission.

cause they need money to buy building materials, they have to get a loan from a bank. They write letters to the local bank explaining what they need. The banker tells them that they need to have some collateral. Of course, Mary and the banker have worked out the scenario. The kids realize that the only thing they have is Mr. Jiggs, the big rabbit who lives in the cage in the classroom. The kids visit the bank and "negotiate the loan." The banker visits the classroom for the signing. He also explains how interest on their loan works and the payment plan he approved.

An increasing number of math educators are realizing the value of writing for a specific audience. Many of the model-building problems of Zawojewski and Lesh (2003) are like simulations where the students act as consultant teams who have a particular "client" with a special problem. The consultant teams must interpret, make decisions about, and then recommend a course of action for the client. The teams write drafts of reports to the client. The drafts are written several times and are ultimately published.

Like many math teachers, incorporating student writing into my teaching was no simple matter. I asked my colleague Jane Moore who has done extensive journaling with kids to tell us briefly what she has learned about this vehicle for student learning.

Journaling

It is common practice today in the elementary school classroom for journaling to occur—students often journal on a daily basis, filling notebooks with compositions, poetry, assigned essays, and dialogues with teachers. The phenomenon is called "writing across the curriculum" and many wonderful combinations of social studies, science, and literature are written about.

The dialogue between student and teacher that occurs in journaling can help children think through ideas and develop

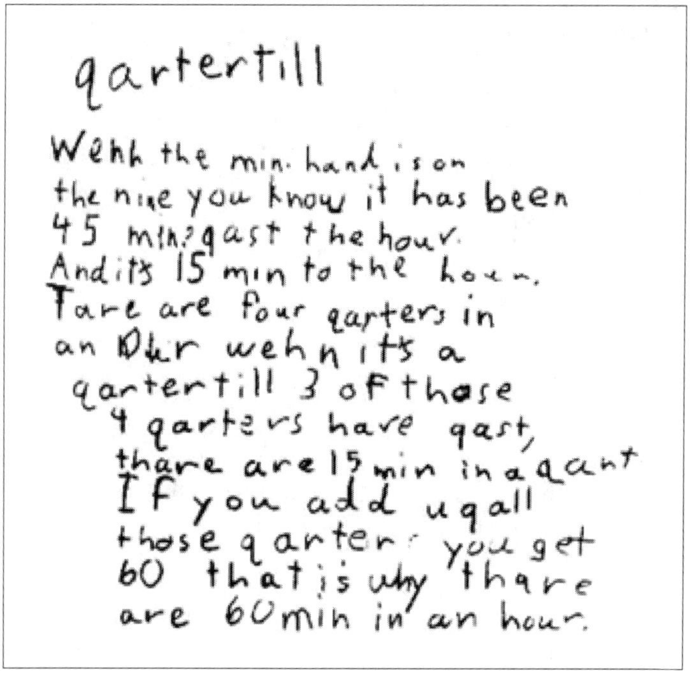

qartertill

Wehh the min. hand is on
the nine you know it has been
45 min. qast the hour.
And it's 15 min to the houn.
Tare are four qarters in
an Ohr wehn it's a
qartertill 3 of those
4 qarters have qast,
thare are 15 min in a qant
If you add uqall
those qarter you get
60 that is why thare
are 60 min in an hour.

FIGURE 6.10

Half Past and how it got it's name

there are 60 min.'s in a howr.
when somebody sais half pa t.
they mean half of 60 min's
that's 30 min's. 30 min's in he
an howr. that's how half Past
got it's name

FIGURE 6.11

concepts. Questioning techniques used in response to student writing allows children as young as second grade to converge on an understanding. Journals have a major advantage: to help teachers know what students know.

I began to implement mathematical journal writing in my second/third-grade classroom with the concept of time. We spent a day full of time-telling projects and I assigned a journal topic of "Why do we use the terms 'half past' and 'quarter till' when we tell time?" The results were quite fascinating, and as diverse as the children themselves.

Some children immediately understood the idea (Figure 6.10) while others were even more concise (Figure 6.11).

Still others required the dialogue I spoke of earlier (Figure 6.12). When student journals are unclear, questioning helps the authors to clarify their ideas. Personal interaction between teacher and student helped children to refine their thinking and sharpen their understandings.

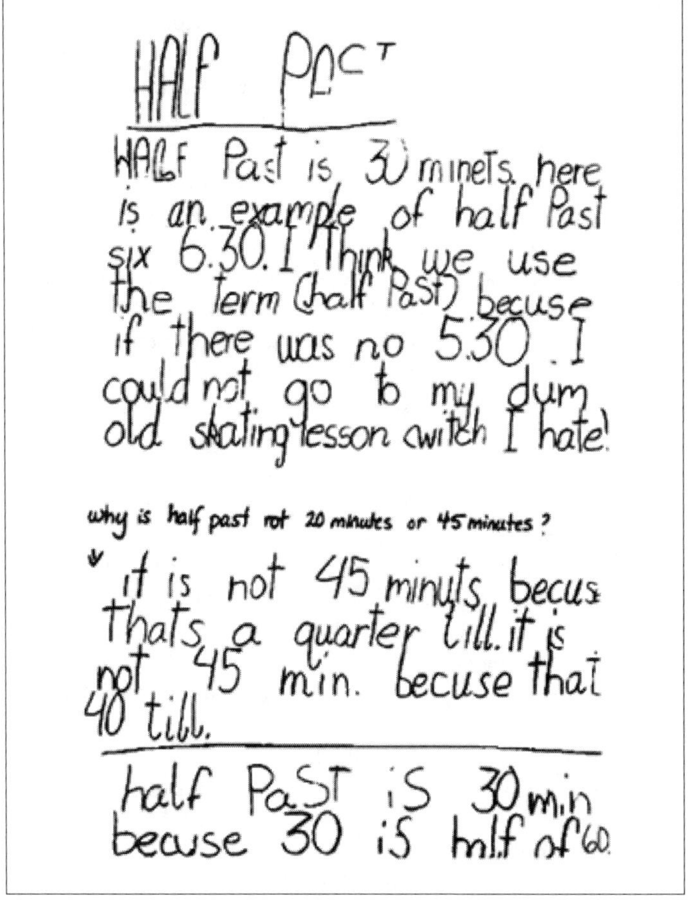
HALF PACT

HALF Past is 30 minets. here is an example of half Past six 6.30. I Think we use the term (half Past) becuse if there was no 5.30. I could not go to my dum old skating lesson witch I hate!

why is half past not 20 minutes or 45 minutes?

it is not 45 minuts becus thats a quarter till. it is not 45 min. becuse that 40 till.

half PaST iS 30 min becuse 30 iS half of 60.

FIGURE 6.12

I asked the children to write about ideas in time telling that are often taken for granted. We followed the individualized questions with a paper-folding activity. I gave each child a round paper clock face. I told them to match the 3 to the 9, make the edges even, and then fold it in half. After all agreed that the clock face was folded in halves, we folded again to make four equal pieces, or fourths. I asked the children to give another name for "fourth" and someone volunteered *"quarter."* Then I asked if the "half hour" and "quarter to" phrases made any more sense. Some of the children who were unable to articulate this earlier in their journals were able to understand it better using the paper clock.

On another day I tried the question, "What is Daylight Savings Time?" This rather abstract question (especially for a teacher who can never remember whether to fall forward or backward) produced many convoluted replies and one delightful response, *"It's when there is a big sale . . ."* Sometimes we just don't ask the right questions!

One way to ask the right questions is to use a good model. The Sum of a Pair of Dice game is a good example. The children work with a partner. They write the numbers 0–12 in a line across one sheet of paper. I give each student thirteen counters. I tell them to arrange the counters on the number line. "You can do this any way you like. You may put one counter on each number. You may stack all the counters on one number, or you can group them in any other way you like."

Once all the counters have been placed, I roll the dice. I call out the sum that came up. If they have a counter on that number, they remove it. "If you should happen to have two or three or more counters on a number I call, you would take off only one of those counters. No rearranging!" As they are playing the game, I stop and ask if anyone is waiting on a particular number. I ask them to think about which numbers came up more often. Then without discussion we play again. Some make a chart that keeps track of the numbers. After the game I have them write about what they discovered.

"I would put the most on seven because there are more ways to make seven than any other number. But not too many. I dare you to put them on 12 or 2 because they have only one combination." Or:

"Now I have understood how 6, 7, 8, and 9 are rolled often. They are rolled often because they have more sums and numbers that add to be them. Now I will put my counters on them."

As I have become more comfortable with math journals, I've asked questions about models, symbols, and strategies for solving problems. I asked one of my boys which fact strategies he used for 9 + 5. (See Figure 6.13.)

We can sometimes find out that a child who appears to have a good understanding of a concept is confused. Consider the an-

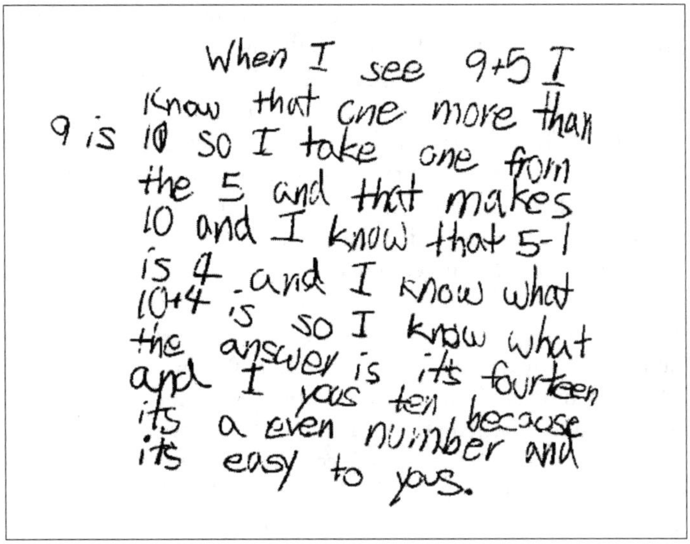

When I see 9+5 I
know that one more than
9 is 10 so I take one from
the 5 and that makes
10 and I know that 5-1
is 4 and I know what
10+4 is so I know what
the answer is its fourteen
and I yous ten because
its a even number and
its easy to yous.

FIGURE 6.13

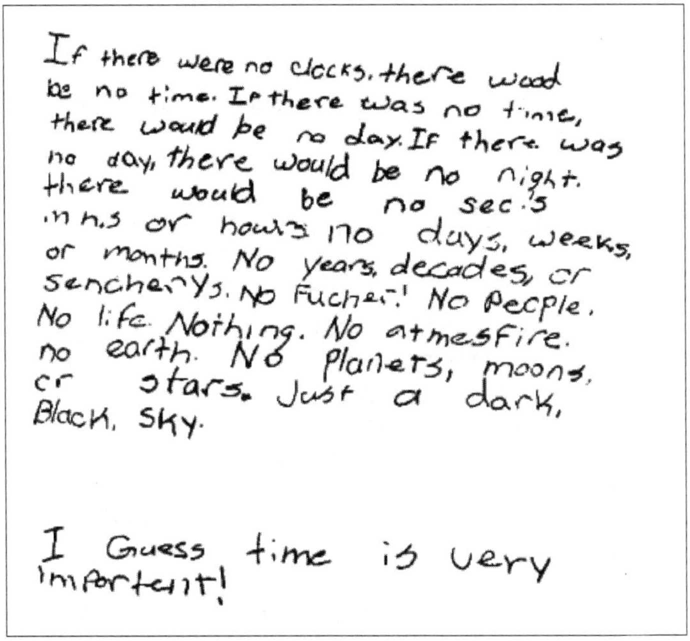

If there were no clocks, there wood
be no time. If there was no time,
there would be no day. If there was
no day, there would be no night.
there would be no sec's
min.s or hours no days, weeks,
or months. No years, decades, or
senchenys. No Fucher! No People.
No life. Nothing. No atmesfire.
no earth. No Planets, moons,
or stars. Just a dark,
Black, Sky.

I Guess time is very
importent!

FIGURE 6.14

swer I got when I asked, "What if there were no clocks or watches?" after we had all removed our time pieces and covered the classroom clock (Figure 6.14).

I thought that she was confused or didn't understand the question. It was several years later that I realized that I had been reading the math journals from a very narrow perspective. I was presenting at a math conference on the use of math journals and used the example above (Figure 6.14). As I was explaining how this was an example of the way a journal can point out a misinterpretation by a student, it suddenly occurred to me that I had been looking for a right answer rather than looking at all the information the student was presenting. In rereading the journal, I saw that this second-grade student had accurately listed all the increments of time in sequence—quite remarkable, and yet I had not remarked on them to her in any of our back-and-forth written dialogues in the journaling we were doing. I learned a valuable lesson at that time: we need to look at what students are telling us and value their responses both in light of our prompts and in light of mathematical learning. When I began using math journals, my hardest task was developing the questions to begin with. Now I find questions everywhere and with them the opportunities for risk-taking, problem solving, making conjecture, and ongoing dialogue that lets me "know what they know."

When I read the response of the student in Figure 6.14, I told Jane that this response reads like a poem. She said that, indeed, this child had gone on to win poetry contests.

SYNTHESIZING MATHEMATICAL IDEAS WITH CHOCOLATE

When I think of math activities that are likely to foster synthesis of the profound kind, one comes immediately to mind: Chocolate Math for intermediate grades and Chocolate Algebra for the middle school. I cooked this up about ten years ago in order to fully integrate (synthesize) the different representations, data tables, graphs (and equations for the older kids) within a real-life situation. It is done in the context of *chocolate* and *money*, two of the seven deadly sins, I believe. From the dozens of different ways I have done it, I'll describe a typical scenario for a class in grades three to five.

I usually have the students work in pairs for these activities. I begin by posing a problem to the class: "If you have \$10 to spend on \$2 Hershey Bars and \$1 Tootsie Rolls, how many ways can you spend your money without receiving change? All chocolate, no change—tax included." I give them stacks of play money so they can have a concrete manipulative to help them think about the solutions. In the first problem, \$10 to spend on \$2 and \$1 chocolate items, I tell them that each \$2 bill represents a \$2

Hershey Bar and a $1 bill, a Tootsie Roll. They can show us a solution by holding up the bills that represent the chocolate items.

After introducing the situation of spending exactly $10 on $2 Hershey Bars and $1 Tootsie Rolls, the students quickly began generating solutions. As expected, most randomly jotted down any combination that popped into their minds. As they shared solutions, it became apparent that we needed an organizational system. I gave each pair a recording sheet, a simple two-column table (or T-chart) to keep the combinations in order. The left-hand column was "# of $2 HBs" and the right-hand column "# of $1 TRs."

I asked them, "Did you find all the possible combinations?" To make it easier to answer, I suggested that they start with the most $2 Hershey Bars they could buy ("the most of the bigger item") and decrease the number of Hershey Bars one at a time. See Figure 6.15.

When making data tables, I emphasize that the numbers in the table are *how many* chocolates of each kind. Not the money. Note the little box in the corner of each cell in the table. I tell the students to enter into the "box in the corner" the cost of the number of items in the cell. Therefore, in the first cell in the table (upper left) the kids enter 5 for the number of Hershey Bars (HBs) at $2 apiece that would cost $10 (the dollar amount goes in the box).

We proceed down the HB column, filling in each row as we go, including the box in the corner for each cell. See Figure 6.15. Along the way I show them another way to think about these boxes. For example, when we went to 3 HBs and we entered $6 in the box as the cost, I asked, "If we spend $6 on HBs, how much do we have left for the TRs?" They would subtract $6 from the $10 and say, "$4." I'd enter that in the TR box and ask, "Okay. How many TRs can we buy with $4?" The purpose of this

# of $2 HB		**# of $1 TR**		**TOTAL $10**
5	$10	0	$0	
4	$8	2	$2	
3	$6	4	$4	
2	$4	6	$6	
1	$2	8	$8	
0	$0	10	$10	

FIGURE 6.15

was to get them used to working with these tables flexibly, not only to record but also to help them analyze and generate solutions. When they use bigger numbers and more complicated situations later, they will need to be able to reason that if they choose a number for either item (actually a value for either variable), they can multiply that number times the cost of one item, get that total cost for all of them, and subtract it from the total to see how much they have left to spend on the other item. They then *divide* the money left by the cost of the second item. If it comes out even, then they've found a solution. So far, this division has not been obvious because the TRs cost $1, which allows the kids to put the same numbers in the TRs cells as in their boxes.

When they complete the table, I ask them to look at the numbers in the table and tell me what patterns they see. Look at the number of HBs and the Number of TRs. In the past kids have said something like, "*One side goes down and the other side goes up.*" Some kids mention the TRs were counting by the even numbers and the HBs were counting down from 5. Others say, "*We're counting up or down.*" Several said things like, "*The HBs are going down by one and the TRs are going up by two.*" I ask if this happens every time; is it a regular pattern? They can see that every consecutive row has 1 less HB and 2 more TRs. I suggest to the kids that we call it the "down by 1, up by 2 pattern." They are fine with that.

Then I ask them, "Why is the pattern down by 1, up by 2?" They usually just stare at me. I say, "Now we know the pattern for the number of candy, but what are the patterns in the money, in the boxes in the corner?" The kids say things like "*They change by $2 on each thing*" or "*The cost of the HBs go down by $2 and the TRs go up by $2.*" As we talk about the money, some kids say, "*I got it. When you buy 1 less Hershey Bar you save $2 but you don't really save it because you give it to the Tootsie Rolls.*"

# of $5 FM		**# of $1 TR**		**TOTAL $27**
5	$25	2	$2	
4	$20	7	$7	
3	$15	12	$12	
2	$10	17	$17	
1	$5	22	$22	
0	$0	27	$27	

FIGURE 6.16

# of $5 FM		# of $2 HB		TOTAL $40
8	$40	0	$0	
6	$30	5	$10	
4	$20	10	$20	
2	$10	15	$30	
0	$0	20	$40	

FIGURE 6.17

# of $5 FM		# of $2 HB		TOTAL $45
9	$45	0	$0	
7	$35	5	$10	
5	$25	10	$20	
3	$15	15	$30	
1	$5	20	$40	

FIGURE 6.18

Other kids say, *"Every time you take $2 and 1 HB off that side, you've got to add $2 on the other side which lets you buy 2 TRs."* They got it.

To extend their thinking, I have them buy $1 Tootsie Rolls and $5 boxes of Fannie Mae with $27. I give them recording sheets. They make tables to show the combinations. Again I ask for the pattern and why. See Figure 6.16. Whenever we do a new table, I ask them what certain numbers are referring to because I do not want them to lose sight of the real-life situation the table is modeling. I want everything connected. I also remind them that each row in the table is a solution to our question of ways to spend all our money on chocolate, with no change.

Then I ask students to shop for $5 Fannie Mae and $2 Hershey Bars with $40. This is a bit difficult because they cannot decrease the number of $5 items by one each time. (See Figure 6.17.) Some are amazed that they cannot use every number for the $5 FM and when I ask the class to explain why, it takes a while for them to see the reason.

Every time they put an odd number of FMs in the cell, they get an odd number of dollars in the box (e.g., 7 FMs cost \$35, 5 FMs cost \$25, etc.). Then when they try to buy \$2 HBs with an odd amount of dollars, they have change, which is not allowed. Therefore the pattern is down by 2, up by 5. Somewhere along the way of looking at patterns, one kid always asks, "*Do you always get this pattern with FMs and HBs?*" So I suggest we look at \$5 FMs and \$2 HBs with \$45 (an odd amount). They are a bit surprised to see the odd numbers, but we discuss the pattern and why once again. See Figure 6.18.

I spend a couple of minutes reviewing the basics of graphing. If they have not done graphing before, I use this as an opportunity to teach it. Then we graph the values in the table in Figure 6.17. See Figure 6.19. Most notice that the solution points "line up" and that they start in the top left and go down towards the bottom right, which is different from their usual graphs that go up from lower left to top right. I ask them why this graph is different. Someone usually realizes that in the table we've been using, one side goes down and the other side goes up. In their usual graphs, both sides go up.

"Take your pencil and put it on the point (8, 0). In the table we saw the pattern down by 2, up by 5. What would it mean to move down?" Someone calls out, "*Move to the left.*" "Yes, we go to the left 2 and we are at point 6, 0. Now we go up five. Where are we?" They are surprised that we are at the next solution in the table (6, 5). These five points are the only solutions. They are on a straight line. Why? What was the pattern in

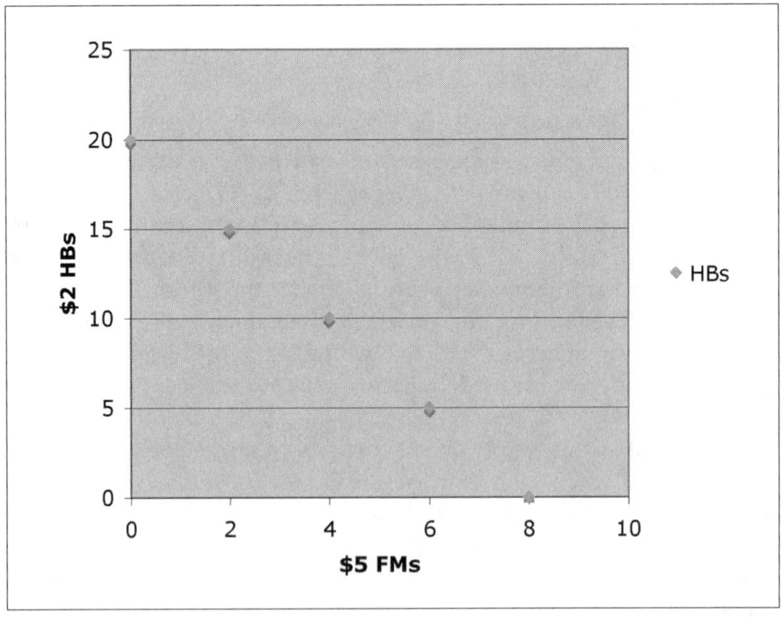

FIGURE 6.19

the table? Down by 2, up by 5. Some students need help seeing why moving to the left 2 points on the x-axis is going "down" (decreasing in value). Then they go up by 5 on the y-axis and arrive at the next point on the graph (4, 10). They continue and are excited to see that the pattern that they saw in the table has a direct counterpart in the graph.

It is a definite step up in abstraction for the students to record these solutions as (8, 0), (6, 5), and so forth, and plot the points in the graph. We want to build full understanding of each representation as well as connections among them for all students. Therefore, we require that the students go back and connect to the real situation by asking them, "What is that 5 talking about? Five what? What does (6, 5) mean?"

A wrap-up for the students in grades three to five usually includes graphing the solutions to the $40 and $45 to spend on the same graph. See Figure 6.20. We use dashed lines to signify that these points are the only solutions and although they are on a straight line, there are no other points of whole numbers that are. A solid straight line depicts continuous

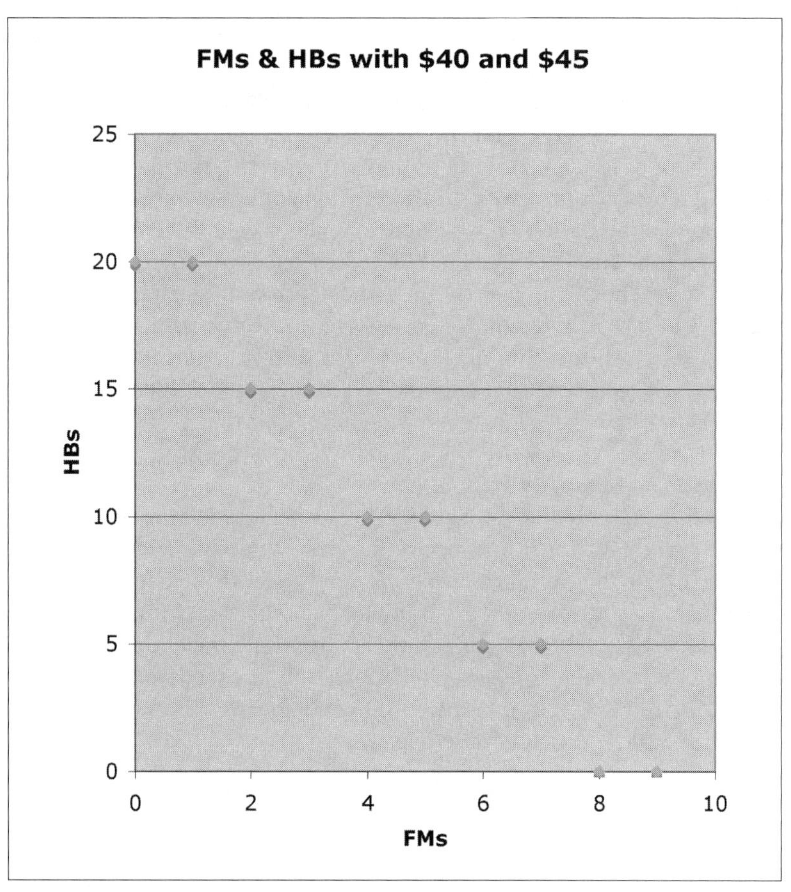

FIGURE 6.20

solutions. When the kids see the two solutions sets in two parallel lines, some are amazed. Others realize that it is logical because they have the same pattern of down by 2, up by 5. With middle school kids I help them appreciate the x and y intercepts and their contextual meaning—all of one candy and none of the other (0, 20), (8, 0), and (9, 0).

The older kids can be shown how to create a two-variable equation using the boxes in the corner. The younger kids stop here. However, they continue several times during the year to work with other situations that have the same mathematical structure. Recall the ISAT problem of how many small sleds for 2 and big sleds for 3 are required to handle 17 kids (Figure 6.8). What is the most big 3-person sleds we could use? With 5 we'd cover 15 of the 17 kids and the remaining two could be in one small sled. One solution is 5 big, 1 small. Are there other solutions? We can't use 4 big sleds because 17 is an odd number, which also will happen with 2 and 0 big sleds. But 3 big sleds will take 9 and 4 small will take 8; so 3 big and 4 small works, as does 1 big and 7 small.

To create the equation I simply ask the kids, "If x is the number of FMs, what would be their cost? What would we put in the box in the corner? What did we do when we knew what the number was?" Virtually everyone realizes the box gets \$5 times x or simply "$5x$." I repeat the question with the number of HBs as y and they tell me the cost is \$$2y$. Then I ask, "What is the total cost of both together and how much money do you have to spend on them?" If they struggle with the question, I ask, "Do you remember how we could add the two boxes in a row together to see if we had the right total we had to spend?" They all see $5x + 2y = 40$.

For all the students who have done this activity with me or with the dozens of teachers who have tried it, the depth of understanding of the concepts and their interconnectedness is astonishing. Each representation is clear and directly linked to the real-life situation from which it sprang. Each representation is connected to each of the other representations. There have been not giant leaps required that so often become chasms that kids cannot traverse. Each step has been built on a solid foundation and properly scaffolded.

How do I know that true synthesis has occurred? One indicator to me is when the younger kids begin thinking with tables, when they are quick to create them and use them effectively, seeing the patterns within them. For the older ones, a good indicator is the ease with which they create equations. Some algebra teachers have done the chocolate activities *after* they have taught linear equations from the textbook. Invariably many of the kids exclaim, "Why didn't you show us this chocolate stuff *first*! This makes so much more sense!"

7 THE POWER OF BRAIDING

Throughout this book I have tried to demonstrate how we help students become more powerful problem solvers and more sophisticated mathematical thinkers by braiding together language (especially reading comprehension), important cognitive processes, and mathematics. Sometimes I feel like I have just scratched the surface of the possibilities for braiding these three. In this concluding chapter, I want to provide an overview of why the Braid Model is so powerful and indicate where this model will lead you if you take up the challenge of committing yourself to doing it, not just a half-hearted try, but serious follow-through. I promise you will not be disappointed. Hundreds of teachers have tried this braiding approach. The vast majority of them have found great success when they adapted it *and did not skip over parts of the process.*

PLANNING FOR PROBLEM SOLVING

In the Points to Ponder sections at the end of each chapter, there are a great many things for you to consider in planning your lessons or units. They are a guide to adaptation and implementation of this approach. Virtually every one of these considerations has its roots in cognitive psychology. The Braid Model incorporates a great many ideas described in *How Students Learn* (Donavan and Bransford 2005) and *How People Learn* (Brown, and Cocking 2000), two reports that synthesized research on cognition, child development, and brain functioning.

Each consideration does not tell you exactly what to do, but rather it flags what you need to think about and then decide how to deal with it in your own situation. When parts are skipped or considerations ignored, the percentage of students who understand plummets, the deep river of understanding dries up to a craggy river bed, and the amount of reteaching needed escalates.

Here is a very real example. In Chapter 3 I described a full, rich set of experiences to build understanding of multiplication with partial products. For many years a particular curricular program showed partial products, *but never showed the rectangles.* Teachers found the lessons confusing and the whole thing made no sense to the kids. We showed teachers not only how to use rectangles, but gave them a full-blown "multi-rep lesson" in which kids translated back and forth across the representations (using yellow and blue base ten blocks and crayons, drawing rectangles on graph paper, drawing the cross-bars, identifying the four smaller rectangles, and so forth). Nearly every teacher who has taken these basic tools and done some version of what is described in Chapter 3 tells me how wonderfully it worked. There are a few teachers who have said it didn't go as well as planned or even that it bombed. When I asked them to describe what they did minute by minute, *every single one had left something out.* And they all said the same thing. "I didn't think they really needed to do that." They do! The second most popular reason it failed was that the teachers thought my way would take too much time. My response is always, "How much extra time do you spend reteaching?" There is no substitute for understanding.

I suggest that you read the considerations in planning before every unit. The full set of considerations is in the appendix. They will give you lots to think about.

TEACHING MATH CONTENT THROUGH PROBLEM SOLVING

The Braid Model of Problem Solving is given in the appendix. It describes what you should help the kids do. Its special power derives from both the specific processes it incorporates and also how it braids them together. Would I be accused of using a cliché if I spoke of synergy? Let me enumerate the components of the Braid Model and also the terrain it covers.

The model easily handles traditional (perhaps timeless) story problems with the givens, goals, and constraints. The questioning process of the KWC gives students a structure by which to analyze these problems. Furthermore, this structure is not a mindless recipe. It is based upon a thoughtful reading of the problem with an eye on the comprehension strategies.

The Braid Model is equally powerful at helping students deal with broader problems and open-ended tasks because the KWC is enhanced by a dozen other probes that further analyze the problem. Visualization helps them imagine the situation and context. Making context and content connections activates their schemata to bring insight and conditionalized knowledge (the most appropriate prior knowledge) into this problem. By illuminating the distinctions between literal and inferential meaning, the Braid Model helps kids avoid unwarranted inferences (and dubious assumptions). The model emphasizes the creation of representations to assist in seeing patterns at the heart of every problem and every concept.

These virtues come about primarily from the braiding—the infusion of the language and thought into the mathematics of the situation (or to create some mathematics for the situation—depending on your philosophy—but now is not the time to get into epistemological arguments. I already admitted I can't get Kant!). Teachers model the kind of thinking they want kids to do through the language they use. If they want kids to use metaphors, then the teachers themselves must speak in metaphors. Teachers also must help the kids become aware (in a metacognitive sense) of important distinctions between modes of language and mindful of their different purposes—descriptive, procedural, explanatory, and reflective language that may lead into the language of reasoning (assume, connect, infer, predict, interpret, conclude).

Teachers and I have often discussed and lamented how difficult it is to help other teachers to incorporate the processes of mathematics into their classrooms. Adding a concept here or there to the long list of concepts in the curriculum is far easier than it is to establish the creation of representations, to build the habit of seeking patterns and connections, and to develop the norms of reasoned discourse. As I worked on this book during the past year, I became convinced that among the many reasons that the math processes are more difficult to enact than curricular changes is the low level of attention to infusing language and thought into the curriculum. I have come to believe that the braiding of language, thinking, and mathematical problem solving has had such success because it helps teachers see what kids need to do in order to understand, and how to do it.

In *The Handbook of Research on Mathematics Teaching and Learning* (2006) the authors of the chapter on problem solving, Lesh and Zawojewski, describe the basic premises and ultimate stalemate of traditional problem solving. The traditional approach consists of encouraging the students to:

1. acquire the mathematical knowledge needed
2. acquire the problem-solving strategies that will help make decisions about what already-known procedure to try
3. acquire the metacognitive strategies that will trigger the appropriate use of problem-solving strategies and mathematical knowledge
4. and finally, unlearn beliefs and dispositions that prevent effective use of problem-solving and metacognitive strategies, while also developing productive beliefs and affect

"Results from research based on these preceding assumptions have been unimpressive" (Lesh and Zawojewski 2006, 88).

There are several serious difficulties with these ideas. Inevitably, everything to be learned gets reduced to a recipe (a list of simple rules or declarative statements). Concept development gets separated from the learning of problem solving because teachers focus on content-independent problem-solving processes. Some curricula lead teachers into believing there are problem-solving skills to be mastered, assuming that problem-solving strategies and skills function in very similar ways across diverse sets of tasks and situations. Then the concepts are left to the old standby of direct, deductive instruction.

If we believe that problem solving is what mathematicians do, that it is at the very heart of mathematics, and that we can have students learn concepts of mathematics with understanding by doing problems, it appears that it is time to broaden our conceptions of what problem solving is and how we do it.

FUTURE DIRECTIONS OF PROBLEM SOLVING

Lesh and Zawojewski point to three significant areas of research that have shown results and will probably shape the character of problem solving in the coming years. These are: situated cognition, communities of practice, and representational fluency. The Braid Model is in a great position because it already takes advantage of all three. You may recall from previous chapters that Lesh is one of the pioneers of a models and modeling perspective on problem solving.

Situated cognition refers to learning and problem solving in context. There are many situations in real life where groups of people have developed significant types of mathematics to handle a particular (local) need. These particular ways of thinking about the concepts and accompanying procedures make perfectly good sense to those who use them, but they bear little resemblance to the mathematics typically learned in school. People who make extensive use of mathematics in their work settings organize their ways of thinking mathematically around situations and problem contexts, not around the abstractions in school math textbooks. The research from situated cognition consistently has shown that virtually everyone engaged in solving problems in their local contexts are able to develop mathematical concepts and powerful conceptual tools for problem situations.

The Braid Model emphasizes context and situations asking kids to imagine, visualize, and connect the math and the context (content and context connections). We encourage teachers to look for (or create) problems where the context facilitates access to the content and is not merely window dressing.

Research on communities of practice has been closely associated with research on situated cognition. Communities of practice emphasizes the fact that humans acquire knowledge through interaction with others. Learning is a social enterprise (e.g., peers learning under the guidance of a teacher). Groups of students are communities of practice that are involved in a mathematical task too challenging for any one individual. The interactions among group members provide opportunities for individuals' conjectures, conclusions, and understandings to be tested, integrated, differentiated, extended, revised, or rejected.

The Braid Model has been used effectively with whole-class instruction, small groups, and individuals. The dozen or so questions can structure the whole-class dialogue. This is actually a good way to start so that the teacher can model and think aloud what each question means. The questions are effective for small groups beginning their attack on a problem by "discussing the problem in small groups," the representational strategy based on oral language. As individual students begin to internalize these questions they use them by themselves during homework and tests.

Representational fluency, also known as metarepresentation, is the capability a student has to construct, critique, and refine a variety of representational forms. It refers to a person creating a representation appropriate for a particular problem, mathematical task, or situation/context and not simply imposing a standard representation. Such highly appropriate representations are, essentially, models. The centrality of representations to the Braid Model should be obvious. Representations have been at the heart of my teaching and learning for two decades.

Students learn to use conventional mathematical language and symbols introduced by teachers, textbooks, and technology but don't get much exposure to the dynamic and changing use of representations in the technological world. The representational media that students get to use in schools often require only passive watching on their parts. Yet it is clear from cognitive science that they need to be able to create with various representational systems so that their creations truly embody their internal images and conceptual systems. Representational fluency is especially valuable in communicating one's conceptions and in flexibly using them to develop solutions to real-life problems.

Researchers have found that, with minimal intervention from a teacher, young problem solvers can develop metarepresentational competence. Developing competence is enhanced by students talking with other students to test representations, getting feedback from peers. Through continual cycles of representing, sharing, critiquing, and revising, kids are able to improve their representations considerably.

A somewhat surprising finding in this research was that there was no relationship between students' metarepresentational capability and students' mastery of conventional classroom-taught representations. When students explained their thinking or presented their work it had little or no influence on their development of metarepresentational capability. However, involvement in the creation, production, testing, and revision of representations for a specific purpose did positively influence metarep growth. That would make good sense; they were practicing the very trait that was to be assessed. It is not enough to copy the representations that the teachers showed. It is much more important to think through how to create something yourself that works for you, something that you understand intimately. I would hypothesize that there is a certain amount of experience and knowledge about representations that needs to be in place, like a minimal threshold, from which, once attained, kids can really take off.

When one combines these three areas (situated cognition, community, and representations), one can see students working in small groups of mathematical tasks and problems emanating from real contexts where there is an authentic purpose. They discuss and hear interpretations of what the problem really is. As their understanding of the problem grows, they create various representations of what is going on, especially to communicate their ideas to fellow team members, the teacher, and other students. They explain their reasoning and use their representations to convince others. When they are satisfied with the quality of one or more of their representations, they present it to their community of student scholars and publish their results.

What a marvelous vision of students learning mathematics this scenario is!

APPENDIX

CONSIDERATIONS IN PLANNING FOR PROBLEM SOLVING

Situation

Big Ideas, Enduring Understandings, and Essential Concepts

What is the concept that I want the students to understand?
To what prior knowledge should we try to connect?
Are there different models of the concept?
Should I break down the concept into its underlying ideas?
Is there a sequence of understandings that the students need to have?
What other mathematical concepts are related?

Authentic Experiences

What are the different real-life situations or contexts in which students would encounter the concept?
Will they see it in science or social studies?
How can I vary the contexts to build up a more generalized understanding?
What version of this situation can I present to start them thinking about the concept?
What questions can I ask to intrigue them and initiate problem solving?

Cognitive Processes in the Context

How do I scaffold experiences for progressive development from concrete to abstract?
How concretely should I start?
How can I encourage initial play and exploration with the materials or ideas?
How can I make the experiences challenging, but not overwhelming?

What questions can I ask or terms can I use to help them visualize or imagine the context, situation, or problem?
Should they work in small groups and discuss the problem or concept in the specific context?

Grouping Structures to Encourage the Social Construction of Meaning

How can I vary the grouping structures: whole class, small group, individuals (with attention to small groups of two to five students)?
How can I enhance small-group discussions for students to develop, refine, and elaborate their thinking?

Language Representations

How do I talk about the concept or ask questions to reveal connections or promote reflection?
How can I model thought processes, strategies, practices to encourage both cognitive and metacognitive processes?
How can I incorporate reading, writing, speaking, and listening into the activities?
How can I help the students use journals to document, reflect upon, and refine their thinking?
How can I help them explain their representations (orally/in writing)?

Other Representations

How do I scaffold experiences to move from concrete to abstract?
What manipulatives or physical objects can help students see what is going on?
Should they draw a picture of objects or of the situation/problem as they imagine it?
Does the situation contain a sequence of actions that students might act out?
Should they record information in a list and later organize it into a table?
What symbols are essential for them to understand? *n*, objects, or pictures?
How does each symbol specifically relate to the situation?

Patterns

What patterns (visual, spatial, or numerical) do I want them to see?
What questions do I ask to help them see patterns?
What questions do I ask to build bridges, helping them make connections?
How do I talk about the other mathematical concepts that are related?
What terms or language could I use? What metaphors or analogies could I make?

What connections are important for them to make as we debrief the activity?
How do I help them move from natural language to more precise mathematical terms?
How do I help them communicate (orally/in writing) their solutions and understandings?

The Braid Model of Problem Solving

Understanding the problem/Reading the story
Visualization
Do I see pictures in my mind? How do they help me understand the situation?
Imagine the SITUATION. What is going on here?
Asking Questions (and Discussing the problem in small groups)
K: What do I know for sure?
W: What do I want to figure out, find out, or do?
C: Are there any special conditions, rules, or tricks I have to watch out for?
Making Connections
Math to Self
What does this situation remind me of?
Have I ever been in any situation like this?
Math to World
Is this related to anything I've seen in social studies or science, the arts?
Or related to things I've seen anywhere?
Math to Math
What is the main idea from mathematics that is happening here?
Where have I seen that idea before?
What are some other math ideas that are related to this one?
Can I use them to help me with this problem?
Infer
What inferences have I made? For each connection, what is its significance?
Look back at my notes on K and C. Which are facts and which are inferences?
Are my inferences accurate?

Planning how to solve the problem

What REPRESENTATIONS can I use to help me solve the problem?

Which problem-solving strategy will help me the most in this situation?

Make a model	Draw a picture	Make an organized list
Act it out	Make a table	Write an equation
Find a pattern	Use logical reasoning	Draw a diagram
Work backward	Solve a simpler problem	Predict and test

Carrying out the plan/Solving the problem

Work on the problem using a strategy.

- Does this strategy show me something I didn't see before now?
- Should I try another strategy?
- Am I able to infer any PATTERNS?
- Am I able to predict based on this inferred pattern?

Looking back/Checking

Does my answer make sense for the problem?

Is there a pattern that makes the answer reasonable?

What CONNECTIONS link this problem and answer to the big ideas of mathematics?

Is there another way to do this? Have I made an assumption?

REFERENCES

Balanced Assessment. No date. http://balancedassessment.concord.org. The website contains a large number of performance assessment tasks.

Beck, I. L., M. G. McKeown, R. L. Hamilton, and L. Kucan. 1997. *Questioning the Author: An Approach to Enhancing Student Engagement with Text.* Newark, DE: International Reading Association.

Bickmore-Brand, J., ed. 1990. *Language in Mathematics.* Portsmouth, NH: Heinemann.

Blachowicz, C. and D. Ogle. 2001. *Reading Comprehension: Strategies for Independent Learners.* New York: Guilford.

Bransford, J. D., A. Brown, and R. R. Cocking, eds. 2000. *How People Learn: Brain, Mind, Experience and School. Expanded edition.* Washington, DC: National Academy Press.

Burk, D., A. Snider, and P. Symonds. 1991. *Math Excursions 2: Project-Based Mathematics for Second Graders.* Portsmouth, NH: Heinemann.

Daniels, H. and M. Bizar. 2005. *Teaching the Best Practice Way: Methods That Matter, K–12.* York, ME: Stenhouse.

Devlin, K. 2000. *The Math Gene: How Mathematical Thinking Evolved and Why Numbers Are Like Gossip.* New York: Basic Books.

———. 2005. *The Math Instinct: Why You're a Mathematical Genius (Along with Lobsters, Birds, Cats, and Dogs).* New York: Thunder Mouth Press.

Donovan, M. S. and J. D. Bransford. 2005. *How Students Learn: History, Mathematics, and Science in the Classroom.* Washington, DC: National Academy Press.

Egan, K. 2002. *Getting It Wrong from the Beginning: Our Progressivist Inheritance from Herbert Spencer, John Dewey, and Jean Piaget.* New Haven, CT: Yale University Press.

———. 2005. *An Imaginative Approach to Teaching.* San Fransisco, CA: Jossey-Bass.

Exemplars. No date. http://www.exemplars.com. The website contains a large number of performance assessment tasks.

Gawned, S. 1990. "The Emerging Model of the Language of Mathematics." In *Language in Mathematics,* edited by J. Bickmore-Brand. Portsmouth, NH: Heinemann.

Gerofsky, S. 2004. *A Man Left Albuquerque Heading East: Word Problems as Genre in Mathematics Education*. New York: Peter Lang.

Harvey, S. and A. Goudvis. 2000. *Strategies That Work: Teaching Comprehension to Enhance Understanding*. York, ME: Stenhouse.

Hyde, A. A. and P. R. Hyde. 1991. *Mathwise: Teaching Mathematical Thinking and Problem Solving*. Portsmouth, NH: Heinemann.

Kamii, C. 1994. *Young Children Continue to Reinvent Arithmetic, 3rd Grade*. New York: Teachers College Press.

Kamii, C., and A. Dominick. 1998. "The Harmful Effects of Algorithms in Grades 1–4." In *Teaching and Learning Algorithms in School Mathematics,* edited by L. J. Morrow, 130–40. Reston, VA: National Council of Teachers of Mathematics.

Keene, E. O. and S. Zimmermann. 1997. *Mosaic of Thought: Teaching Comprehension in a Readers' Workshop*. Portsmouth, NH: Heinemann.

Lakoff, G. and R. E. Nuñez. 2000. *Where Mathematics Comes From: How the Embodied Mind Brings Mathematics into Being*. New York: Basic Books.

Lehrer, R. and L. Schauble, eds. 2002. *Real Data in the Classroom: Expanding Children's Understanding of Math and Science*. New York: Teachers College Press.

Lesh, R., and J.S. Zawojewski. 2006. "Problem Solving and Modeling In *The Handbook of Research on Mathematics Education*. Reston, VA: National Council of Teachers of Mathematics.

Mack, N. K. 1990. "Learning Fractions with Understanding: Building on Informal Knowledge." *Journal for Research in Mathematics Education,* January, 16–32.

Miller, D. 2002. *Reading with Meaning: Teaching Comprehension in the Primary Grades*. York, ME: Stenhouse.

Miura, I. T. 1987. "Asian Languages Aid Mathematics Skills." *Science News*. Vol. 132, September 19.

———. 2001. "The Influence of Language on Mathematical Representations." In *The Role of Representation in School Mathematics*, edited by A. A. Cuoco. Reston, VA: National Council of Teachers of Mathematics.

National Council of Teachers of Mathematics. 1989. *Curriculum and Evaluation Standard for School Mathematics*. Reston, VA: National Council of Teachers of Mathematics.

———. 2000. *Principles and Standards for School Mathematics*. Reston, VA: National Council of Teachers of Mathematics.

Palinscar, A. S. and A. L. Brown. 1984. "Reciprocal Teaching of Comprehension—Fostering and Monitoring Activities." *Cognition and Instruction, 1 no. 2:* 117–75.

Public Education and Business Coalition. 2004. *Thinking Strategies for Learners*. Denver, CO: Public Education and Business Coalition.

Raphael, T. 1982. "Question Answering Strategies for Children." *Reading Teacher* (36)2: 186–190.

Steen, L. A., ed. 1990. *On the Shoulders of Giants: New Approaches to Numeracy.* Washington, DC: National Academy Press.

Sun, W. and J. Y. Zhang. 2001. "Teaching Addition and Subtraction Facts: A Chinese Perspective." *Teaching Children Mathematics*, 7, no. 2: 28–31.

Van de Walle, J. A. 2006. *Elementary and Middle School Mathematics: Teaching Developmentally*. New York: Longman.

Wickelgren, W. A. 1974. *How to Solve Problems*. San Francisco: W. H. Freeman.

Yakimanskaya, I. S. 1991. *The Development of Spatial Thinking in Schoolchildren.* Reston, VA: National Council of Teachers of Mathematics.

Zawojewski, J. S. and R. Lesh. 2003. "A Models and Modeling Perspective on Problem Solving." In *Beyond Constructivism: Models and Modeling Perspectives on Mathematics Problem Solving, Learning, and Teaching*, edited by R. Lesh and H. M. Doerr, 317–28. Mahwah, NJ: Lawrence Erlbaum Associates.

INDEX